FAITH WALK

Living Each Day by the Power of Faith

Bob Peterson

ACKNOWLEDGMENTS

First and foremost I must acknowledge and thank my Lord and God. This study is not about my wisdom or insights. It is something God put on my heart for the purpose of sharing with others. Any benefit or blessing you receive from it is to God's glory and His alone. I would, however, like to say thanks to some others who have been a tremendous help in writing this study. I would like to thank all those who were willing to share their stories with me. I know it was not easy, and I thank God for your courage and willingness. I want to say a special thanks to Andy Smith and my wife, Michelle. If it were not for your help and insight, this study would not have been possible. I appreciate you more than you know. I would also like to thank my church family at Dufur Christian Church for their encouragement and support. May God bless you all.

I have tried to document any time I have used someone else's words or ideas, but I know one study in particular should receive more recognition. The study "Experiencing God" has played such a part in my understanding of faith, that at times, it is hard for me to tell where Henry Blackaby's teaching ends and my own thinking begins. So for any of Mr. Blackaby's ideas I have failed to acknowledge, I hope this will serve as one big footnote.

All Scripture quotations come from the NASB unless otherwise noted

First Printing

CONTENTS

INTRODUCTION

"for we walk by faith, not by sight--" (2 Cor. 5:7)

Faith is one of the most powerful forces known to man. Christ taught that even a tiny amount of faith has the power to move mountains.[1] Unfortunately few of us find that to be a reality in our lives. Even those who see faith to be important seldom see its power transforming their lives. I am convicted that this is not because faith has lost its power, but because we have lost its meaning.

Faith is just as powerful today as ever, and still holds the ability to change and enrich lives. But we need to understand what scripture is talking about when it speaks of faith, and we need to be willing to try to put that into practice in our lives. That is the goal of this study, to help us understand what it means to walk by faith. Not just because this is something that we ought to be doing, but because it is what brings life to our Christianity.

There is a story of two men who were discussing the costs of Christianity. One of them was complaining of how the preacher always seemed to be asking them to give money, time, or service. He felt it was asking too much. The other man replied, "You know, I once had a son, and when he was young it cost a lot to raise him. He always seemed in need of shoes, clothing and food. As he got older the cost grew even more. We sometimes wondered how we could afford the cost. A few years ago my son died. Now he doesn't cost us anything. I would rather he was alive."[2]

This study is not about an easy faith or a cheap grace. It is about a faith that involves sacrifice. It will cost you, but the benefit we receive is more than worth it. What kind of faith do you want, one that costs you very little but is also very dead, or one that can stretch you to your limits, but is alive and growing?

If you are walking in faith, then it is my hope that this study will help you deepen and enrich your faith. If you are struggling in your faith, then the goal will be to give you some direction and to give you something to stand on so that your faith will become more meaningful to God and to you. If you have never committed yourself to Christ, the goal will be to introduce you to a faith that is real and that has meaning both for eternity, and for the here and now as well.

A walk of faith will push us beyond our comfort zone. But it is real and it involves a relationship with Christ that is alive and meaningful. It is not about ritual and rules. It is about learning what it means to walk with God. Some times it can seem to move too fast. Other times it can seem to take forever. But the rewards of a walk of faith are not just found in reaching a certain end, but in the journey itself.

Faith Walk is divided up into thirteen chapters. Chapters One and Two lay down the foundation of what it means to live by faith. Chapters Three through Eleven look at how walking by faith plays out in our lives, in the everyday challenges we face. Chapters Twelve and Thirteen look at how walking by faith should affect a congregation as well as the individual.

Each chapter is broken up into four sections:

THE QUESTION OF FAITH - This section looks at a person from Scripture and how they dealt with faith in regard to the subject of the chapter. This section is written in the first person narrative form. The point here is not to say this is what was really going on in that persons' mind. Rather it is to help us see beyond the recorded actions and get an idea of what struggles the person must have faced as they had to make the choice of faith.

A CLOSER LOOK - This section discusses the insights and the instructions that we find in scripture in regard to the area of faith the chapter is discussing.

DIGGING DEEPER - This section looks at the more practical aspects of how walking by faith works in regard to the subject of the chapter. This section is also designed to facilitate discussion. It has questions aimed at getting the reader to look into the Bible and think about how it might apply in their life.

LIFE EXAMPLES - This section is a testimony of a real life person and how they had to deal with the issue of walking by faith in regard to the subject of the chapter.

May God bless and enrich you as you go through this study.

Chapter 1
FAITH IN OUR FAITHFULNESS
"I believe; help my unbelief."(Mark 9:24)

The Question of Faith
The father of the demon-possessed boy - Mark 9:14-29

My son turned and looked up at me with questioning eyes. Though his tongue could not speak his eyes clearly asked, "Where are you taking me?" A simple question, one that Isaac asked Abraham on the day Abraham displayed his great faith. But I had no such great faith. I'm not sure I had much faith at all. The fact was I was scared and desperate. It was because of my desperation that I was taking my son Micah on this journey. Somehow I had to help him. As I looked down into his trusting eyes, I was reminded of how precious he was to me, and how little I deserved his trust.

I remember how scared I was when Micah was first born. There was so much that I didn't know about being a father. Would I do it right or would I be a failure? I was scared, but I was excited as well. Somehow, I thought, it would be okay. My father hadn't been the best father, but I turned out all right. I would do better. I would be a good father. That is what I told myself then. But now I know better.

At first things had gone okay. Micah was a healthy boy, a boy any father could be proud of. My wife took on the major role in caring for him. But as he got older she began pressing me to spend more time with my son. It is not that I didn't want to, but I was busy. I had a business to run. What did she expect? In order to have the things we were accustomed to, it meant there had to be some sacrifices. We couldn't have all the things we wanted without paying a cost. But I never imagined what it would cost Micah.

To be honest I now realize it wasn't just the work. I began to get involved in things that I shouldn't have. They were mostly innocent, or at least that is the way they seemed at first. I would tell myself, that they weren't that bad. Others were doing things far worse. It had been so pleasurable and hadn't done any harm. At least that's how it seemed. As time went on I was drawn deeper into my folly. I continued to deny that there was any harm, but inside I knew differently. I just chose not to see. It wasn't that long before the pleasure began to fade. To get the same feeling I had to go a little further, and a little further. Eventually nothing seemed to bring much happiness, but I couldn't stop. I slowly became the kind of person I never thought I would become. I kept telling myself, "It was okay, I just need a little more right now. But soon everything will be all right." It was a lie I chose to believe. It wasn't until I finally saw what it was doing to my family that the truth came crashing in. I had been able to blind myself to my wife's misery, but when it tore into my son I couldn't deny it any more.

At first I thought it was just some kind of sickness he would get over, but he didn't. He got worse. His hearing diminished and his speaking became confused and muffled. Eventually he lost entirely his ability to speak or hear, but that was not all. He began to have seizures and they became more frequent and violent. One moment Micah would seem quite normal, and then his face would lock into a mask of agony. His mouth would open as if to scream but no sound emerged. He would drop to the ground with froth bubbling from his mouth. His body would begin to flail in all directions. He seemed to be fighting an unseen foe that I was powerless against. I could do nothing to help my child. When it was over, I would gather his limp body into my arms. I would hold him close, rocking back and forth, whispering, "It's all right son, it's all right now." But it was a lie, and we both knew it.

I tried to help him. At first I was confident I would be able to fix things. I tried healers and priests. I tried potions and charms. I tried every remedy I could find. But as failure lead to failure, I began to lose hope. Nothing seemed to help. We tried to keep Micah's problem quiet, but we never knew when it would happen. Soon he became the talk of the town. We had to deal with the shocked indignation, the pitying looks, and with so many well intended suggestions that I grew to avoid talking to people. For a time, I must admit, I was even ashamed of Micah. But that shame turned against me instead. It wasn't his fault, it was mine.

It became apparent that this was no common illness. I could feel an evil intent in the seizures as they sought to destroy my son. I t would throw him into water, or fire, or any place that could do him the most harm. Micah was being tormented by a demon. My son had done nothing to deserve this, so I knew where the fault lay. I didn't know if this was God punishing me through Micah, or if this was just the natural result of my own foolishness. When you let the Devil in, I guess you shouldn't be surprised when he starts making himself at home. Whatever the cause, all I knew was that I just wanted it to end. I wanted my son back, and I was willing to try anything, which brings me back to why we were on this journey.

Where were we headed? In truth I didn't know. Oh I knew the location we were going to but where it would lead us I hadn't s clue. I wanted to say something encouraging to Micah. I wanted to tell him that we were going to see a man who could help him, but I didn't know how. I didn't know who to get through to him. The rudimentary hand signals we had developed to communicate with Micah couldn't convey all I wanted to say. I wanted to tell him how much I loved him. I wanted to tell him how sorry I was, and how much I wanted to make things right. I wanted to tell him all the things I should have said before but didn't, but now I didn't know how. How could I tell him of this man name Jesus who people say can do miracles? How could I share with him my hopes and fears of what might happen when we found Him? I didn't even know if He would be able or willing to help us, but we had to try. All the things I wanted to say stayed locked up within me, so I just smiled down at him with a smile I didn't really feel, and ruffled his hair feeling once again like a failure.

When we got to the place, we found that Jesus wasn't there. Most of His disciples were there, as well as a number of other people, but no Jesus. I tried to get them to tell me where I could find Him, but they told me He couldn't be disturbed. "Couldn't be disturbed?" This was my son, for God's sake. Perhaps they could help me, they suggested. They assured me that they had done this kind of thing lots of times. I was not convinced, but felt I had little choice. So I agreed. They put their hands on Micah and they prayed, and they prayed, but nothing happened. Finally, I was told that they were sorry, but my son couldn't be helped. It might be better if I went on home. One more failure, one more disappointment, but as I looked at Micah I just couldn't give up yet. "Please," I begged, "Can't you just tell me where I can find Jesus?"

"So sorry," they said, "maybe next time."

It was then that I lost my control. I was desperate, and Jesus was my last hope. I began yelling, and some others around joined in. Things were getting pretty hot when Jesus showed up. He came walking up with three of His disciples. When I saw Him, I ran to Him and dropped on my knees. "Please," I cried, "please, Lord, have mercy on my boy. He's my only son." I told him of how my son suffered.

Jesus asked, "O unbelieving generation, how long shall I be with you? How long shall I put up with you?"

I was sure He must be speaking of me. I bowed my head in shame, afraid He would send us away. Instead, Jesus called for my son. As he came, the demon struck again. Micah was slammed to the ground so hard, that it knocked the breath from him. His body convulsed as if it was in the grip of some savage beast.

Jesus looked upon him and quietly asked me, "How long has he been like this?"

"For years now," I replied, "Ever since he was a child. It throws him into the water and the fire, seeking to destroy him. Please," I said begging Him, "If you can do anything, won't you please help us?" Jesus turned and looked at me with eyes that seemed to bore straight through to my soul. I suddenly became afraid as I realized He knew me. He knew my past, my sin, and my shame. He knew it all. I thought, now He will despise me and refuse to help my son. Once again Micah would pay for my sin. I closed my eyes and cried. But as it turned out, it was not my sin Jesus was bothered by, it was my doubt.

"If you can?" Jesus said, "All things are possible to him who believes."

All things are possible? Even this? Even my son? But I am such a weak man, and my faith is so small. I looked at Him and said, "I believe; help my unbelief."

Jesus turned back to Micah and said in a commanding voice, "Spirit, I command you, come out, and leave him lone." Micah's body gave one tremendous jerk and he screamed in anguish and then he was still. For a moment no one moved or said a word. Some of those standing around thought he was dead, but then Jesus walked over to Micah, took him by the hand, and raised him up.

Jesus turned to me and said, "Here is your son." Micah looked at me with an amazed smile on his face and then he spoke. "It's gone," he said. "Father, it's gone, and I can hear." I staggered to my feet and rushed to my son. I grabbed him in my arms and could only cry as Micah whispered to me, "It's alright Father, it's alright now."

Scripture gives us no further information about this man or his son. We only get this one glimpse of a man who in desperation for his family, cries out to Jesus. We are not told that this was a good man or that he had great faith. In fact, he admitted that he struggled with faith. But even a little faith, when it is placed in Jesus, can have a great impact on our lives and the lives of our families.

A Closer Look

Webster's New Collegiate Dictionary:
Faith: "1 a: allegiance to duty or a person: LOYALTY   b: fidelity to one's promises"[1]
Faithful: "1: full of faith"[2]

"I believe; help my unbelief." Have you ever said those words or something like them? I know I have. Most of us have read or heard of faith that can do wonders, that can heal the sick, open up prison doors, and move mountains. That kind of faith seems like a wonderful thing, only for most of us it does not seem to have much connection to the kind of faith we experience. We believe, and yet healing seems to allude us. Nor can we seem to find freedom from the prisons that lock us in. The doors will not budge, and our mountains stubbornly refuse to move. In fact, even the mole hills seem to trip us up. You may wonder, "Did that faith stuff ever really work, has it lost its power over time, or is it just me?"

Well if it is you, you're not alone. I would say most Christians today struggle with the issue of faith. Faith may indeed be important to them, but how it works and what it is about is far from clear. The faith which they experience in their lives has little resemblance to the faith they see in scripture. The problem, though, is not with scripture. God's Word has proven itself true. And if it were not, then our faith would not be worth anything anyway. If man's opinion is the source of authority then truth has no meaning. Everything is up for grabs. I f our faith is based on our opinion rather than the truth of God, then it is about as valuable as a counterfeit three dollar bill. It may make us feel better to hold on to it, but in the end it won't get us anything.

God's Word is true, and a faith that is based on the strength and faithfulness of a living God holds meaning and power. I am convinced that faith is just as powerful today as it was in the time of Jesus, and that miracles continue to happen today. But the goal of this study is not to learn how to do miracles, or to develop a faith that demonstrates its power in wonders that may happen now and again. The goal of this study is to learn how to develop a faith that demonstrates its power in the mundane, day to day struggles we face. One that continues to have power when we are at work, or when we are at home, and has an impact on our relationships, our finances, and our future. We need a faith that has power not just when things are going good, but when things fall apart as well. We need a faith that continues to help us even when we fail, and sin. That is reality. That is where we live, and that is where we need a faith that works. That kind of faith makes our Christianity meaningful, and is the kind of faith that Jesus wants us to have. It is available to us, but first we must understand what faith really involves.

Our understanding of faith today often lacks the fullness and depth of the faith that scripture speaks of. The words that scripture uses for faith carry with them not only the idea of belief, but also of faithfulness. We often separate these ideas. We have a tendency to see belief as an intellectual agreement about something. "Yes, I believe that to be true." We also see faith as not just believing about something, but committing our trust in it as well, relying upon it. "I have faith in you." But we see faithfulness as being something completely different. It is demonstrating loyalty and staying true to one's commitment. "He really shows faithfulness." Scripturally though, there really is not much distinction between these three words.

In the New Testament, belief and faith are used interchangeably.[3]

> "And without faith it is impossible to please Him, for he who comes to
> God must believe that He is and that He is a rewarder of those who seek
> Him." (Heb. 11:6)

The Greek word for "believe" (pisteuo) is basically just the verb form of the word for "faith" (pistis). When the Bible tells us "to believe" it is telling us to do or to demonstrate faith. Scripturally, you cannot believe in something without acting upon it. To say, "I believe in Jesus" or "I have faith in Jesus" but not demonstrate that faith in how we live is a lie. When scripture says those who believe in Christ will be saved,[4] it is actually saying, those who demonstrate faith in Christ will be saved. That is what the word means. And in actuality, it means even more than that. The Greek words for believe and faith both come from the same root word (peitho) which not only has the meaning to believe in, trust in, depend upon; it also has the meaning to obey and follow.

In fact, not only can the Hebrew word that is translated "believe"[5] (aman) also translated "faith,"[6] but it is the same word that is translated as "faithful."[7] It is all the same word. It is all the same idea. If you believe in someone you strive to be obedient, to be faithful to them. Believing in someone means committing yourself to them.

For years people have debated whether salvation comes by works, or by faith, or by combining works and faith. Well, it's not a matter of faith or works, or even faith and works. The faith that scripture speaks of has works as an integral part of it, or it is not real faith. James makes this very clear.

> "But are you willing to recognize, you foolish fellow, that faith without
> works is useless? . . . For just as the body without the spirit is dead, so also
> faith without works is dead." (James 2:20, 26)

Faith is not passive; it is very active. While there is nothing we can do to earn our salvation, we are told there are some things we need to do to receive it. Let me use a story to illustrate this.

> Let's say there was an owner of a sports team who wanted to reward the fans
> who were loyal to his team, so he announced that everyone who wore a team hat
> could get into the big game for free. Some people came wearing team hats and
> were let in. Others came, but for whatever reason, did not have a hat, but did
> come dressed in the team's colors. Would they be let in? By rights they would
> not deserve to, for they would not have done what was asked of them, but if the

owner was a gracious person he would probably still let them in because it was the loyalty he was looking for. Now let's say some other people came wearing neither hats nor team colors, but saying they too were loyal to the team. They claimed they were loyal within, or had worn a hat a few years ago, and therefore thought they should be able to enter. Would the owner let them in? Probably not, for true loyalty is demonstrated.

None of the people would have earned the right to enter. It was only the generosity of the owner that allowed the people in. Doing what was asked of them only enabled them to receive the gift.

What God requires of us is faith[8] or belief[9] in Christ. Again, the word for belief means not just an intellectual agreement, but it involves committing one's self to Christ. God looks into the heart, but faith that is not demonstrated is not faith at all. Scripture tells us of a number of things that are needed for salvation; repentance,[10] baptism,[11] obedience,[12] confessing Christ as Lord,[13] and endurance.[14] These things are not a substitution for faith, or even in addition to faith. They are all a part of what faith is. None of us are perfect in all these areas, but God does not require perfection, what He wants is faith.

We are not talking about a "work's righteousness." Paul makes it very clear that no one can be justified by works of the Law.[15] We cannot earn our salvation by what we do, not even by working at being faithful to God's Word.

> "For by grace you have been saved through faith; and that not of
> yourselves, it is the gift of God; not as a result of works, so that no one
> may boast." (Eph. 2:8-9)

Our salvation is only by the grace of God. But that grace comes to us through faith, a faith that is real, and is demonstrated in how we live. Without faith there is no grace. Paul tells us that it is faith, not works, that save us, but he also talks about the importance of obedience in faith.[16] When Paul is accused of saying, that grace allows us to go on sinning or living as we please, he responds by saying, "May it never be!"[17] Or in other words, "No way, that doesn't work!" He goes on to say:

> "Do you not know that when you present yourselves to someone as slaves
> for obedience, you are slaves of the one whom you obey, either of sin
> resulting in death, or of obedience resulting in righteousness?"
> (Rom. 6:16)

Faith in Christ is directly connected to being faithful to Christ. And this really should not be any surprise. After all, can you live in truth and yet not be truthful? Can you live in joy and yet not be joyful? For us to living in faith means that we strive to be faithful. However, as "faithfulness" needs to be a part of our understanding of what it means "to believe," so should "belief" be a part of our understanding of what it means to "be faithful." Being faithful does not mean to do everything right or to never fail. Being faithful just means to try to live a life that demonstrates faith. In Luke 18 we find the parable of the two men praying in the temple. Jesus said it was not the man who did so many right things that was acceptable to God but the sinner who realized his unworthiness, and so turned to seek God's mercy

The whole reason faith is necessary is because we do not have the ability live like we are supposed to. Faith is not another means by which we earn salvation. Faith is what we cling to because cannot earn it. Paul points out that a righteousness based on our own efforts will never work, for we simply are not good enough. Our only hope is in the grace we receive through Christ Jesus. When we commit ourselves to Him, when we put our faith in Him, His righteousness covers us. We are acceptable to God, not because of what we do, but because we belong to Christ. But if we truly belong to Christ then it will be seen in what we do.

> "So then, you will know them by their fruits. Not everyone who says to
> Me, 'Lord, Lord,' will enter the kingdom of heaven, but he who does the
> will of My Father who is in heaven will enter." (Matt. 7:20-21)

The importance of our actions, or our "fruits," is not in their perfection, or in what they achieve in and of themselves. Their importance is in their testimony as to who is truly Lord of our life. If Christ is our Lord then that will be apparent by our trying to serve Him. And because we belong to Him, then even if we are imperfect in our attempts, even should we fail, His grace covers us.

Now, why spend so much time on trying to establish that faith involves striving to be faithful? For two reasons: First off, there are a lot of people out there who claim Christ in name, but are not seriously trying to live for Him. Maybe they started well but then fell asleep spiritually,[18] or as Paul says, they have "gone astray from the faith,"[19] or "suffered shipwreck in regard to their faith."[20] Maybe they never really understood what was expected of them in the first place. Whatever the case, they are living a Christianity that is mostly in name only and they need to know before it's too late that this kind of faith will not save them. This may sound rather harsh, but it is far better to face it now than to wait and face it on the judgment day.

Secondly, there are a lot of Christians who truly want to live for God but are struggling with their Christianity. Their faith is important to them but it seems so weak. "I believe, help my unbelief." Well the good news is, it can change. You can have a faith that has power not just in church but in your life, in your work, in your family, in your finances, in all areas of your life. Even if you have faded away from God, there is still hope. God has said, "Return, O faithless sons, I will heal your faithlessness."[21] We can grow in our faith, and it can become a power in our lives, but it takes time and work. It is not something that comes naturally. It is something we learn. That kind of faith involves faithfulness. Faithfulness not to a set of rules, but to a living Savior. This is what makes the difference between living according to a dry ritual and living according to a walk of faith. A walk of faith is not about rules. It is about learning how to follow God's lead, so that we might come to know Him more, and experience His power and presence in our lives. A walk of faith is a walk with God that is worth getting excited about.

Digging Deeper

1. Where does the ability to have faith come from? (Rom. 12:3)

Faith does not just spring up from our own goodness. It starts with God. He has put within us the ability to believe in something beyond what we can see. Not everyone uses this ability to put their faith in Christ. There are many other things people put their faith in. God gave us the capability of faith, but it is up to us to choose what to do with it. This is not to say we can walk by faith through own ability. We are too weak, and by our efforts we will fail. It is God who, through Christ and the Holy Spirit, first reaches out to us, and it is His power and grace that enables us to walk by faith. But for us to put our faith in Christ, we first must come to know of Him.

2. Where then does Christian faith begin? (Rom.10:17)

3. The Word of God can become very powerful in our lives. It can instruct, convict, guide, and enrich. This, however, is not always the case. While some people read the Bible and hear God speak to them, other read it and it does nothing for them. What is the difference? (Heb. 4:2)

4. Keep in mind the word "faith" here means not just to accept as true but to also act upon. The word did not profit those who did not unite it with faithfulness. What did Jesus say was the difference between the wise man and the foolish man? (Matt. 7:24-27)

Read Luke 17:3-10.

5. What is it Jesus tells the disciples they need to do? (vrs. 3-4)

6. How do the disciples respond? (vr. 5)

7. Why do you think they asked Jesus to increase their faith?

There are a lot of things that our Lord asks of us that we find difficult to do. Forgiveness especially in regard to repeated offenses, is one of those things.

8. What are some other commands of Christ, or things you know you should do, that you find especially difficult to be faithful in?

There are a number of things that I struggle with, and some times I just wish that God, would make me stronger. Make me more loving. Make me more faithful. Lord increase my faith. This request makes more sense when we understand that faith is not just about believing something, it is about being faithful in regard to our service. "Lord, this seems too much for us, help us to be more faithful."

In looking at Jesus' response, (vrs. 6-10) at first it does not seem to fit the request.

The disciples ask: Jesus responds:
     increase our faith   A little faith is enough to move a mountain
                                       A servant should serve without expecting to
                                       be patted on the back.

9. How do these responses answer the disciples' request?

We may be able to understand the first part of Jesus' response. The disciples want more faith. Jesus tells them they don't need a lot of faith to do what needs to be done. This makes some sense, but it does not seem to help the disciples much. Nor does it seem to connect with the second part, unless one keeps in mind that faith also means faithfulness.

The disciples wanted Jesus to just give them greater faith, but Jesus let them know that is not how it works. They did not need Him to magically endow them with greater faith. They just needed to use what they had. The faith they already had was sufficient for them to respond in obedience to God's direction. No, it was not easy, but it is not supposed to be easy. We are servants of Christ and we are to be faithful even when it is not easy. In fact, the most beneficial time for us to be faithful is when it is not easy.

10. When do you think God is most pleased with our faithfulness?

Jesus was not just telling the disciples, "Stop whining boys. You've got to be tough if you're going to follow me." He is answering their request. He was telling them how their faith might be increased. When the challenge is hard, and yet we still choose to act in faith (in faithfulness), not only does it please our Lord, but it is also more effective in enabling us to live in His power. Our obedience opens the door for God's power to work in us. And as we see God working in response to our obedience, we become encouraged and it helps to strengthen our faith. As our faith gets stronger we are then able to act with greater faithfulness in the future. It becomes a cycle that brings us closer to God. And it works not through our ability or our great faith, but in our commitment, even in the midst of our inability, to try to act in a faithful manner. "We are unworthy slaves; we have done only that which we ought to have done."

So the way our faith increases is for us to strive to be more faithful. This tells us what we should do, but does not necessarily tell us how we are to find the strength, will power, or the faith to do it. If you are feeling inadequate for the task, there is good news. First off, you are not alone. We all feel inadequate. Secondly, God does not expect us to have the ability to be faithful. That is why he sent Jesus.

11. What things do we receive from Christ? (1 Tim. 1:14)

The source of our faith is in Christ. When we try to be faithful on our own, we will eventually fail. But the more we rely upon Christ, upon His mercy and strength, the more we will find that He can do in us. We may not be faithful, but Christ in us can help us to become faithful.

12. Keeping in mind what we have learned in this lesson, how you would deal with the following scenarios?

A. You are someone who goes to church, but struggles with many areas in your life. What can you do to help your faith to become stronger in those areas?

B. You have a friend at work, who is a nice person, but lives a very worldly life style. They come back from a funeral and tell you that they believe in Jesus, but do not are uncertain if they will go to heaven or not. What can you say to them?

13. What does will it mean for you to walk by faith?

14. What is one area you can work on walking by faith in?

Life Examples
Bob[22]

I remember the winter of 1981-82 as being exceptionally cold in more ways than one. I was cold, hungry, and feeling so lost and alone that I wondered if it might not be better if I were dead. Just that last summer life had seemed so easy. I had been living and working with some friends doing yard work and odd jobs. We made enough money to make ends meet, and had plenty of spare time to do as we pleased. Life was easy, although not very meaningful. Somehow I had forgotten my desire to be involved in ministry. While I had plenty of spare time to play, I couldn't seem to find time for prayer or reading God's Word. Sunday mornings were spent in bed or in front of the TV far more than in church. It wasn't so much a conscious choice to rebel as it was a lack of commitment. The result was still the same. I called myself a Christian, but in truth, I had stopped living it. Although I still claimed to have faith, I was not being faithful. I knew better. I was raised in a Christian home. I knew the things I should be doing but couldn't quite find the motivation to do them. And as I stopped doing the things I knew I should, I found it more difficult to resist the things I knew I shouldn't.

As summer turned into fall, and fall into winter, life became less enjoyable. The yard work faded away, and with our country in a recession, jobs were not easy to find. The winter that year in Seattle was one of the coldest they had had for a long time. The temperature dropped well below freezing and stayed that way for weeks. The house we were staying in had no insulation, and we could not afford heating oil. The only heat we had was an open fire place. At night, wrapped in sleeping bags, we would huddle around it like moths to a flame. We kept the fire going by feeding in what ever scrap wood we could salvage around the neighborhood. In the mornings we would have to break the ice in the toilet before we could use it. Our meals went from three a day, to two a day, to a bowl of oatmeal once a day.

I know that others have had it much more difficult, but for me, it was the lowest point in my life. But it wasn't the outward difficulties that bothered me as much as the inward emptiness. As I turned away from God, I left a vacuum in my life that all the good times in the world couldn't fill. As long as I kept myself busy seeking pleasure, I could hide from the emptiness. But when everything else got stripped away, I could hide no longer. My life was leaking down the drain with nothing to show for it. It was benefiting neither God nor those around me, and I sure wasn't enjoying it. If it hadn't been for my upbringing, I may have turned to suicide, but instead I turned back to God.

Ever since I had drifted away from God, I no longer felt very close to Him. I even began to doubt if He was really there, or if He cared about me. I tried praying but it didn't seem to help. Finally in desperation, I sat down one day and said, "Listen God, I am at the end of my rope. I don't even know what to pray." I remembered then someone saying that in prayer we should talk less and listen more. So, since I didn't know what to say anyway, I just said, "God if you're there and if you're listening, I could really use some answers. I'm just going to sit here and listen." I sat there with my eyes closed.

At first nothing happened. My mind just seemed to wander back and forth as usual. Then two visions appeared in my mind's eye, clear and sharp. The first one was of a scroll. It began to unroll, and as it did, I could see that it had writing on it. The writing at first was legible, but as the scroll continued to unroll, even though I could see that it continued to have writing on it, I could no longer read it. The second vision was of a bunch of gallon sized food cans. They were stacked in a pyramid, and one by one they were moved and stacked up into another pyramid. Then they were moved back to where they had been at first.

I felt certain that this was a vision from God, for not only was the vision clear, but I knew exactly what it meant. The visions were answers to the questions I needed but hadn't even known how to ask. The first one was in answer to the question, "Does my life have any meaning and is there a plan for it?" The answer was, "yes." God had a plan and a purpose for my entire life. Right now I could only see a small portion. There was more, but I was not able to see it yet. The second vision was in answer to the question, "What am I supposed to do now?" The answer was, that I was to do the small, mundane, seemingly unimportant things that I already knew I should be doing, but wasn't. I felt a joy within me just knowing that God was there and that He cared enough to reach out to me. I prayed then and there, "God I will follow You where ever you lead me, I just want to be with You.

The temperature at that moment didn't suddenly warm up. We still had little to eat, and it was a couple of months before I finally found a job, but from that day on, life has been good. Not that there haven't been bad times, or that I have always felt close to God. But I know I have a God who cares for me. I know there is a plan for my life, even if I can't see it just yet. And I now have a goal and purpose for my life. My goal is to do the desire of my Master.

I had been baptized years before that day, and I had been going to church and trying to be a good Christian, but I still count that day as my new birth. For not only did I get a second start on life, but from that point on my Christianity changed. No longer was I merely trying to do the right things, trying to follow the rules. From that day on, the motivation for what I did was that I might please my Lord and come to know Him more, in the small things as well as the big. I wish I could say I have always been faithful in my commitment, but I haven't. But my Lord is also my savior and my redeemer, and His love and grace covers me. My Christianity was no longer about doing the right thing. It was about a relationship with Christ. It was no longer a walk of rules. Instead, it became a walk of faith.

Would I have been saved if I had died while not living in faithfulness? I don't know. God's grace covers our sins, so we don't have to be perfect to be saved, but God's grace comes to us through faith.[23] I claimed to have faith in God, but I didn't live that way. The kind of faith I was showing that the time looked a lot like the kind that Jesus said would not be acceptable and would not save us.[24] There is a difference between a kind of faith where one tries to walk in faithfulness but struggles and fails from time to time, and a kind of faith that is in name only. The kind of faith in which one claims to have in God, but ignores God's will for their life, and instead lives by their own desires.

Would have been lost if I had died then? I don't know. I'm not here trying to argue against the concept of Eternal Security. I merely trying to share what was real, and the reality was, I was lost. I felt so very lost, hopeless and alone. And I was dead, or at least dying. The life within me was smoldering to nothing. It started slowly but as I turned away from God, I no longer experienced His presence within me. I no longer had His strength, or His wisdom. I was living life on my own. I thought I could handle it, but I was wrong. I know that some of my circumstances I brought on myself by my own folly, but I also believe that God, in His grace and love, allowed me to fall to such a situation so that I might see my folly before it was too late. Then He drew me out of the ashes and breathed life into me again.

I thank God for that cold winter, for in the midst of the misery I found not just a God, but a personal friend and Savior. And I found a Christianity that wasn't a religion or ritual, but was a relationship. I never want to go back to the way things were. I never want to harm or lose that relationship, and that is why, even though I am still a sinner, I will continue to strive to walk by faith.

Chapter 2
FAITH IN OUR WALK WITH GOD
"... what does the LORD require of you ... to walk humbly with your God"(Mic. 6:8)

The Question of Faith
Moses - Exodus 32:30-33:17

I stepped outside my tent and looked up at the angry clouds above. They swirled and churned with threatening menace. Here and there patches of cloud glowed with momentary brilliance as lightning flickered within. The air was charged with tension, but no rain descended from the heavens. I shifted my gaze down to the tents that stretched out around me. The people were beginning to stir, preparing for the day, but they moved about with an uneasy stillness. There was tension here as well, mingled with fear and uncertainty. People hurried about with their daily tasks but the usual morning sounds seemed muted. Most moved with eyes cast low, occasionally taking anxious glances to the mountain of God or stealing a quick look in my direction. The people were afraid, and they had good reason to be.

It was hard to believe that only yesterday I had been standing on the holy mountain glorying in God's presence. In the midst of His instruction He suddenly stopped. His spirit that surrounded me became charged with anger. The joy I had been experiencing changed to alarm. Something was terribly wrong. "Go," He told me. "You must return to the people for they have turned aside from My commands and are even now worshiping a gold calf." The anger of the Lord burned so fierce that it nearly overwhelmed me as I heard Him say. "I shall destroy them."

I knew the people to be foolish and fickle, and at times I wanted to destroy them myself, but not now, not after so much. "Oh Lord," I cried," please after all You've done for the sake of Your people, do not destroy them in Your anger." I went on, trying to come up with reasons for why God should not wipe the people away. I think that in the end what saved them was not so much my words but the fact that the Lord God is a gracious god, ready to forgive. He does not desire to destroy us even when we deserve it.

As I went down the mountain I could hardly believe that the people would be so foolish. How could they so quickly go back to idols after they had repeatedly seen the power of the hand of God? What were they thinking? I was half way down the mountain when the truth of God's words became evident. The sound of the people's debauchery could be clearly heard. The closer I drew to camp, the louder the noise increased and the angrier I became. As I rounded the last corner I saw before me the people dancing and worshiping a golden calf.

I had been carrying the stone tablets that were inscribed with the commands of God, and as I looked and beheld the people making a mockery of those commands, my anger filled me. I lifted the tablets above my head and I hurled them down to the ground. The tablets shattered into pieces. I tore my robes and ran as a wild man into the camp, screaming at the people to get away from the calf, shoving them back.

"What are you doing?" I yelled. "Have you all lost your senses? Do you not know that our God is a jealous god? Would you mock Him by worshiping an idol in His very presence? You fools, do you want Him to destroy us all?" How could they so easily turn back to that which only enslaved them? Had they so quickly forgotten what God had done for them? Did they truly wish to exchange the presence of the living God for the emptiness of immorality and idolatry?

Those around me stood frozen as in a trance. They stared at me with confused expressions, unsure at what they should do. I turned to Aaron, my brother, who of all people should have known better. I pointed to the calf and said in a voice of barely contained fury, "Burn it! Do you hear me? Burn it! Burn it now!" Even after the calf was destroyed it was not easy getting the people back in order. Once you give in to sin, it is very difficult to go back. In the end blood had to be shed, and there were much suffering before order could be restored.

All this had taken place the day before. The noise and chaos of the night were gone but its dark shadow still remained. Now as I stood outside my tent, looking around at the camp, there was an unnatural quiet that hung upon it. The stillness was almost as tangible as the ominous clouds over head. It was the calm after the storm, but the people were still afraid of what storms may wait ahead. They had seen the hand of God and they knew of its frightening power. They now wondered if that power would fall upon them.

I summoned the people together, and when they had gathered I raised my hand. A hush fell over the crowd. As I looked out at the sea of faces few eyes would meet my gaze. "You have sinned," I called out, "and your sin is great, but I will now go before the Lord and see if atonement can be made for your sin."

I turned to go and the people parted and made a path for me. I could feel their eyes on my back as I moved toward the tent of meeting. Their future hung in the balance and they knew it. The pillar of cloud already hovered above the tent. Joshua, standing guard, opened the flap for me and I walked into God's presence. There is nothing in this world that can compare to standing in the presence of God and feeling His glory all about you. It is something like jumping into a cool spring on a hot day and feeling your entire being come alive. But this time I could not bask in its joy for my heart was heavy.

I knelt down before God, and though I could not see Him, I could feel Him in a way that is more sure than sight can ever be. With my head bowed I said, "Alas my God, the people have committed a great sin. They have turned from You to make themselves a god of gold, but I pray that you will forgive their sin. If you can not, then may you punish me as well."

When God spoke, His words seemed to penetrate my flesh reaching to my soul. "It is the one who sins," said the Lord, "who shall be punished. The day will come when the people will know my punishment, but for now you are to lead them on to the land of milk and honey. I will send an angel to help you and to prepare the way, but I will not go with you, for you are an obstinate people. I would most likely destroy you on the way. Have the people cast off their jewelry. Have them humble themselves and I will decide what I shall do with them."

I got up and went out of the tent, and as always when I left God's presence, it felt as if a part of me died or at least began to fade away. Once again I called the people together. As I looked out at them I could sense both their anticipation and their apprehension. They hoped for forgiveness, but feared they would receive something far worse. I raised my hand and silence fell on the crowd.

"The Lord has spoken," I told them. "He has said He will not destroy us but will allow us to go on to the Promised Land. He will even send an angel to help us." The people were barely able to believe their good fortune. They turned to each other with smiles and began to talk with excited voices. "But," I shouted, raising my hand to quiet them, "He has told me that He will not go with us. No longer will we share in His presence for we have shown ourselves to be a sinful and an obstinate people."

The people were silent for a moment as the meaning of my words sank in. No longer would God's spirit go with us. No longer would we feel His presence as we went into battle. His strength would no longer support us. His love would no longer surround us. Someone in the crowd began a mournful cry, and it was soon picked up by others. Some of the people tore their robes others fell to their knees and wept. They had wanted their pleasure, but they had not realized how much it would cost them.

Once again I lifted my hand and signaled for silence. "We have one hope." I said, "The Lord has said that we should put away our ornaments and then He will decide what He shall do. Let us humble ourselves before God and seek His mercy and maybe He will change His mind. Go now, go to your tents. Remove your finery, and seek the Lord."

The people began to disperse and I, too, turned to seek the Lord. I headed back to the tent of meeting that I might plead with God, for I could not bear the thought of being cut off from Him. It was strange how only a few months ago I had been unaware that one could share in God's presence. I had been living my life based on my own wisdom and strength and had not known there was anything more. If I thought about God at all it was as some distant being, unconnected to my life. But God had reached out to me. Why, I could not imagine, but He called me by name. He wanted to know me and for me to know Him.

When I opened myself to Him, He began to fill voids I hadn't even been aware existed. The idea of now being cut off from Him filled me with a sense of dread. Now that I knew there was so much more to life, I didn't want to lose it. At one time I had thought that being comfortable and well off was all one could wish for. Gaining the Promised Land would have been all I could want. But now even the idea of being given the Promised Land held little interest if God was not with us.

I entered the tent once again and bowed down before the Lord. For a moment I just knelt there in silence, my soul trembling within me. Then I lifted my face to the heavens and spread my hands out to God. "You have told me," I began, "that I am to lead the people up to where they are to go, but who is to lead me? How am I to know the way if You are not with me? You have said that You know me and I have found favor in your sight. If I have truly found favor in Your sight, then I pray, show me Your ways. Let me know You. It is You I desire, to know You and to please You. Do not leave me and do not leave Your people, oh God. If Your presence will not go with us then do not send us forward. If You are not there, then I don't want to go. It is being with You that makes us who we are. Apart from You, we are nothing. My Lord and my God, please, I just want to be with You."

God heard Moses' plea and He agreed to stay with the people and to continue to dwell in their midst. Moses never got to enter the Promised Land. Because of an act of rebellion, God told him he had to remain outside. Moses could have ignored God's instruction and gone on into the Promised Land anyway. After all, why should he be kept out when others were allowed to enter? But one thing Moses had learned through his journeys was that it is better to be in the desert with God, than to be in a land of abundance without Him. The true blessing is not found in reaching a certain destination in life, but in the company we keep along the way. When we walk with the Lord, then where ever He may lead us is the "land of promise."

A Closer Look

Moses had a different kind of relationship with God than anyone before him. God spoke to others and revealed His name to Abraham, Isaac, and Jacob. But with Moses God chose to reveal Himself.[1] With other prophets God used visions and dreams to communicate. But with Moses God spoke mouth to mouth,[2] face to face, as one would speak to a friend.[3] Why did God pick Moses for this honor? We do not know. When God appeared to Moses in the form of the burning bush, Moses did not have much that would seem to qualify him for a friendship with God.

Earlier in his life Moses had been given privileges and opportunities that he had squandered by bad choices. Now he was an eighty year old underachiever living out in the wilderness watching goats. When God called Moses, he did not really even know who God was. Still God chose to make Himself known to Moses. One thing we do know about Moses is that he was humble.[4] The two most important qualities for someone to have to be used by God are humility and patience. A humility before God that says, "I will follow You and put my trust in You rather than seek to do things my way, and a humility before others that is demonstrated in a willingness to lift up and encourage others even we may not feel like it. Patience is not just the ability to wait, but the willingness to find our contentment is serving the Lord where we are at and not worrying about what may be ahead. It may have been that through Moses failures he came to understand his unworthiness and this helped him to appreciate God's friendship all the more. Most of the Israelites served God out of a sense of duty, fear, or self-preservation. But Moses came to serve God because he valued his relationship with the Lord more than anything else.

It is this kind of relationship that Christ wants to have with us, to walk with us and speak with us, not as some distant entity but as a friend.[5] He reaches out to us not because we deserve it but because He loves us in spite of the fact that we don't deserve it. He is not only the friend of the righteous but He is also the friend of the sinner as well.

But for us to share in this relationship we must seek it above all else including friendship with the world.[6] We can not hold on to sin and the desires of this world and share in a relationship with God at the same time.[7] To be a friend of Christ means our desire is to please Him and to be obedient to His commands.[8]

To walk with God means to walk in obedience to His will. Walking with God or walking in His ways, is directly connected with walking in, or keeping, God's statutes and commands.[9] But this is not talking about following a rule book, or living by law. It is talking about a relationship: to obey God's voice,[10] to love Him,[11] and to be wholly devoted to Him.[12] These are all a part of walking with God, or walking in His ways.[13]

> "Now, Israel, what does the LORD your God require from you, but to fear
> the LORD your God, to walk in all His ways and love Him, and to serve
> the LORD your God with all your heart and with all your soul, and to keep
> the LORD'S commandments and His statutes which I am commanding you
> today for your good?" (Deut. 10:12-13)

Walking with God means we strive to be faithful to God's will for our life, not because it earns us something or because we are afraid of being punished, but because we love Him and trust Him. These, you may notice, are the same things involved in walking by faith. The Old Testament describes men, such as Enoch and Noah, as men who "walked with God."[14] The New Testament describes them as men of faith.[15] Walking by faith and walking with God is essentially the same thing. But what does it look like for us to walk by faith? In Psalms 23, David gives us some beautiful imagery to help us see what it means to walk with God.

> "The LORD is my shepherd, I shall not want." (Ps. 23:1)

The metaphor David uses for the Lord is not that of some distant being, or even that of a lofty ruler, but that of a shepherd. The shepherd lives with the sheep. He is their guide, physician and protector.[16] As the sheep grow to know the shepherd, they come to know His voice.[17] They find security in His presence. But this is not just a one-sided relationship. The shepherd is there to take care of the sheep, but the sheep must be willing to follow the shepherd. David says, "I shall not want." This is not only a statement of trust that the Lord will take care of his needs. It is also a vow that David will find his sustenance in the Lord. He will not look elsewhere for his fulfillment. He will not sneak away, but rather, he will stay with the Lord. The Lord is truly our shepherd, but the question is, are we truly His sheep?

> "He makes me lie down in green pastures; He leads me beside quiet waters."
> (Ps. 23:2)

When we walk with God there is a peace and a comfort that come from knowing that God is the one in control that He has a plan, and that His plan is the best possible one for us. It can take a load off of our shoulders and bring a sense of serenity, like that of walking beside quiet waters. But David shows us that walking with God can mean other things as well. Sometimes God makes us lie down in green pastures. What is the problem with that? The problem is we may see a different pasture as being greener, and we do not always want to lie down. We want to be going and doing, and can get very frustrated when God says, "Wait."

Years ago when we first started in the ministry, my wife and I decided it was time to start a family. We thought we could just make this happen, but we were wrong. We went through months, and then years, of frustration and fading hopes. The doctors had no explanations or answers, and our prayers seemed to go unheard. We wanted to walk with God, but we also wanted a child. We could not understand why God was not answering our prayers.

We eventually came to accept the situation even if we did not understand it. Then five years after we had started trying, suddenly and unexplainably we could have children. For a long time I could see no reason for why God made us wait. Then one day it was as if God opened my eyes to His wisdom. I saw that while we thought we were ready for a family, God, in His wisdom, knew better. At that time, not only was I a full-time seminary student, I was also trying to pastor three churches. Not only were we short on time, we were also short on money. With my school bills and low paying job, we were going in debt, even with Michelle working.

On top of this, God knew that during those five years there would be some times of high stress that would be very trying for us. At one point I was even ready to leave the ministry. God knew this was not a time for us to have the added stress of children. Was it just coincidence that the very week I graduated from seminary, when our financial and time strain was lessened, that suddenly Michelle became pregnant? We were not satisfied with the green pasture that God had provided. We wanted children, and we wanted them in our timing. But God, in His love and grace, said, "No, wait."

"He restores my soul; He guides me in the paths of righteousness for His name's sake." (Ps. 23:3)

If we walk with God, He will lead us down the path of righteousness, truth, and integrity. This may indeed be the way we want to go, but it is generally not the easiest of paths to follow. In fact, it is often the path we would just as soon avoid. For us to follow this path means confessing our sins when we would rather hide them, standing up for truth when it would be easier not to, going out of our way to help others, and letting go of our pleasures in order that we might please our Lord. If we are going to walk with God, sometimes that will mean He will lead us down paths we do not want to go.

And we may ask ourselves, "Why should we?" Following these paths may not seem to bring us much earthly benefit. In fact, sometimes it may be rather costly. To follow the path of righteousness may mean we lose an opportunity for something we want, or even need. Sometimes even when we follow God's leading, things may not go well for us. Sometimes the bad guy wins. Sometimes we end up getting stepped on.

Does this mean our faithfulness was wasted? No. While it is true that God knows best, and following Him will usually be to our benefit in the long run, that is not the point. The point is that we glorify God, and live in His presence. The reason for following God is not earthly rewards. It is for living in God's presence and being pleasing in His sight.

What if we choose not to follow God's lead? Will God strike us with lightning? Probably not, but just as with a sheep that refuses to follow its shepherd, we would bring problems upon ourselves. We may think we know what is best for us, but if it is in opposition to God's leading, it will only end up bringing us harm. And the biggest harm is that it cuts us off from God's presence. No longer do we have His strength and wisdom to protect and lead us. We may think, "It is just this one thing, then I will get back on the right track." But without the power of God, we are not strong enough or smart enough to follow that track on our own. Fortunately for us, our Lord is not only the one who shows us the paths of righteousness in the first place, He is also the one who can restore our soul. If we cry out to Him, He can bring us back and renew our soul. He can put us on the path of righteousness once again, and give us the strength we lack to go forward.

> "Even though I walk through the valley of the shadow of death, I fear no
> evil, for You are with me; Your rod and Your staff, they comfort me."
> (Ps. 23:4)

Sometimes walking by faith can be a very frightening thing. Other times, it is life that is frightening and walking by faith is what enables us to go on. Whatever the case, from time to time we will face the valley of the shadow of death. It may be a threat to our own life, or a threat to someone or something we care about. Walking with God will not keep us from having to face these valleys, but it will help us make it through them. For as long as He is with us, we will be okay, whatever the outcome.

The rod was a club the shepherd used for defense against wild animals and enemies, and the staff was a walking stick that he used to direct the sheep where they should go. It is a comfort to know that our God is more powerful than any foe we may face. It is also a comfort to know that the ground on which stand is solid ground. We may not always like being kept in line. God's Word does not always tell us what we want to hear, but if we follow His leading, not only can we have the assurance of His presence, but we can also have the assurance of knowing we are where we need to be.[18]

> "You prepare a table before me in the presence of my enemies; You have
> anointed my head with oil; my cup overflows." (Ps. 23:5)

The table represents blessing, celebration, and joy. While these are things we generally associate with being among friends, David points out that when we walk with God we can enjoy them even in the presence of our enemies. This may mean that God will overcome our enemies for us, or it may mean that though our enemies are all around us, they will not be able to steal the blessing of God's presence from us. Walking with God can take us into some difficult situations, but as long as we are with Him we can still experience God's blessings, no matter what men may do. The anointing, which may be a symbol of the Holy Spirit, is also a symbol of blessing and favor. When God anoints us with His Spirit there is an overflowing of joy that can be with us no matter what the circumstances may be.

> "Surely goodness and loving-kindness will follow me all the days of my life, and I will dwell in the house of the LORD forever." (Ps. 23:6)

When David speaks of dwelling in the house of the Lord forever, he is not speaking of being with God someday in eternity. The Hebrew word translated, "forever," literally means, "for the length of days." In other words, David is just using a different phrase to say the same thing as, "all the days of my life." David is talking of being with the Lord, here and now, and continuing to do so all his life. And he is not talking about camping out in the temple. The temple had not even been built at this time. He is talking of living in God's presence, walking with the Lord. This was David's ultimate goal. Wherever it took him, whatever he may face, David's desire was to walk with God. For in God's presence is goodness and loving-kindness.

Digging Deeper

Choosing to walk by faith with our Lord, Jesus Christ, is no small matter. It is an entirely different approach to life. It carries both great rewards and great costs. We will begin by looking at the rewards of living by faith.

1. What are some of the rewards of faith or faithfulness that we find in these passages?

A. 1 Peter 1:9

We are saved by the grace of God, but it is our faith that gives us access to that grace.[19] It is faith that enables us to become sons of God,[20] and to receive the inheritance of eternal life.[21]

B. Matt. 17:20

Faith not only gives us access to God's grace and eternal salvation. It also gives us access to God's power working in our lives here and now. It can bring healing,[22] increase the effectiveness of our prayers,[23] give us wisdom and insight,[24] help us to resist the attacks of Satan,[25] and bring peace to our lives.[26]

  C. Acts 15:9

A life lived in faith not only changes our eternal future, it changes us - or rather, God changes us. When we strive to walk with God in faithfulness, He cleanses our hearts,[27] He justifies us even though we do not deserve it,[28] He forgives our sins and sanctifies us.[29] When we choose to walk by faith, we become children of God,[30] not because our faith earns us that position, but because God chooses to bestow it upon those who live by faith.

  D. Prov. 28:20

All throughout the Old Testament God continued to tell His people that if they would be faithful and walk in His ways, He would show His loving-kindness to them and bless them in all aspects of their life,[31] that they might succeed in all they did.[32]

  E. Eph. 3:16-17

This is the greatest benefit of all. When we walk by faith, we live in fellowship with our Lord. It is our commitment of faith that allows us to receive the Holy Spirit.[33] It is walking by faith that allows us to live in His presence. God has promised that not only will He dwell with those who are faithful to His ways,[34] but they will be His delight,[35] a treasured possession.[36]

2. Can you think any instances in scripture where someone acted in faith and then was blessed?

3. Can you think of a time you have acted in faith, and then experienced God's blessing?

The rewards are great for truly walking in faith, but so are the costs..

4. What were some of the costs for those who lived by faith that are found in Hebrews 11?

      11:8-9

      11:17

      11:24-26

      11:35-37

5. Can you think of any other costs of faith, either from scripture or from experience?

In the New Testament Jesus does not lower the cost; in fact, He raises it.

6. What will it cost us to walk with Jesus? (Luke 14:26-27, 33)

Large crowds would gather to Jesus to get something from Him or because it had become the popular thing to do. When this happened Jesus had a tendency to use some harsh or confusing statements. He apparently did this to test and see just how committed they were to Him. It is doubtful that Jesus actually meant that we should hate our families for else where in scripture we are told to honor our parents,[37] have compassion for our children,[38] and love our wives.[39] Part of our faithfulness to God is our loving our family. This is not to discount what Jesus said. He wanted to make it clear that no relationship to any person, or any thing, was to stand before our relationship to Him.

7. How does Paul describe, "Living by faith?" (Gal. 2:20)

8. How is living by faith sometimes like being crucified with Christ?

This is a lot to ask, especially if our life belongs to us. If our life belongs to us, then we are free to do with it as we please. Sacrificing it would seem to be a foolish thing to do. However, if our life belongs to us, then we have neither Christ's presence, nor His salvation. If we own our life we own our sin as well, and it is we who must pay the price. If our life belongs to Christ, then whatever He may ask of us is not too much. We may have to go through hardship, but we will go through it with Christ. Even should we die we will live again with Him.[40] The motivation to walk by faith, it is not the fear of God's wrath, but the joy of His love.[41] Our motivation to walk by faith is not that it is easy, but rather that the reward is worth the cost.

9. What does Paul see as being more valuable than any worldly gain? (Philip. 3:7-8)

As costly as walking by faith can be, not walking by faith can even be more costly. All of the promises that God gave to those who would faithfully walk in His ways were turned to curses for those who were unfaithful.[42] God's blessing would not be with them, and even their successes would turn to failures. Not only do they lose God's blessing, but they lose His presence as well. God said, "I will hide My face from them . . . in whom is no faithfulness."[43] One does not have to be doing "evil" things to lose God's favor. To God, when we do not walk in faith, we are walking in sin.[44]

There is a difference between a person who is trying to live in faithfulness, but fails from time to time, and a person who lives in unfaithfulness. If we are trying to live for the Lord, His grace will cover our sins. But this does not mean obedience is not important. Even one act of unfaithfulness can have a big impact on our life. Any sin puts a barrier between us and God,[45] and until it is dealt with, it will cut us off from experiencing the fullness of His presence and power. Without God's power we are more vulnerable to Satan's attacks. Thus, one sin can make us more susceptible to fall for the next. This is why it is so important that we deal with any act of unfaithfulness by confessing the sin, repenting of it, and asking God's forgiveness. This allows us to be forgiven and to have our relationship with God renewed. But even when we are forgiven, there still may be a cost for our unfaithfulness.

In Numbers 20, the Hebrew people complain for lack of water, so God told Moses to speak to the rock so it would bring forth water. God had brought the people there for a reason so they could see how God could provide for them. But instead of doing what God had instructed him to do Moses instead claimed to have power to bring forth water from the rock and struck it with his staff. This may not seem to be a big deal to us, but to God it was disobedience and unfaithfulness. I think Moses had been stung by the people's criticism of his leadership and wanted to impress them with his ability. At first Moses got what he wanted. The water came forth and the people were impressed, but Moses did have to pay a price.

10. What is the price Moses paid? (Deut. 32:51-52)

In Numbers 13 when the people had an opportunity to act in faith and go into the Promised Land, they choose not to because of the difficulties that they saw. This one choice meant that they would never get a chance to have a part in the wonder and blessing that God had planned for them. Instead they would live their lives in the wilderness. When they changed their minds and decided to go into the land, it was too late. God told them they were forbidden to go into the land. They decided to try and go in anyway, believing God would help them. This may have looked like an act of faith, but it was not, because it was not done in obedience to God's will. God did not help them. When they asked for forgiveness, God forgave them, but their opportunity was gone forever.

11. Who else suffered because of the people's lack of faith? (Num. 14:33)

We are told that our sins may have impact on our children for three or four generations,[46] but our faithfulness can have impact for thousands of generations.[47] God continued to have mercy on Israel even when they did not deserve it because of the faithfulness of Abraham, Isaac and Jacob. God's plans for us are always the best for our life. When we walk in faith, He will bless not only our life, but the lives of those around and after us as well. When we act in unfaithfulness, we may very well lose the opportunity for that blessing.

12. Keeping in mind what we have learned for this chapter, answer how you would deal with the following scenarios?

    A. You have a friend who thinks that Christianity is all about following rules. They ask you why you would want to be involved is something like that. What would you tell them?

    B. You have been going to church for some time, but still do not feel God's presence in your life. What are some things you might need to look at changing?

---

13. What does will it mean for you to walk by faith in a relationship with God?

14. What is one area of your relationship with God you can work on?

Life Examples
JOE[48]

"No problem. You may use it. And I hope Fanta gets well soon." Mr. Bangura borrowed my bike. Neighbors do that sort of thing often here in West Africa. Few have cars. Some have motorcycles. My neighbor did not even have a bike on which to visit his sick wife across town. So I lent him mine.

He returned it once. He returned it twice. But the third day "He'll prob'ly return it tomorrow morning," thought I. Tomorrow came and went. No bike. I need my bike. You see, diesel is much more expensive than rice. I save money and stay in shape by pedaling across town rather than driving. "After Bible study," I announced to my wife, "I'm going to Bangura's to get my bike back!"

Once a week, I would go to another neighbor's place to read and discuss the book of Luke. That day, bikeless, we happened to be in Luke chapter six and discussed this passage:

> Give to everyone who asks you, and when a man has taken what belongs to you, don't demand it back. Treat men exactly as you would like them to treat you and if you lend only to those from whom you hope to get your money back, what credit is that to you? Even sinners lend to sinners and expect to get their money back. No, you are to love your enemies and do good and lend without hope of return. Your reward will be wonderful and you will be sons of the Most High. For he is kind to the ungrateful and the wicked! (Philips; underline mine)

Now I had a problem. I wanted my bike and Jesus said, "Don't demand it back." Some people may assign this coincidence to chance. I will not argue with them for it is more than either of us can know. But what if God arranged for me to see this Scripture just before getting my bike so that I could, if I chose, become more like Him in character? What if this coincidence was God getting up, so to speak, and saying, "Joe, come on, let's take another walk together"? If so, my subsequent actions - were they translated into words - would say something like, "Isn't there anything better to do, Father?"

After the Bible study, I went straight home. I didn't ask for the bike; I was not yet sure what to do. The next day, another neighbor asked to borrow my bike. "Hmm," thought I, "Maybe I can have my cake and eat it too. I will ask him to ask Bangura for the bike and get it back that way? Self, you are a genius!" But then I remembered that the text said, "lend without hope of return." "Bother!" I said inwardly, "I am not even supposed to expect my own bike back!" So I told my other neighbor that someone else has the bike and that neither one of us can use it now.

"Oh! Hang it all!" I prayed the next day, "I can't pretend I don't expect the bike back. I want it back; I should get it back; it's mine for crying out loud!" Then, I employed all my training in Linguistics and Bible translation to find a loophole. I got my grammars, looked at lexicons, conjugated and cogitated. In the end I was disappointed to find that all 11 of my English Bibles and all 4 of my French Bibles and the Maninka translation done by my colleagues were indeed faithful to the Greek text.

Next, I conducted some ethnographic interviews to determine if borrowing and lending in Maninka culture were significantly different than that of Jesus' own culture. I wanted so much to be able to honestly say something like,"In the Maninka culture, the borrower is expected to keep the item in order to guarantee a continuation in the relationship with the owner who must one day ask for his or her item back. If the owner fails to ask for the item back, it means that the relationship in his or her mind is not even worth the value of the item borrowed." But no, borrowing in both Jesus' culture and Maninka culture is the same. Jesus' teaching applies to me, Bangura, and my bike.

So there was no loophole. I could not ask for the bike and have a good conscience. So I determined to remain mum. But it was not easy. Bangura was my neighbor. A typical morning greeting before my bike was borrowed went like this:

Bangura: [Smiles] Ousman, [that's what they call me], I ni soo ma. Joe, you and the morning!
Joe: [Smiles] Nba, I ni soo ma. Hey! You and the morning!
Bangura: Tana ma sii? Was there no evil in last night's sitting?
Joe: Tana si te. There is no evil at all.
Joe: Tana te i ye? Is there no evil for you?
Bangura: Tana si te. There is no evil at all.
Joe: Tana te I moso la? Is there no evil with your wife?
Bangura: Tana si te a la. There is no evil at all with her.

It was more and more difficult to be at peace. One day I was walking to town in the African sun. My legs were logs and my forehead was a waterfall of perspiration. Zip! My bike passed me by with Bangura on it! He said nothing. He saw me but chose not to acknowledge it. There was no, "Oh my neighbor you must be wilting in this sun. Take your bike back. I am so sorry!" Nope. All I heard was an angry growl coming from deep within myself. Now see what morning greetings were like without my bike. [The words in brackets are my silent thoughts.]

Bangura's wife: (long since recovered from her illness and having returned home, smiles.) Ousman, I ni soo ma. Joe, you and the morning!
 Joe: (not smiling) Nba, I ni soo ma. You and the morning.
Bangura's wife: Tana ma sii? Was there no evil in last night's sitting?
Joe: Tana si te. There is no evil at all. [Except that every night I have to pray for your scoundrel husband!]
Joe: Tana te i ye? Is there no evil for you?
Bangura's wife: Tana si te. There is no evil at all.
Joe: Tana te I ke la? Is there no evil with your husband? [angry growl!]
Bangura's wife: Tana si te a la. There is no evil at all with him.
Joe: [oh that is too bad!]

Clearly something was wrong. The produce of my obedience to Jesus should not be [angry growl] malice. So I asked God what the problem was and returned to Luke 6. And there it was. How could I miss it? "Then [when we lend without expecting to get anything back] your REWARD will be GREAT, and you will be sons of the Most High "Jesus has a great reward in mind for us. It is a joy to be a child of the Most High! But my heart was set on a cheap bike made in China. I had not thought about becoming like my merciful Father and enjoying Him forever; I wanted my bike back! "Hello Joe!" s aid my soul, "Forget the bike! There is something bigger and Someone better here!"
So there is. I know because peace returned. There is no more growl. And best of all, I want to keep walking with my heavenly Father and become just like Him.
What? Did I ever get my bike back? Are you still thinking about that?

Chapter 3
FAITH IN OUR WORK PLACE
"...whatever you do, do all to the glory of God." (1 Cor. 10:31)

The Question of Faith
Daniel - Daniel 6:1-28

Slowly I made my way up the stairs to the roof. There I paused and gazed across the expanse of the city of Persepolis, the capital of Persia. All around me houses and buildings spread out, testifying to the great wealth and might of the Persian Empire. Those who wished to flatter me said this was my city. They said, next to the king, I was the most powerful man here, or in the whole empire, for that matter. But I knew I was just a man like any other man, and in some ways even less. I am a stranger, a foreigner. Although I had lived here or in the city of Babylon for most of my adult life, my heart would forever be in Jerusalem.

Jerusalem had once been such a great and beautiful city, and most important of all, it had been the city of the temple of God, the house of the Lord. In my mind's eye I could still see its beauty and splendor. But it was the presence of God that had always filled me with awe. As I thought of the temple, I felt heaviness within my heart, for I remembered its destruction. It was gone now, destroyed years ago by the Babylonians when I was but a lad. Now Jerusalem was only a mockery of what it once had been before the fall. Even though the first group of returnees (who had gone back to rebuild Jerusalem), had been there a number of years now, it was still said to be little more than a clutter of huts amongst a heap of ruins. Yet even with all of the conveniences and comforts that I enjoy here in the capital city, I would give them all up in a moment to live there in the ruins of the city of God. I let out a soft sigh, for even as I thought of going back to Jerusalem, I knew that I could not. My place was here, and here I must stay. It was here that I could best serve both my king and my God. My position of authority had its responsibilities as well as its privileges.

I turned and walked through the door that leads into the room which I thought of as my prayer chamber. In reality it was nothing more than a small enclosure I had constructed on the roof of my house. It was neither large nor plush; in fact, it was rather bare. It could become extremely hot during the heat of the day, but I didn't come here to relax. I came here to pray. I came here because this room had something that made it ideal for my purposes- solitude.

With all the pressures and responsibilities, it was extremely difficult for me to find the time or the space to be alone. Something always seemed to demand my attention. I eventually learned that if I was going to have time or a place to pray, I was going to have to make it happen. So I had this room built, and set aside three times a day to talk with God. At first things had often gotten in the way, but I learned the hard way how vital it was for me to have this time with God. The servants by now knew that when I went up to this room, I was not to be disturbed unless the world was coming to an end, and maybe not even then.

As I had done so many times before, I knelt down to pray. Only this time it was different. This time I was breaking the law. It's not that I made a practice of breaking the law. In fact, I worked very hard to avoid anything that might bring dishonor to God's name. I tried to be very conscientious in my service to the king, and to do my best. I did this, not to gain praise or promotion, but so that I might honor God. I make no secret of my belief in God, but neither do I try to force my views on others. Rather I try to show them what a life dedicated to God looks like. I then try to use the opportunities God provides to share His truth. My one goal is to please the Lord. Because of this, He has blessed me in all I've done and had brought me favor with those I serve.

Not everyone, however, viewed me with pleasure. While some have been drawn to the Lord, others resent me and my God. They don't like the fact that I am different from them. They see me as strange and suspicious because my unwillingness to indulge in the same things they do. They accuse me of being a self-righteous, narrow-minded, fanatic fool. They resent my good fortune. They do not see it as God's blessing, but as undeserved luck, and they are determined to drag me down. I have known of their animosity, and I do my best to be at peace with them. But I know that even if I try to appease them, to become like them, they won't be satisfied. I also know that I can not become like them and still be pleasing to God. So I carry on as best I can and trust that God will take of me.

It isn't always easy to let go of worry. I know my enemies are seeking to destroy me. They have tried to entice me into immorality and dishonesty. Sometimes the attacks had been blunt and obvious, while other times they had been subtle and very appealing. I have only escaped by determining not to take even one step in the wrong direction, no matter how small that step might seem. Having failed in their attempts at trapping me, they began to dig into my actions, both past and present, to find something they could twist around and use to accuse me. I have had to be extra careful, so that my actions could stand the closest scrutiny. But most of all I pray. I know where my real source of strength and protection is found; and the more I feel attacked, the more I pray. Through it all, God not only protected me, He continues to bless me as well.

Lately though, it seems that my enemies may have gotten the upper hand. They have taken my strength and turned it into an apparent liability. They have convinced the king to make a law that forbids the praying to anyone or any god except the king for one month. Any violators are to be killed by being thrown into a pit filled with hungry lions. This has presented me with a dilemma. I know that not only does God desire me to spend time in prayer with Him, but that is also where my strength is found. God's law enjoins me to continually seek Him.[1] It would be wrong for me to go without prayer for even one day, let alone a whole month.

On the other hand, to continue on in prayer would be a violation of the king's law. I know Darius to be a good king, and that the law has probably been duped upon him by my enemies, but that didn't change the fact that it is law. Once a Persian king has signed something into law, it can not be changed. If I were to be found praying, even my position in the court and friendship with the king couldn't save me.

I was faced with some difficult choices: 1. I could disobey God's law and stop seeking and praying to Him for a month so that I could obey the king's law. This, to me, is unacceptable. I can not deny my God. I could try and justify it by saying that it would only be for a while, but I know it would still be a betrayal against God.

2. I can go to the king and complain and try to force him to change the situation for my benefit. I'm not sure it would even do any good, but I might be able to find some loop hole I could take advantage of. This was possible, but I felt this demand for special treatment would compromise my witness for God. Besides, I had discovered long ago that when I tried to take matters into my own hands, I usually just made a mess of things.

3. I can try to hide my prayers so I can fool others into thinking I am obeying the king's laws while secretly being disobedient. This might work, but I feel it would be dishonest. I would be living a lie. I would be disobeying one of God's commands in order to obey another. This would not be right, and it would show I had little faith in God. This left only the last choice.

4. I can continue to do what I believe to be right. I won't flaunt my prayers, but neither will I hide them. I will put my faith in God, and demonstrate it by continuing to be obedient to God's will, trusting that He will take care of me. If I have to pay the price, I will do so willingly, and pray that I might give God glory through it.

As usual, I started my prayers with praise then I brought my concerns before God. I asked God for wisdom and deliverance. I quoted David from the Psalms:

"As for me, I shall call upon God, and the LORD will save me. Evening and morning and at noon, I will complain and murmur, and He will hear my voice. He will redeem my soul in peace from the battle which is against me, for they are many who strive with me."[2]

As I continued to pray, loud voices from below began to drift up to me. The officials who had devised the plan to bring me down had barged into the house, and were ignoring the protests of my servants as they made their way to the roof. I thought of what I should do and decided to continue to pray. One the officials swung open the door to my prayer chamber and said in a falsely pleasant voice, "Oh, Daniel, we were just passing by and thought we'd stop in." Then he stopped, and with a mock look of surprise said, "Daniel are you praying to your God? Surely you know of the law against such an offense." He mimicked a look of despair and said in a mocking voice, "Although it grieves us deeply, I'm afraid we will have to report this to the king." Then, with smiles on their faces, the officials made their way back out of the house, already congratulating themselves on my demise. I neither looked up nor made any comment. I just continued to pray.

It took a little longer than I had expected for the summons to come requiring me to report to the king. Darius must have been stalling, hoping to find a way to spare me. But I was sure that the officials who had written the law had left no loop holes for me to escape through. So in the end the king was force to arrest me. I decided to make no excuses as I stood before the king. Instead I said, "You, oh great Darius, are my king, and it has been my pleasure to serve you, but I must obey my God." I could tell that Darius was distraught at condemning me, but he had no choice. Surprisingly, I was not afraid as they led me to the lion's pit. God's peace was with me. I knew that He could deliver me if He so chose. But even should He choose not to I will die giving glory and honor to Him. As the guards grabbed me to throw me to the lions, I decided to neither plead nor fight. Instead, I decided to pray.

Daniel's prayer did not spare him from the lion's den, but God did protect him in the midst of the lions. God sent an angel that closed the lions' mouths and Daniel was not harmed. The next morning King Darius had Daniel taken out of the pit and restored him to his position with even greater honor. Then it was Daniel's enemies who were thrown to the lions. Their wickedness ended up costing them their lives. Darius then made a decree that the entire kingdom was to fear and honor Daniel's God. [3] Daniel's faith not only protected him in his time of need, it ended up glorifying the name of God across the entire Persian Empire.

A Closer Look

Sometimes trying to live out our faith in the workplace can seem like being thrown to the lions. For Daniel this was a literal experience. It may have appeared that Daniel was foolish to continue to pray when it would have been so easy not to. Why would he put his faith in God, or to remain faithful in his service to God, when it could cost him so much? It could have cost Daniel not only his position, his means of income, and his comfort. It could have cost him his life. Why would he do such a foolish thing?

Now when we look at the rest of the story, we see that it was not a foolish thing after all. Not only did God spare Daniel's life, but through this experience God bestowed upon Daniel even more blessings, while at the same time destroying his enemies. God did not spare Daniel the experience of being thrown into the lions' pit; rather, He displayed His power in the very midst of the pit. And because of this, not only was Daniel delivered, but God's glory was displayed for all to see. It may have been easier for Daniel if God had kept him from having to face the lions in the first place. But because of Daniel's willingness to act in faith God's glory and power were proclaimed far and wide. What if Daniel had played it safe? What would have been lost had he chosen to bow to the pressure?

From our perspective of the story, it is easy to see that Daniel made the right choice, but Daniel made that choice before it was evident that God was going to deliver him. Daniel made the choice expecting that he would probably be torn apart. Why would he do that? Because Daniel had one primary goal for his life, and it was not for his own personal well-being or comfort. Daniel's primary goal was to glorify God. If glorifying God meant being thrown into the lion's pit, then so be it.

When we look at Daniel, we see a great example of what it means to live by faith in the context of one's work or occupation. Daniel's example doesn't start with the willingness to die; rather it starts with a willingness to live in a manner that gives glory to God. For Daniel this meant that he must start with striving to do the best he could at the tasks he was given. Daniel was known for being faithful in his service, not just to God, but to the king as well.

This did a number of things for Daniel. First off, it gave him a more sympathetic audience. We are told that Daniel found favor with those who were over him.[4] Daniel was not a slacker or complainer. He did not just do his job, he did his best. Because of this (and God's blessing) when he asked for consideration in regard to his beliefs, Daniel generally found a favorable response. Secondly, it gave credibility to Daniel's witness. When Daniel's enemies sought to find something to use to discredit Daniel, we are told they came up empty-handed. They could find nothing to blacken Daniel's name, no corruption or negligence. They were unable to find anything for one simple reason- Daniel always did his best. He did his best, not for promotion or reward, but for the glory of God. Daniel's goal was to give God glory, and that was what determined how he did his work. He did not just seek his own pleasure, he sought God's pleasure. Because of this, God blessed him in his work.

For Daniel, living for God meant more than just working hard, it also meant demonstrating his commitment to God. Daniel did not do this by preaching to those around him. He did it by showing them a life that was holy to God. When others were indulging in a luxurious lifestyle, Daniel determined not to defile himself with things that were not of God.[5] At first the others thought him to be foolish, but as God blessed him, the others began to see the wisdom of Daniel's choices. He also made sure to give God the glory for any successes he enjoyed, and for the abilities with which God had blessed him.[6] All of this came back to Daniel's goal for living. It was not about gaining wealth or privilege. It was not about receiving glory or honor. His goal was to give God glory.

Daniel did not have to force his opinions on those around him. Because of his lifestyle and because of the way God blessed his life, when others faced situations they did not know how to deal with, they came looking for Daniel to seek his advice.[7] When Daniel was asked, he spoke the truth of God - even when he knew it would not be popular. Daniel lived God's truth and spoke God's truth, and let God take care of the results. If they listened to his advice, he gave God the glory. If they ignored his advice, he gave that over to God as well.

As far as we know, Daniel never preached one sermon. Yet because of his witness and because he put his faith in God, even in difficult situations, the Lord was able to use him in mighty ways. Because of Daniel's witness, God's glory and honor was proclaimed throughout the entire Persian Empire. This did not happen right away. Daniel went through years of toil without any apparent result. At times he was ridiculed or persecuted for his faith. God did not keep Daniel from being thrown into the lion's pit. He did, however, protect him in the lion's pit. Did Daniel have times of doubt, times of frustration, times of weakness, and even failure? Probably, he was, after all, human like us. But through it all Daniel continued to remember what his goal was. He was there to glorify God. The people that worked with Daniel knew him to be a servant of God.

There is one other thing we see in Daniel's life that played a major part in Daniel's success in his life and work- prayer. Even with the demanding responsibilities of Daniel's life, he set aside three times a day to pray. I believe that much of Daniel's courage, wisdom and fortitude came out of his times of prayer. Daniel understood the power and the necessity of prayer. When he had no place to pray, Daniel made a place. When he did not have time to pray, Daniel made time. Prayer became so important to Daniel that even when it came down to a choice between prayer and life, Daniel chose prayer. When there was a choice between comfort and holiness, Daniel chose holiness. When there was a choice between truth and popularity, Daniel chose truth. And because of Daniel's choices, God not only used him in a mighty way, God blessed his work as well.

Digging Deeper

What does walking by faith in the work place look like in the 21st century? There are many things that have changed since the time of Daniel, but many of the principles are still the same. It all starts with one central question; "What is the goal of your life?" Now you probably have a number of goals for your life, as I do for mine. Some of them are noble, and some of them not so noble. But if we want to walk in faith, then it all starts with one central goal - that my life would honor and glorify God. If this is the goal of our life, then it will affect everything we do, including how we function at work.

Why would we make such a goal? For three reasons: 1. Until we surrender out life to Christ, we will never experience the power and joy of Christ living and working within us. That is where Christianity really begins, not in being good or going to church, but in giving our life to Christ. 2. Striving to please God is the natural response of someone who experiences the life-changing result of having a personal relationship with Jesus Christ. We want to please Him, not only for what He has done for us in the past, but because of the benefit we receive now. 3. What God owns, He blesses. Surrendering our life to God not only pleases Him, it is what is best for us.

Glorifying God may be our desire, but doing that in the work place can be very difficult. Let us start by looking at our motivation for work.

1. What is your motivation for work?

Read Colossians 3:22-25 and Ephesians 6:5-8.

Paul here is speaking to slaves, or servants, and while we are not slaves (although it may feel like that at times), many of the principles are still the same.

2. What is the motivation Paul gives for us to work hard?

3. God's Word tells us that He wants us to be in subjection to those in authority over us,[8] but how should we deal with employers who are unfair or unjust? (1 Peter 2:18-19)

One might wonder why God would be interested in how we fill out paper work, dig a ditch or fill an order. Well, it is not the work itself with which God is concerned. God is not nearly as concerned about the benefit our work brings to our employer as He is in the benefit it brings to us. I am not talking here of money or promotion, but of our character and our witness. When we humble ourselves before others, even those who don't deserve it, this is pleasing to God. It allows Him to work in our lives to shape and mold us. God is able to work, even through non-Christians, to change our heart if we allow Him to. It also gives Him an opportunity to touch the hearts of those around us.

4. What is the motivation Paul gives for obeying those under whom we serve?
(1 Tim. 6:1)

Employers are going to be more lenient with a good employee than they are with an average or poor employee. This then may allow you more freedom in being able to express your faith at work. It will also give your words more credibility. If you are not showing integrity, commitment, and a willingness to sacrifice for others in your own life, then people are not likely to listen to you when you speak of living for God. Working hard will give you more opportunities, but that in itself will not glorify God. It is what you do with the opportunities that will give God glory or not. Nor is it only employees that God gives direction to.

5. What are some instructions God's Word has for employers or managers? (Prov. 3:27; Eph. 6:9)

Daniel not only worked hard, he also demonstrated his faith at work. You do not have to preach or lecture to people to express your faith; in fact, it is generally better if you do not. How we live our life is usually the best testimony we can give. Now I am not saying that we should not share the gospel. We should, God wants us to proclaim His gospel. But that generally is not the best place to start, especially not at work. Showing them a life that is different is where we need to start. But this requires that you live a life that is different from the rest of the world, and that you show it at work. God tells us that our lives are to be holy because He is holy, but what does a holy (set apart) life look like? Let us start by looking at the Ten Commandments.

Read Exodus 20:2-17.
Let us look at each of the commandments, and try to apply them to our work.

6. What will it mean at work for you to have no other Gods but God? (Ex. 20:3)

7. What things may become idols for us at work? (Ex. 20:4-6)

8. To use God's name in vain, means to lower its dignity. What are some things we might do at work that lowers God's name? (Ex. 20:7)

9. How can we make sure to have time for rest and worship amidst the demands of our work? (Ex. 20:8-11)

10. How can our work sometimes prevent us from honoring our parents or taking care of our family? (Ex. 20:12)

11. Jesus tells us in Matthew 5 that the command not to murder not only refers to taking a person's life, but of taking a person's dignity by what we say. What are some of the behaviors or types of speech found at work that can drain the life from people? (Ex. 20:13)

12. Jesus also let us know that the command not to commit adultery forbids more than the actual act of adultery but the mind set that leads to it as well. What can you do at work to protect yourself from falling into this sin? (Ex. 20:14)

13. Keeping in mind that Jesus told us that these commands deal not just with the actual act, but the attitude as well, what are some different ways that people can steal from: employers, other employees, costumers? (Ex. 20:15)

14. How can the demands of work pressure us to compromise on the truth? (Ex. 20:16)

15. How did Daniel handle it when he was told to do something he felt was wrong?

16. What kind of things can we find ourselves coveting at work? (Ex. 20:17)

These commands do not cover all the multitude of challenges and decisions we may face in the work place, but they do give us an idea of what God is looking for from us. It is true that we are not under the old law, but we are under the law of faith,[9] or the law of Christ.[10] This means that for us the question is not, "Is this something the law forbids?" The question is, "Is this something Christ would have me do?"

Daniel decided to cut himself off from things others indulged in, not because they were necessarily evil, but because they would interfere with his relationship with God. He had a right to them, but he gave up that right so that he might please God.

17. What are some things you have a right to, but that can interfere with your relationship with God?

In dealing with others, the standard God has set up for us is not, "What is required under law?" But rather, "What is required under love?" Christ told us that the second greatest commandment is that we would love our neighbors, or in this case; our fellow workers, our employees, or our employers.

Read 1 Corinthians 13:4-7.

If you are like most people you probably have room for improvement in many areas of showing love. Rather than trying to fix everything, focus rather on one area at a time. Pray and ask God to point out what area He wants you to work on. When He convicts you of where you need to improve, focus there and be patient with yourself. The standard God sets is high, but He is patient and forgiving. Remember that how we deal with failure can at times be just as valuable of a witness as doing it right in the first place.

---

18. What is one area of love you can work at improving this week at work?

We must also remember that the standard God sets is for us. It is not our job to judge those around us. That is God's job.[11]

19. Whose job is it to convict the world of sin? (John 16:7-8)

If there is a Christian brother or sister who is acting in a manner that is bringing shame to the name of Christ, then we may need to confront them, but even that must be done in humility and love.

20. What does Jesus say is our primary job? (Matt. 5:13-16)

21. What does it mean for us to be salt and light in our work place?

If you are working at showing love and demonstrating a different kind of lifestyle, then you are not going to have to corner people to tell them about Jesus. When they run into situations they cannot handle, they will come to you. Then you will have the opportunity to share the truth of God's Word. Do not preach or judge, just respond to their questions with God's truth, in humility and love, and you are not likely to offend them.

They may not follow your advice, but leave it in the hands of God. When Daniel was called in to interpret the dream of King Nebuchadnezzar, he humbly told the king that God's message was a warning. If the king did not humble himself before God he would be struck with madness. Daniel advised him to turn from his sins before it was too late. Because of how Daniel presented the message, the king did not react negatively to Daniel, but neither did he follow Daniel's advice. It was not until later, when God actually struck him for a time with the madness, that the king acknowledged the truth of Daniel's wisdom.[12]

22. What is God's promise to those who strive to be obedient to Him? (Deut. 28:8-13)

This is God's promise. But keep in mind that it may take time, and it does not mean that we will not face difficult situations. We must remember our main goal. Walking in faith in the work place may bring you ridicule and discomfort. It may cost you privileges, promotion, and even your job. But like Daniel, if we remain faithful, God can use our difficulties for His glory, and we will receive His blessing in the end.

23. Keeping in mind what we have learned in this lesson, how you would deal with the following scenarios?

A. You have a co-worker who you know desperately needs to hear of the love and forgiveness of God. You do not feel comfortable preaching to them, so where do you start?

B. You have been reading your Bible at break times, and your supervisor comes up and tells you that someone has complained. He tells you that he wants you to stop so that you will not offend the other person. What should you do?

24. What will it mean for you to walk by faith in the work place?

25. What is one area at work that you can work on?

Life Examples
Tom[13]

"I know that God has placed me in the school working as a custodian so that I, along with Pastor Andy, can help the kids at this school and encourage them to not take the path that I chose some 25 years ago. It was in this very town and this very school that I started drinking and doing things that were wrong and definitely not what God wanted for me. I spent the next 16 to 18 years living a life without Jesus or love in my heart.

I now know that everything I went through during that time, and every job that I have had, is now being used for His glory, that I might help the youth of this very same community and school today. This job I have is not merely a job, but it is the mission field that God has placed me in to bring Him glory and honor. And maybe, just maybe, save some of these kids from taking the path that I did, and therefore saving them from the life I know oh, so too well.

1. Why am I at this job?
    A. I am here because God placed me here!
    B. I am here to first and foremost bring glory to God.
    C. God has put me here to let others see the love of Jesus through me to all people.

2. How do I let others see Jesus through me?
    For me, I am not just another staff person at the school. I am there to be a man of God (who is real) that the kids as well as my co-workers can see and come to for help. This help may be through guidance, advice, a shoulder to cry on, and even being someone that they can come to just to complain about their bad days or home issues.

3. How do I keep my faith at work?
    A. First and foremost, it starts in the morning at home. That is my personal time with Jesus. I start with devotions and prayer. I read the Word everyday before anything else. I spend time in prayer -- I ask for forgiveness for my sins from the day before and ask for help with whatever the day may bring ahead. The biggest thing I have learned to ask for is for the Spirit to be with me instantly when needed. I have found at work especially, I don't have time to run and find a place to pray about things that happen at work which I have to react to right then. This is when I need God's Spirit the most. I need His Spirit to guide me to do what will be the right thing for God and for me, as well as others. (Instant decisions are the toughest.)
    B. The second thing I do is when I get to work I try to say a prayer alone in the building. I ask for God to bind Satan from my workplace today, that His Spirit will fill the building, and all who enter will see and feel His presence, whether through me or not. I try to do this before I get started for the day at work.
    C. Thirdly, I have to remember that when things happen they are not a personal attack on me! (I struggle with this a lot.) It is Satan attacking what Jesus is doing in and through me. If I am in a good and strong personal relationship with Jesus, then I can know when things happen they are not aimed at me. It is about Christ in me. That is what I can understand and feel better about. (Note: I learned this last year from Max Lucado's book, "It's Not About Me," which I strongly urge everyone to read.)
    D. At work with people I am in contact with I really try to look for opportunities to help them. This means I don't just do my job, but I really try to help those around me, seeking an opportunity to do something for them that normally wouldn't happen. I try to greet people and get to know them by talking with them (this is God stretching me). I try

to be positive when others are being negative. There is always something to say positive about anything. I try to be there to comfort and console when someone is in a crisis. If the opportunity arises, I pray for them, or at least tell them I will pray for them (then do it). I check back with them later to see how they are doing. Always following up with them shows them you still care. We have to build relationships with the people around us before we can reach out to them.

E. I do not go preaching at people on how they should be living, or on how they should be doing this or that. But I try to let those around me see Jesus in me by my actions (I am a terrible speaker and talker.) I have found my actions speak louder than words. We have too many hypocrites for me to just say I am a Christian, or I believe in God. I try to show my Christianity by being a "doer," and helping others in need. Showing the love of God leads to opportunities for me to then share about my faith.

F. When I have done something wrong, or felt I reacted wrongly, it usually bothers me all the rest of the day (sometimes through the night). I will make an attempt to apologize to that person. (As soon as I have gathered the courage or Jesus has worked on me long enough.)

G. This I have found at every job I have ever had! DO NOT HANG OUT WITH GOSSIPERS. Gossip is the most damaging thing in the workplace. Fight all gossip. It will only lead you into an ugly situation and bring you down. Those who hang in that circle can never really be good at sharing their faith, and expect others to believe it.

H. And when I get up in the morning, it is a new day with a fresh, clean slate.

Chapter 4
FAITH IN OUR HARDSHIP
"But as for me, I trust in You, O LORD, I say, 'You are my God.'" (Ps. 31:14)

The Question of Faith
Silas - Acts 16:1-30

It was hard to tell if my eyes were even open or not. It was so dark that no matter how hard I strained, I couldn't see a thing. The darkness seemed to press in upon me from all sides, trying to crush me beneath its weight. While my eyes were of no use to me, the rest of my senses were working all too well. The stench of the place was over whelming. There was a musty dampness that seemed to hang in the air, but surpassing even that, was the odor of men held in captivity for too long. There were no sanitary or washing facilities here. The smell of bodies was mixed with the smell of fear, hopelessness and death. At first the odors kept me on the edge of sickness, but eventually I became accustomed enough to them that I could push them to the back of his mind. The sounds, however, were another matter entirely.

From the other cells lost in the darkness, I could hear some of the other prisoners. Some were moaning in pain from the injuries they had received while being interrogated. Others were weeping softly or talking to themselves in the sing-song voice of the half insane. Still others were cursing or shouting insolence. Worse than the voices of the other prisoners, was the sound of scurrying little feet in the darkness all around me. I had never liked rats when I could see them, and I liked them less now that I couldn't. It made my very skin crawl and it was all I could do to keep from screaming at them, for all the good that would do. From time to time I could feel one of them run across my legs or brush against my arm. I tried to strike out at them, but the rats seemed to know just how far my chains would let me reach.

I could hear Paul shift about on the hard floor beside me trying to ease some of the discomfort and pain. It did him little good. His feet, like mine were secured in stocks that chafed against our ankles. Our arms were locked in manacles chained to the floor, the cold steal cutting into our wrists. We were secured in such a way to prevent us from being able to lay back. At the present this was just as well anyway. Our backs were swollen and bleeding from the beating we had received a few hours before. They had stripped off our cloths and lashed us with rods. Each stroke brought searing pain and left an angry welt upon our back. Under the continual blows the welts eventually broke open leaving our backs raw and bleeding. The pain had been almost more than I could bear.

This was not quite how I had envisioned this journey in the service of the Lord. I had imagined this journey as a grand and glorious adventure, winning souls for Jesus. And if I were to suffer for Christ's sake, I would be noble and brave. It had seemed so easy back then. Only now I didn't feel so noble or brave. I felt dirty, hungry and tired. I hurt all over and I was afraid. No, this was not what I thought serving God would be like at all. I had been so excited. When the Paul came to me and said, "Silas how would you like to accompany me on a journey?" I was eager to go and I must admit, even a bit proud at being the one Paul had chosen. Now I as sat in my pain and my fears, tears running down my cheeks, I felt anything but proud. Maybe it would have been better if Paul had chosen someone else.

The journey began well enough. Paul and I traveled from one city to the next, visiting the churches Paul had established earlier. Although the travel had been hard, it had been an exciting time. I remember thinking, "Now this is what serving God is all about." Then things started going wrong. Travel arrangements fell through. We ran into sickness and other obstacles. I began to wonder if this had all been a big mistake. Maybe we should just go home, but Paul had said, that God had been clear about us going on the journey, so this must be God's way of telling us we needed to go in a different direction. We needed to continue on and pray for God to give us guidance.

When we got to Troas, a city in the very northwest corner of Asia Minor, we ran out of road, and I felt that we had run out of options as well. But that very night, Paul received a vision that we should continue going northwest across the Aegean Sea to Macedonia. When we got to Philippi, the leading city of Macedonia, Paul began to share the gospel. A slave girl who was possessed by a demon began following us, crying out that we were bond servants of the Most High God. This wasn't so bad at first, but as she continued to do it day after day, it got on my nerves, and even Paul lost his patience. He commanded the demon to come out of her, and it did.

At first this seemed like a great thing. The girl was overjoyed at being freed from the demon; and all people were amazed and impressed. All that is, except the girl's masters. The demon, while tormenting her, had seemed to give her the power to foretell the future, which in turn had brought in a lot of income for her owners. Without the demon, the income was gone and the owners were not happy about it. They dragged us before the authorities and put forth a number of charges against us. It was then that we were beaten with rods and then taken to our prison cell that we might enjoy all its joys and comforts.

As I sat here, I began to wonder what the future might hold. It didn't seem very promising. How could God have allowed us to come to such a predicament? Had we not been serving Him as best we knew? It seemed like such a waste that we should be stuck here in prison when we could be doing great things for the Lord. It just didn't make any sense.

I turn to Paul, or at least to where I assumed he was, and asked, "What do we do now?"

Paul was silent for a moment and then replied, "Well, I think dancing is out of the question, but I suppose some singing might be in order."

At first I could not believe my ears. Had I heard wrong, or had the beating driven Paul from his senses? "Sing?" I said, "Why would we want to sing?"

"Well," Paul replied, "I have found that singing helps to take my mind off of my problems. Besides, it is my favorite way to give God praise and to offer up thanksgiving."

I didn't want to sound ungodly, but I've got to say that at that moment, I was having a hard time finding anything for which to be thankful. I said to Paul, "You know that I want to be a man of faith, but it's so hard, especially right now."

"Yes," Was Paul's gently reply, "it is hard. It's hard for me as well. But let me ask you something Silas, when you gave your life to Christ and vowed to serve Him, did you only mean that for when it would be easy?" I felt stung by the question and tried to reply, but Paul cut me off, "No, of course you didn't. But really it's not quite as hard as it may seem. Listen Silas, why did you come with me on this journey? What is your goal for this trip?"

I thought for a moment and then said, "Well, I must admit that some of it was for the excitement of going, but mostly I wanted to serve and glorify God."

"Is that still your goal?" Paul asked.

"Sure," I said, "It's my life's goal. Christ is Lord, and I want to please and glorify Him."

"Good," Paul said, and though I couldn't see him, I could tell he had a smile on his face. Paul then went on to ask, "Would it be your opinion that we have been following God's will up to this point?"

I thought about it and then answered hesitantly, "I think we've tried to, at least as far as we knew anyway. We may have made a wrong turn now and then, but I think we've tried our best to follow God's will."

"And I would agree with you." Paul went on, "Now let me ask you. Do you believe that God is able to deal with anything or anyone who stands in His way?"

"Of course," I said with no hesitation this time. "There is nothing impossible with God. You're the one who told me that."

"So I did," Paul said with a chuckle. "It's nice to know you've been listening. Let me ask you one last question. Do you believe God loves you?"

"How can I doubt it," I responded, "with all He has done for me?"

"Alright then," Paul said, "if we've been following God to the best of our abilities, then we must also believe He has led us here to Philippi, and even to the encounter with the slave girl and her masters."

I decided that made sense and nodded my head, not that Paul could see it. He went on, "And if we believe God is able to overcome any obstacles then we must also believe that He has brought us to our present situation, or at the very least has allowed it to happen for His purposes."

I was uncomfortable with this, for it seemed to me rather harsh, but before I could think of a response Paul continued on, "And if we believe that He loves us, then His purpose must not be just to let us suffer. He must have some bigger plan. What that plan is, I must confess I haven't a clue as yet, but our past tells us it will be for our benefit."

"Our past?" I asked. "I'm not sure I follow you."

"Think back on our journey," Paul said, "and even before that. Has God not always taken care of our needs? Has he not stepped in when we faced difficulties, and guided and protected us? Has He ever failed us Silas?"

I thought of all the different times God had come through right when we needed Him to. "No," I said, "I suppose He hasn't."

"Nor will He now," Paul asserted. "God has not changed. He has not abandoned us, and He never will. So, not only can we be thankful for what He has done for us in the past, we can be thankful for His deliverance to come."

I thought of the chains on our legs and arms, of the gates and doors with their guards and asked, "How is He going to deliver us from this?"

"I have no idea," Paul replied. "That's His job to work out. And even if He doesn't, even if we end up stuck here and have to continue to suffer, or even die, we can still be thankful."

I shook my head and said, "I'm not sure I understand. It is true that with the way I'm feeling just now, death doesn't sound like such a bad thing. But why should we be thankful for suffering?" I asked Paul, "What do we have to be thankful for, sitting in this dungeon?"

"Silas," Paul said, "try to understand. There must be a reason we are here, and because of what we know about God, it must be for our benefit. Maybe it is to teach us something. Maybe it is to prepare us for some challenge ahead, I don't know and I don't need to know. You said yourself, our job is to please and glorify the Lord. If it is His desire that I am here, then this is where I want to be, and I will seek to glorify Him here. You see, we can either just suffer, or we can suffer for the Lord."

I thought back on my dreams of dying a glorious death and said, "I can understand the value of suffering for the Lord, but we weren't locked in here for proclaiming Christ. We've been shut up in this black pit because of the greed of the slave girl's owners, and because the authorities refuse to listen to reason. Not only can I not see any sense in it, I can't see how Christ is glorified, either."

"Our enemy, Silas, may wear different faces," Paul patently explained, "and he may use different means or reasons for his attacks, but he is still the same enemy and he is still trying to do the same thing. He is trying to keep us form serving and glorifying our God by taking our eyes off of the Lord and fixing them on ourselves. You see, suffering for the Lord isn't just about why suffering comes upon us, it is even more about how we respond to the suffering. How we got here isn't near as important as what we do now. If we focus on our problems, then we will accomplish nothing more that making ourselves miserable, and our suffering will have no benefit. On the other hand, if we can focus on honoring God, even in the midst of our suffering, then regardless of the cause of the hardship, we will be suffering for the Lord."

I guessed that made sense, but asked him," Couldn't we go for a different option, one that doesn't involve suffering at all?"

"I suppose we could try," replied Paul with a laugh, "but I doubt it would do any good. Hardship happens to us all. Your only real choice is how you are going to handle it. Take a moment," Paul said, "and listen to the voices around you."

I stopped and listened and over the whispered movements of our furry little cell mates, I could hear the other prisoners. Some were moaning and weeping, others were raging and cursing. It seemed I could even hear the silence of those who had given up, and were just waiting to die.

"Despair," Paul went on, "never really helps anyone. Not only does it make you and those around you miserable, it is a statement of disbelief in God. Defiance also usually gets us nowhere. But even should we, by our own efforts, be able to free ourselves from this prison, what will it have really gained us?"

"We would be free." I said, thinking this should have been clear to Paul as well. "We could be preaching and serving God

"True," Paul acknowledged, "and I'm all for leaving if that is God's will. But have we not already reasoned that God must have brought us here for a purpose? If God wanted to free us from this situation He could do it at any time. If it is God's will for us to be here at this time, then we will be far more pleasing to Him locked in these stocks than preaching on the streets. Is our goal and desire freedom, or pleasing God? As for serving Him and giving Him glory, we can do that in whatever situation we are in."

"How," I asked, "are we suppose to serve Him locked up in here?"

"We can serve Him," Paul answered, "by demonstrating our trust and faith in Him, and praising His name. The choice is up to you. You can weep in self-pity and despair, you can rage in defiance and determination or you sing out in praise and faith."

I thought about all Paul had said; about how God must have allowed us to be here for a reason, and that He must have a plan even now. I thought of the pain and discomfort I was in, and then of all that Christ had done for me. I thought of what I wanted most in life, and then I quietly asked Paul, "What song should we start with?"

Their voices began softly, but grew in strength and feeling as they sang. They went from praising God with their lips, to praising Him with all they had, including even their chains. As their voices swelled with warmth and emotion, the other prisoners grew still. The sound penetrated even the minds of those half mad, and brought a sense of peace that had long been lost. In the darkness and despair their songs became glimmers of light and hope. As the joy and praise penetrated the deepest corners of that prison, the Spirit of God filled the darkness, and the walls began to shake.

God caused an earthquake that opened the prison doors and made the chains to fall from Paul and Silas. The jailer, thinking they had all escaped was going to kill himself, but Paul intervened. He was then able to lead the jailer and his entire family to Christ. Paul and Silas' faith in the midst of hardship opened the door for God's praises to be heard far beyond their prison walls.

A Closer Look

What do you do when the world seems to be crashing in upon you? How do you walk in faith, when it seems that the God in whom you have put your faith, has turned His back on you? Dealing with hardship is something we all have in common. It is true that some people have faced more hardship than others, but fear, depression, and anxiety are not restricted only to the "big" problems. In fact, the actual size of the problem often has little to do with the amount of stress it may cause. When we feel overwhelmed by a problem, little or big, it has a tendency to dominate our life. This is true for all of us. The question of how to deal with hardship is equally important to us all, for we all have to face it from time to time.

The key to walking in faith in the midst of hardship is the same for small problems as it is for big ones. The place to start is not looking at the size of our problem, but at the size of our God. Henry Blackaby, in his study, Experiencing God, tells us that it is essential that we do not base our understanding of God from the context of our situation, but rather that we view our situation from the context of what we know of our God.[1]

Our situation is very unstable. It is continually changing. It is like a roller coaster: sometimes things are going up, and sometimes they are going down. If we base our understanding of God by how things are going for us, then we will never have a clear understanding of who God is. He will seem fickle and undependable. Sometimes He will seem good and caring, other times He will seem cold and distant. The truth is that God is always the same.[2] Our situation does not change who God is. It merely changes our perception of Him. If we start with what we know about God, and let that influence how we see what is going on in our lives, then not only will we have a clearer understanding of God, but we will also have a clearer and more reliable perspective on our life.

What then do we know about God? First off, scripture tells us that God loves us. He has demonstrated His love for us through the sacrifice of His Son.[3] Why would God love us so much? It is not because we deserve His love, but because love is a part of God's nature.[4] We are His creation and He loves us even though we do not deserve it. We do not have to earn God's love. He already loves us completely. Nothing we could do could make God love us more, for He already loves us 100%, right now. It also means that nothing we can do will remove that love. No matter what we do it will still be 100%. God's love never fades.[5] Our sins may put a barrier between us and God,[6] so that we can not feel His love, or experience the benefit of that love, but it is always there.

God's love for us is stronger than we will ever be able to understand, but it is not a soft love. Even in the midst of our sin God still loves us, but He loves us too much to let us remain there. God knows the damage sin does to our lives, so He disciplines us,[7] to bring us back to Him. God's discipline does not remove His love; rather, it is a part of His love. God knows the damage sin brings to our life, both for the here and now, and also for that which is eternal. Therefore, His love continues to draw us away from sin, even if it must cause us pain to do so. He may also allow hardship to prepare us for something ahead knowing that the blessing we will receive will out weigh the hardship we endure. This too is God's love.

Secondly, scripture also tells us that, God is all powerful. He created the heavens and the earth,[8] and in Him all things are held together.[9] There is nothing impossible with God.[10] There is no obstacle God can't overcome. There is no enemy that can stand against Him.[11] Nothing can happen apart from God allowing it to happen. This is not to say that everything that happens is God's will. God has given us the freedom to choose to follow Him or not.[12] Should we choose to ignore God's will, there are consequences for our actions. God allows them, but that does not mean they are His desire for us.

There are many other things scripture can tell us about God, but these two things alone can help us as we seek to understand what it means to walk by faith in times of hardship. Since God is all powerful, we can know that whatever it is that we face, God has allowed it to happen. God may purposely allow it to test us, to teach or to prepare us for some challenges ahead. It may also be that our trials were not a part of His will for us. They may be a result of our own rebellion and sin, or they may just come as a part of living in a fallen world. For whatever reason they came, they could not have happened if God did not allow them. This lets us know three things:

1. God is still in control. No matter how bad things look, they are not beyond God's ability to fix. If God allows something to happen, He has the power to bring solutions to the problem as well. Sometimes in the midst of a storm it is hard to see that there is any hope, but our Lord has the power to calm the storm with just one word. Sometimes all He is waiting for is for us to come to Him in faith and ask.

2. God has a plan. Nothing catches God off guard. Whether He causes something to happen or just allows it, He knows it is coming in advance, and He has both a plan and a purpose for what we are dealing with. This is why we may ask God to remove a hardship from us, but not get the answer we want. His answer may be, "No," or "Not yet," or we may not seem to get an answer at all. This does not mean God has forgotten us or that He is not concerned with our pain. It just means that removing the problem at this time would work against what God is trying to accomplish. Maybe there is some sin we have not dealt with. Maybe there is some lesson we have yet to learn. Maybe it has nothing to do with us, but involves what God is trying to do with someone else. Whatever the case, if God says, "No," or "Not yet," He has a good reason to do so.

On the one hand, this may seem to make it harder on us. God is not always going to answer our prayers the way we want Him to. He will answer our prayers, but He is not bound by our will or our reasoning. If our desires go against God's plan, it is our desires that will need to change. On the other hand, this actually makes things much easier for us. For it is not up to us to find the solution. We do not need to worry and fret over how to deal with the problem. God already has a plan.

3. God can work the situation out to our benefit. Since we know that God loves us with a love that never fades or changes, then we can know that He will not just hang us out to dry. He is not just playing with our lives for His amusement. God has a plan and His plan is for our benefit.

> "And we know that God causes all things to work together for good to
> those who love God, to those who are called according to His purpose."
> (Rom. 8:28)

Notice it says, "all things," not just the things God originally planned for us, but even the problems we brought upon ourselves. God has a plan for taking whatever we face and using it for our good. Our good, however, does not necessarily mean our pleasure. Paul goes on to say that we may still face persecution, famine and even death, but even these things cannot take away our victory that is found in the love of God.[13]

While most people remember the first part of Romans 8:28, it is the second part that is the key. God's promise to "work all things to the good" is contingent upon our loving Him and seeking His purpose for our lives. If we love ourselves more than the Lord, or if we are set on our own purposes for our life, then we have no promise that God will work our problems to our good. This is not because God no longer loves us, but because; 1. God is not going to help us down a path that is leading away from Him and to our destruction. 2. It is our seeking His will in our life that opens the door for God to bring about the good He has in store for us.

The key to dealing with hardship is not in running from it, or even in understanding why it has come upon us, but rather in what our focus is in the midst of it. If our focus is on us and on our desires, then our problems become monsters that we must slay before they destroy us. The more we think about them, the bigger they become until they threaten to overwhelm our lives. If our focus is on God and His will for our lives, then our problems are things God has allowed to come for a reason, and we can be confident that they will turn out for our benefit. Our job is not to fix the problem, but to seek God's will in the problem. We then put the situation in His hands, trusting He will do what is best for us as we seek to glorify Him.

In Matthew 26 Jesus is in the garden of Gethsemane preparing for what is to come. This is no small matter. Not only is He facing torture, humiliation and death by crucifixion, but He also has to face having the sin and guilt of the world being placed upon Him. For the first time in His existence he will be cut off from the Father. Jesus told his disciples, "My soul is deeply grieved, to the point of death."[14] In Jesus' prayer to the Father we see a good example of how to walk by faith in hardship.

> "And He went a little beyond them, and fell on His face and prayed, saying, 'My Father, if it is possible, let this cup pass from Me; yet not as I will, but as You will.'. . . He went away again a second time and prayed, saying, 'My Father, if this cannot pass away unless I drink it, Your will be done.'" (Matt. 26:39, 42)

We see here there is nothing wrong with asking God to help us with our problems, or even asking Him to remove them. God wants us to bring our problems to Him, but He wants us to learn to surrender them to His will. Jesus did not want to face the trials ahead, but His first priority was to glorify the Father and be obedient to His will. He knew the Father was in control and knew what was best. But Jesus still had to choose to surrender to the Father's will. That was the battle, and it was also the victory. When Jesus entered the garden he was grieved to death, "His sweat became like drops of blood."[15] After Jesus surrendered the situation into the hands of the Father, He had the strength and composure to face what was ahead. Most of the trial was yet ahead of Him, but the victory was won in the garden.

If our ultimate aim is to fulfill our own desires, then surrendering our situation to God would make no sense. But if our ultimate aim it to please and glorify God, then surrendering our situation to Him is the best thing we can do. When we surrender our hardships into the hands of God, not only is He free then to work matters out according to His will (and our good), but He also gives us the peace and strength we need to face whatever may come. The victory is in the surrender, and in the obedience that comes out of the surrender. For that is what pleases our God, and that is what opens the way for the power of God to move in our lives in whatever situation we may be in.

Digging Deeper

Difficult times come to us all. Some problems we bring upon ourselves by our bad choices or sin. Others may be attacks of Satan or just the result of living in a fallen world. Some may come from the hand of God. We may never know why problems come upon us, but we do know God allows them for a reason.

1. What is one reason God may bring hardship upon us? (Lev. 26:18-21)

2. Is there any benefit for us in punishment? If there is, what is it?

One of the reasons for hardship is for punishment. Some people may think this is the main reason God brings hardship, but the truth is, this is rarely the reason for our difficulties. God is not just looking for opportunities to try to make our lives miserable. We know this because our God is not a god of anger or vengeance, but a god of love. God is, however, a just god, and He cannot overlook our sin and rebellion forever. By rights we should have been destroyed long ago.

3. Why does God delay our punishment? (2 Peter 3:9)

Even when God does bring punishment, it is still done out of love. When God brought the plagues upon the people of Egypt, it was not just to destroy them. God said if He had wanted just to destroy them, He could have done that with a sweep of His hand. Instead, He chose to demonstrate His power that they might come to know that He was God.[16]

4. What are some other reasons God may allow us to face hardship?

   Deut. 8:2-3

   Prov. 3:11-12; Heb. 12:5-12

   Zech. 13:9; 1 Peter 1:6-7

   John 15:2

   John 9:2-3; 11:4

   1 Cor. 11:29-32

   James 1:2-4

5. Which reason do you think is the hardest to deal with?

With so many different reasons for hardships, we may never know why we have to face a difficult time. But asking ourselves why might still be a good idea.

6. What problems might arise from asking, "Why is this happening to me?"?

When we focus on, "me" our problems just seem to magnify, and we can feel overwhelmed. When we shift the focus to God, then asking why may have some benefit.

7. What benefit might we get from honestly asking, "Why has God allowed this to happen?"?

In the 1 Corinthians 11 passage, some of the Christians were experiencing difficulties because they were partaking of the Lord's supper in an irreverent or unworthy manner. They were ignoring the reason why Jesus instituted the meal and had even combined it with pagan practices. Paul said they had become guilty of the body and the blood of the Lord. Because of this, some had become weak, and others sick. It was important that these Christians should ask the question, "Why?" Paul said they needed to examine themselves, for until they recognized their error and changed their ways, they would continue to experience the same problems, or even worse.

In the study Experiencing God, we are told that when we run into difficulties we should first ask ourselves if there is any sin in our lives, or any bad decisions that we need to deal with,[17] and ask God to reveal them if there are. If we find any areas of rebellion, in our life, then we need to deal with them. If we are not aware of any rebellion and we are seeking to be obedient to God's will as best we know, then we should continue on and assume that God has a good reason for allowing us to face the difficulties we are in.

8. In facing problems, what other questions should we ask besides, "why"?

While understanding why we may be facing hardship may be helpful, what is most important is what we do in the midst of hardship. We do not usually have a choice as to whether or not we will face difficulties, but we do have a choice in how we respond. We can worry or despair, but this only makes matters worse. We can try to force things to happen our way, but we usually only make a mess of things. Even should we succeed in our plans, we will miss out on the benefit and blessing God is trying to bring to us.

Examples in scripture can help us find some keys to dealing with hardship.

9. What key or keys do you find in Matthew 26:38-39, and Philippians 4:6-7?

Prayer is always a good place to start. No matter how big or how small, God wants us to bring our problems to Him. But there is far more power in prayer when we humble ourselves and submit to God's will, than there is in trying to dictate to Him what He should do. We will see far more benefit in trusting and obeying, than in whining and controlling. Not only is submission something that God desires, it is also what opens the door for God's power to work in our lives.

10. What key or keys do you find in Romans 8:18, and Philippians 3:8?

Keeping our goal in mind helps us to have a clearer perspective on the difficulties we face. If our goal is a nice comfortable life, then we are doomed to failure. Sooner or later it all comes to an end. If our goal is to please and glorify God, then times of trial are not things to avoid at all cost; rather, they become prime opportunities to deepen our faith and our relationship with God.

11. What key or keys do you find in Psalms 119:50?

Often in times of trial, Satan tries to get us to pull back within ourselves, neglecting fellowship, prayer, and God's Word when we need them most. God's Word is not only a source of strength, it is the way God can speak to us the clearest. In times of trouble, cling to the Word of God.

12. What key or keys do you find in Acts 16:25-26?

Praise takes our attention off of ourselves and puts it where it needs to be. Even if God should slay us this day, He would still be worthy of our praise. But praise is not just for God's benefit it lightens our load as well. As we focus our mind on praise, the Spirit of God begins to fill the voids in our being. There is power in praise. It pushes the darkness back and brings light to our situation.

While these keys can be a great help in dealing with hardship, they are not an easy four-step plan for removing our problems. There is no guarantee that God will remove our problems, no matter how much faith we have. Sometimes submitting to God's will means living with burdens we do not want. It is not just the weak who may feel like crying out, "My God, my God, why have you forsaken me?"[18] Hardship is no fun for anyone, even when we trust in God. The weight can at times seem to be more than we can handle. God has not promised to remove all our heartaches, but He has made us a number of promises to help us to deal with them.

13. What are some of the promises God has made in regard to our afflictions?

   Ps. 9:9

Ps. 30:5

Ps. 46:1-2

Ps. 50:15

Ps. 55:22

Is. 41:10

Heb. 4:15-16

Heb. 13:5-6

James 1:12

14. Which of these promises are most encouraging to you?

Someday the Lord will wipe away all our tears. There will be no more sorrow, no more pain, no more fear. But until that time He says, Trust me, seek me, honor me, and I will lift you up. I will share your tears and your sorrows. I will ease your pain and your fear. I will be with you no matter what you may face, and together we will rise above it all.

15. Keeping in mind what we have learned in this lesson, how you would deal with the following scenarios?

A. A friend of yours is going through some very difficult times. They feel as if God has abandoned them. How would you help them? What would you tell them?

B. You have really been having a hard time at work. You have been praying that God would provide a different job, but nothing has come. What are some of the steps you should take in dealing with this frustration?

16. What will it mean for you to walk by faith in hardship?

17. What is one area of hardship that you can work on walking by faith in?

Life Examples
Virginia[19]

     I have attended Dufur Christian Church all my life, and was baptized when I was eleven. During the summer of 2005 I started to feel I wanted more from my religion. I was tired of being a 'wall flower' Christian, and prayed God would make my faith come alive. I had no idea what I was asking for.

     My daughter, Jennifer, had just completed her freshman year at college and was looking forward to her sophomore year. Jennifer was working towards a degree in business, and would be able to take Accounting, Business Law and Economics, which pertained more to her area of interest than the general classes she was required to take her freshman year.

     Early in Jennifer's elementary and high school years she learned how to work hard for her grades. She had always done all the extra credit, gone in before and after classes, spent hours and hours on homework, and gone the extra mile to keep her grades up. It had paid off because she maintained A's and B's in all her classes. But we quickly learned that college is different than high school. You don't have the personal connection with the professors, and to most of them you are just one more face in a sea of 50 to 100 other faces and, too often, they really don't care if you pass their class or not.

     The very first day of winter term we realized that passing was going to be hard. But Jennifer started doing all the things she'd learned how to do, such as; sit in the front of the class, make sure her professor's knew her by name, asking for clarification after class when needed, meeting with her professor's one-on-one during their office hours, not skipping any classes, etc. She studied for hours and worked, but still she struggled. She managed to get her grades up to passing, except for Accounting. It seemed regardless how hard she studied and prepared, each test produced another 'F', and the F's began to stack up. Needless to say, she was devastated.

As a parent, I felt frustrated and helpless! Jennifer was looking to me for answers and help . . . and I had none. When she was in high school I had the ability to help her deal with some of the challenges she faced by talking to her teachers, making arrangements for her to do extra work, etc. But now my daughter was an adult, and I faced the fact that I couldn't "fix it" anymore. I felt powerless, and turned to the only thing I knew I could do. I prayed, and I prayed, and I prayed. I became a praying machine, but I still felt helpless as I watched my daughter spiral downward. In the mean time Jennifer had gotten her third 'F' on her accounting test, and 70% of her grade came from her tests. You can do the math. She was in a world of hurt. If she didn't pass this Accounting class she would not get into the Managerial Accounting class Spring Term, and both accounting classes were required to get her degree.

Then the Church started this Faith Walk study. With all my years of being a Christian I had never been a part of a Bible study. I found the nerve to ask my husband if I could take part in this study - - it would only take one hour, one evening per week - - and I was surprised and elated when he said I could. In the first week's lesson there was a verse that just JUMPED off the page the first time I read it. I sat there and read it over and over again. "All things are possible to him who believes". Wow!! I got those eight words at the very same time I was going through this struggle with Jennifer. Those eight words kept echoing in my head. That morning when I e-mailed Jennifer I gave her those words. When she called me after class I told her "we just have to pray. We just absolutely have to believe and we have to pray." And she said . . . "Mom, it doesn't do any good any more. I have prayed and I have prayed and I have prayed and the Lord doesn't hear me." Again I felt desperate. My daughter is a very strong Christian and she had hit a wall with God. I laid in bed that night and the tears rolled down my cheeks. I thought, God, Lord, where are You? I believe in You. I know You are there. You've said that all things are possible, so where are You?!?

In the midst of this, life continued to go on for me in other areas of my life. I am a member of the worship team that leads the singing on Sunday mornings. That fall the worship leader came up with the idea we should all have a prayer partner. Well - - I already had a prayer partner and I didn't see the need for another one, but when you are part of a group you sometimes have to 'roll with the flow. Sometimes you take part in things that really aren't 'your thing' just because it's what the group is doing. So, I thought, "Okay, fine, I'll just participate as much as is required of me and leave it at that." When we drew names my partner turned out to be a lady named Laura. I'd known Laura most of my life, but I must admit I really didn't know her personally or feel particularly close to her. I took her Prayer Partner sheet home, but didn't think any more about it. I never called Laura and she never called me, and a couple of months passed by. Then, one evening towards the end of January, Laura calls me.

She said, "Virginia, I just got this piece of paper from our team leader that says you're my Prayer Partner." Laura said a note attached indicated the sheet had gotten lost in some papers so the team leader was sending it late. She continued, "What are we supposed to do with this?" I really wasn't sure what to say, but responded "I guess we kind of pray for each other." So, we shared all the generic information, such as birthdays, anniversaries, and general information that we each could pray about. At the end of our conversation she asked if there was anything else she could pray about, and suddenly my mouth opened and I heard myself telling her about Jennifer, her struggles with her Accounting class, and how desperately helpless I felt. Laura told me she would pray about that, and also told me she had lived and gone to school in La Grande, where Jennifer was attending college. She said she knew some people up there and she would make some phone calls. She would call me the next morning. I hung up and didn't think a lot more about the call.

The next morning, at 9:00, Laura called me at work. She said, "I tried to contact a couple of my professors from high school and college. I wasn't able to get in touch with one of them, but the other one is John. He is a retired CPA, and retired Accounting Professor. His number is ***-**** and he is expecting your call." For a moment I was stunned! The day after my daughter called to tell me she would probably fail Accounting, and she didn't know where to turn, my prayer partner - - which I thought I didn't need - - calls me to say she knows someone who can help - - and to top things off, the guys a CPA / Accounting Professor. The class Jennifer is flunking. I immediately called Jennifer. "You've got to call this person," I said. "Here is his name and phone number, and he is waiting for you to call." Jennifer was afraid to call, but she found the strength, through God, and she went up to meet with John.

That night when Jennifer called us she was so excited. John met with her for over 3 hours. He was an awesome person and was very encouraging. He spent a lot of time trying to catch Jennifer up to where she needed to be to understand the assignment. John said the work her professor had her and her classmates, doing was so advanced that he would not have taught it except to 3rd or 4th year students. Jennifer and I both knew God's hand was totally in our finding this fellow. I thought, finally, this is the answer. God is going to use this man to help Jennifer get past this class. But even with John's tutoring Jennifer still struggled with the class. Her next test she failed as well. This was very discouraging for both Jennifer and me. "Why," I cried to God, "does it have to be so difficult." I could not understand what He was doing. Finally I came to realize God wanted us to rely not on what we could do, or what others could do for us, but solely on Him. So once again I gave Jennifer, and her class, to the Lord.

At the end of the term Jennifer checked her grade with her professor. She just knew she had failed the class. When she looked at her grade she saw that she had been given 20 extra credit points. Along with her perfect attendance and daily work, she would pass the class. The problem was, Jennifer had not done any extra credit paper. When she told me about it, I told her they had to belong to someone else and she must talk to her professor the next morning. It wouldn't be honest to accept points that weren't hers, as tempting as it could be to just say nothing at all. Jennifer agreed, and although it was very hard, she went in to tell her professor that the extra credit was not hers. The professor showed Jennifer the paper, and it had her name on it.

Jennifer is still sure she didn't write the paper. We both know that God was showing us that He can take care of any situation that we face, without our planning or understanding. Through this we have both learned "all things are possible to him who believes". God wanted us to let go, and believe. He wanted us to have faith in Him, and it wasn't until God took every other avenue away from us that we finally were forced to give it ALL to Him. And then he rewarded us with his faithfulness. Jennifer passed the term with a C.

Chapter 5
FAITH IN OUR RELATIONSHIPS

"Little children, let us not love with word or with tongue, but in deed and truth." (1 John 3:18)

The Question of Faith
Ruth - Ruth 1-3

Somewhere in the distance I heard a jackal cry out its lonely call. I stopped and looked out into the night around me. In the moonlight I could see the fields which had been recently harvested. Everything appeared calm and deserted, but just the same I could not shake my sense of uneasiness. I pulled my cloak a little tighter about me and continued on. It was unlikely that any wild animals would come this close to the town, but one can never be sure. Besides, for a woman alone in the dark, there were other dangers to be concerned with as well.

With each step I took, I could feel my fear rising up within me. I was tempted to turn around and flee the way I had come, but I knew I couldn't turn back now. If there was only myself to be concerned with, that would be one thing, but there was Naomi to think of as well. I knew I was committed to this path that lay ahead of me. I smiled as the realization came to me that I had, in reality, been committed to it for some time, even before I had left Moab.

Life certainly hadn't turned out as I had expected. As a little girl, I had always assumed that I would get married and raise a family there in the same village in which I had been raised, and my parents before me. But life has a way of making a mockery of our plans. I guess the changes started with the arrangement of my marriage to Chilion. He was an Israelite, a foreigner in the land of Moab. I remembered how frightened I had been as the wedding neared. Not only was Chilion a stranger to me, but I just knew he would have all kinds of strange customs I would have to learn and follow.

As it turned out, Chilion was little different from the other men of my village. Although his family were Israelites, neither he nor his brother Mahion put much importance in following the Israelite customs. They both readily accepted the customs and beliefs of Moab. Naomi, my mother-in-law, however, was a different matter. Not that she made things difficult for me; in fact, I must admit that she was a very pleasant surprise. Naomi was kind, and made me feel welcome from the start. What struck me most about Naomi was the peace and confidence that she seemed to derive from her God.

Naomi found joy in worshiping her God. She had an inner strength that intrigued me. She would speak of God's protection and mercy. Mercy was not a concept I was familiar with, especially in relation to the gods. The gods I had grown up serving were beings you had to serve so that no calamity would befall you. There was no joy in our worship of the gods, only fear.

While Naomi continued to cling to her God, Chilion and Mahion soon began to make sacrifices to Baal, Asherah, and other gods for their protection and prosperity. We were not able to have children, and Chilion had prayed to Baal to give us a son. I now see how foolish he was to leave the one true God for gods that did him no good.

Chilion came down with a sickness, and it was only a few days before he died. Mahion came down with the same sickness and died as well. Suddenly we were three women all alone, with no protection and no income. It wasn't so bad for Orpah or me. We could always go back to our families. But I worried about what would become of Naomi.

Elimelech, Naomi's husband, had died a couple years before, and now she had lost her only two sons. I was afraid that my mother-in-law would fall apart, but instead she was the strong one. The more I got to know Naomi, the more I came to love and respect her. I felt drawn to her and her God as well. Even in the midst of her sorrow, Naomi had something that I knew was missing from my life. It was something I had not seen in my family or neighbors. It was something I knew I wanted, something I knew I needed.

I remember the day when Naomi announced she was returning to her home in Israel. The famine which had driven them to Moab was past, and Naomi wanted to be back among her people. She had always felt that coming to Moab had been a mistake. Elimelech had been sure it was the right move, so Naomi had gone along with him. He was a proud man, sure of himself, as were Chilion and Mahion. Naomi later told me that she felt it was their pride and their turning from God that had caused their deaths.

Orpah and I tried to dissuade Naomi from going. We told her that the journey was a long and dangerous one. But she was not to be deterred. "There is nothing here for me," she said. "The hand of God is against me. I will return to my people and my God, even if He has turned His back to me."

I was confused and asked Naomi, "How can you continue to follow a god whom you believe to be responsible for the death of your husband and sons? I don't understand how you can still hold on to Him."

Naomi paused for a moment and then responded, "I do not follow the Lord God because it is easy. I follow Him because He is real. Yahweh is not a tame god. If you spurn Him and serve false gods, as my husband and sons did, there are consequences. I prayed that they would see their folly, and I tried to encourage them to turn back to God, but it was their choice. You can't control those around you, even those you love, or maybe especially those you love. All you can do is try to be faithful in what you're supposed to do. The rest you must leave in the hands of God, and trust Him even when is seems there is no hope."

With this, tears began to flow down Naomi's cheeks. Orpah and I both went to her and helped her to sit down in a chair. I didn't know what to do to comfort this woman I had come to care so much for, so I just knelt beside her and held her hand. After Naomi regained her composure she went on. "I loved my husband and sons, and the ache of their loss is almost more than I can bear. When they died, a part of me died with them." She paused again, but Orpah and I said nothing. We merely rested our heads on her knees and silently wept as Naomi continued on. "I must admit," she said, "that I am angry with God for taking them from me." Naomi then lifted our heads and looked into each of our eyes, and said, "But my children, He is still God. He is still my hope and my strength to go on.

There are many things I don't understand, but I know that God has proven Himself faithful to me time and time again, so even though I don't understand, and my pain threatens to overwhelm me, I will put my faith in Him. What else do I have?"

"Come now," Naomi said, standing, raising us up and making a brave attempt at a smile, "it is time you two said goodbye to this old woman." The thought of leaving her was a shock to both of us, and we started to protest, but Naomi put her fingers to our lips and said, "Hush my daughters. You two have both been a blessing to me, and are dearer to me than you know. But you have no future with me. You need to go back to your families so they might find you husbands to quell your grief, fill you hearts and help you make a new start. Where I go, you will have no family. There will be no one to arrange a marriage for you, or to provide for you. So wish me well and say goodbye."

She reached out and gathered us into her arms, and together once again we shared our tears, our grief, and our love. Naomi then gently pushed us away and said, "It is time." Orpah nodded her head. She wiped her tears away and kissed us both on the cheek, then turned away to gather her few possessions. When she finished, Orpah stopped to look at us once more. None of us could find any words to speak, so she gave a small wave, and then she was gone.

Naomi then turned to me and said, "Now, dear one, it is your turn to return to your home and your old life."

But I had been doing some thinking. I didn't want my old life. Ever since I had come to live with Naomi, I had felt more at home than ever before. It wasn't just Naomi. It was the presence that seemed to be around her. My life before had been rather empty. I had tried to find meaning and happiness in the things others seemed to find so important, but I had never been content.

I hadn't known what it was I was missing until I had seen it in my mother-in-law. If Naomi could still find peace and hope in Yahweh, even after all she had been through then I knew I wanted to know Him as well. As Orpah had been preparing to leave, I had come to a decision. I would go with Naomi and watch over her. It would mean hard work and uncertainty. I realized that to do so may mean I might never have a family of my own. I had no idea where we would live or how we would survive, but if Yahweh could take care of Naomi, maybe He could take care of me as well. I knew I was taking a risk, but I was desperate for something more than what I had now.

When Naomi turned to me and told me it was my turn to go, My mind was already made up. I stood up straight and looked at my mother-in-law with all the determination I could muster, and said, "No Mother, my home is with you. Where you go I will go, and where you stay I will stay. Your people will be my people, and your God will be my God. I vow to you by the Lord God that I will care for you in life and in death." At first Naomi just looked at me. I thought she was going to try to dissuade me, but then I guess she realized there would be no talking me out of it. Her eyes began to fill with tears and she reached out her arms to gather me in. After a moment she let go of me, straitened her dress and with a smile looked at me and said, "Well then, we had better start packing." Later on she told me how relieved she had been at my decision. Once again God had taken care of her. He had taken her sons, but He had given her a daughter. Together we packed up what little there was and started for a town called Bethlehem.

The journey to Bethlehem was a tiring one, but as soon as we arrived, I set right to work. The house had been long dormant and needed cleaning. Soon the harvest started, so I went out to glean in the fields, looking for anything the harvesters may have left behind. It was long, back-breaking work, but with no one to help us it was the only way we could find to survive.

All of these memories were going through my mind as I walked through the darkness. Then a jackal called out again and brought my thoughts back to the present. It was in these very fields that I was passing that I had done most of my gleaning. I stumbled over a stone and nearly lost my balance, and decided I had better pay more attention to where I was walking. I slowed down a little, but my thoughts ran on ahead. Further on in the moonlight I could make out the threshing area. It was there I was headed this night. There amongst the piles of wheat and chaff the men of the village slept, guarding their harvest. It was one of those men who was now the focus of my thoughts, worries, hopes, and uncertainties. His name was Boaz.

I had first met him when I had been gleaning in this very field, one of his fields as it turned out. Gleaning is not only hard work it can also be frightening at times. One never knows how the owner or the workers will treat you. Being a foreigner and having no one to rely on for protection, I was at the mercy of strangers. But God's hand had been with me and had guided me to start in a field belonging to Boaz. I hadn't known it at the time, but Boaz was actually a close relative of Naomi. When he found out that I was her daughter-in-law he showed kindness to me and allowed me to work right among his harvesters.

When I told Naomi about Boaz and his kindness she feel on her knees and said, "Praise be to the Lord, God. He has not abandoned us. He continues to show His mercy and blessing even unto the likes of us. You must stay in the fields of Boaz," she said to me, "for he will protect you from harm." And so it turned out to be.

Today was the last day of the harvest. When I had got home from the fields Naomi told me she had a plan for our future welfare. She said I should bathe and put on my best clothes. Then tonight, after the men had finished doing the threshing and gone to sleep, I should seek out where Boaz was sleeping, and go lay down at his feet. This would be a sign of submitting myself completely to Boaz's care and authority. He then, being one of Naomi's closest kin, might be willing to take care of us.

Naomi seemed so sure of the idea that I had agreed to go along with it, but now as I made my way across the field, I couldn't help but have some second thoughts. What did I really know of Boaz? He was neither young, nor particularly handsome, but he had been kind. How would he respond when I put myself at his mercy? Would he be angry at my boldness? Would he reject or even abuse me? I had to fight to keep the panic from overwhelming me. It was no small thing I would be asking of him - to provide for Naomi and myself. Would he accept, or would he think me a fool? Naomi had said that Boaz was a godly man, and she was sure God had pointed me to him for a reason. This may be, but to submit myself under someone else's authority is a frightening thing to do.

Then I remembered that it was not Boaz whom I needed to rely upon. It was God. In the short time I had been following the Lord, I had already seen Him provide for us a number of times. Even when things had been uncertain, I had felt the continual comfort of His presence. Right now though, in the midst of the uncertainty, I wasn't finding it so easy to trust in God. In the darkness things seemed even more frightening, but I reminded myself that God had always proven Himself faithful in the past. I would just have to believe He would do so again.

Reaching the threshing floor all of my doubts seem to rise up before me like spirits of the night. I could hear the sound of sleeping men all around me and vaguely see their shapes. Once again I felt the urge to flee. I was too frightened to take another step. What if someone should see me? What if . . . ? I stopped myself, closed my eyes, and repeated in my mind, "God is good. God is strong. It is going to be okay." After I regained my composure, I opened my eyes and looked around. I knew where Boaz had been working, so now, as carefully as I could, I headed in that direction. As I approached, I could see his sleeping form resting against a pile of grain. I paused and stood silently for a moment, remembering what Naomi had told me back in Moab. "All you can do is try to be faithful in what you're supposed to do. The rest you must leave in the hands of God." I prayed once more for God's protection, and then stepped forward whispering silently, "Okay, Lord, here we go."

Ruth chose to leave behind her hopes for a future and a family so that she could take care of Naomi. In leaving behind her plans for the future, and stepping out in faith, she became a part of God's plan for the future. Boaz agreed to marry Ruth and provide for her and Naomi. God not only provided a husband for Ruth, but He gave her one that was kind and godly. God also blessed Ruth with children. Ruth goes on to have grandchildren and great grandchildren. One of those is a boy named David who goes on to become the king of Israel, and from his line comes the Messiah. In leaving behind her hopes of a family and putting her trust God, Ruth became a part of the greatest family of all.

A Closer Look

Dealing with relationships can be a very complicated and confusing process. There are many different kinds of relationships: husband and wife, parent and child, friends, siblings, co-workers and so forth. Throw into this is the fact that no two people are the same. Everyone has their own way of seeing and doing things. Some people are easy to get along with and others are not.

While it is true that figuring out relationships can be very complicated, walking by faith in regard to relationships is not. In walking by faith, we do not have to try to figure out the other person. I n fact, our behavior is not to be based on who the other person is, but rather on who we are supposed to be. Dealing with relationships by faith is not about trying to please everyone else. We only have one person we need to please. That person, however, is not us. It is the Lord.

The Lord is very interested in how we deal with relationships. The second greatest commandment deals with our relationship to the people around us.

> "The second is like it, 'YOU SHALL LOVE YOUR NEIGHBOR AS YOURSELF.'" (Matt. 22:39)

1 John tells us that if we do not learn to love those around us, then our love for God is a lie.[1] Our relationship with God is directly tied to our relationship with those around us. Some might say, "But we cannot control how others react to us." This is true, but it misses the point. The point is not that we have good relationships with everyone. The point is that we learn to deal with our relationships according to God's will.

We cannot control how others treat us, but we can work on controlling how we treat others. Walking by faith means we commit to treating others according to what God tells us in His Word, and we leave how others treat us to the hands of God. If we follow God's plan for relationships, we will find that He really does know what He is talking about. But even if things do not go as we would like, it does not mean we have failed. Success or failure is found in our obedience to God's will, not in how others respond.

There will be times when we act in faith, but the other person will not respond as they should. They may take advantage of us, or even abuse us. If our motivation was centered on what we get out of it, then we may conclude that God's way does not work and we will take measures so that it will not happen again. As the old saying goes, "Burn me once, shame on you. Burn me twice, shame on me." However, if our motivation is to please the Lord, then how the other person reacts is irrelevant. In fact, Jesus says that if we are acting in a manner that is in obedience to God's will and others mistreat us, it is a cause for celebration.

> "Blessed are those who have been persecuted for the sake of righteousness, for theirs is the kingdom of heaven. Blessed are you when people insult you and persecute you, and falsely say all kinds of evil against you because of Me. Rejoice and be glad, for your reward in heaven is great. . ." (Matt. 5:10-12)

Let's look now at just what it is that God wants us to do. We have already established that God wants us to love those around us. Admittedly though, this is easier said than done. Much of the time we may not feel love for those around us, and no amount of trying to do better is going to change the feeling. Fortunately, the love God is speaks of is not about how we feel about someone else, but how we treat them.

When someone asked Jesus what it meant to "love your neighbor," He answered them by telling the parable of the good Samaritan.[2] The story demonstrated that loving your neighbor does not mean you are best pals. It does not even mean you necessarily like them. It means when you see someone in need you put aside the excuses, ignore the cost, and do what you can to help. Jesus said we are even to love our enemies and people who treat us poorly.[3] Why should we want to do that?

> "so that you may be sons of your Father who is in heaven; for He causes
> His sun to rise on the evil and the good, and sends rain on the righteous
> and the unrighteous. For if you love those who love you, what reward do
> you have? Do not even the tax collectors do the same? If you greet only
> your brothers, what more are you doing than others? Do not even the
> Gentiles do the same? Therefore you are to be perfect, as your heavenly
> Father is perfect." (Matt. 5:45-48)

The word perfect here means to be full, complete, not having any holes in it. God is always God, no matter who He is dealing with. His character is always the same. We are always to be Christians, or children of God, no matter who we are dealing with, whether it be our kids, our spouses, our neighbors, or even our enemies. We are not to allow how others act to change who we are.

1 Corinthians 13 shows us what love is to look like. Regardless of how others treat us, we are to be patient, and kind. We are not to be arrogant or proud. We are not to be rude or to let others provoke us it to acting in an unchristian manner. Now for most of us, this is beyond our ability. That is why this chapter is "Faith in our Relationships," not "Our ability in Relationships." Faith involves doing the best we can to be obedient to God's will, but it also involves recognizing our weaknesses, and learning to rely on Christ. We are not to wait until we have the ability to love others before we commit ourselves to doing so. Rather, in faith we give ourselves to Christ and then commit to strive to be obedient to His will. We understand that the only way it will work is if it is Christ who works in and through us.

Will we fail? Almost certainly, and probably many times. But it is not our ability God is looking for. He knows we do not have the ability. What He wants is for us to rely on Him and step out in faith, and should we fail, to get up and try again. It is not the ability God is looking for, but the faith. If we choose to walk by faith, it will not be easy. It will mean some inconvenience, but there will be rewards as well.

1. We are pleasing to God. Since it is our faith that God is looking for, when we choose to act in faith we are pleasing to Him, even if our ability is not up to the task. Like a father that wants his child to learn to walk, He says, "Take my hand and walk with me." The father is pleased when the child makes the attempt, and should they fail, he is there to catch them.

2. We are not under judgment. From time to time all of us fail in the area of love. All of us have times when we become selfish, rude, or impatient. If we are trying to live by our abilities, then we will be judged by those abilities. But if we are walking by faith, then we will be judged by grace. Faith opens the door to grace.[4] Like the father teaching the child to walk, if he is a loving father, he will not condemn the child when he stumbles and falls. Rather, he helps the child up and says, "Let's try again."

3. We will experience the benefits of God's wisdom. God's will for our lives really is best for us. When we treat others in a kind manner we will find that it usually ends up benefiting us.[5] When we are patient we will find things really do work out better.[6] When we learn to humble ourselves and act in love, we will find that we will have a lot better results in our relationships.[7] Pride, selfishness, and anger only bring us more problems. Humility opens doors that arrogance leaves locked. It is true that if we step out in faith and act in love, there will be times when it does not seem to benefit us, at least not at that moment. But if we act in faith, there will be benefit, this God has promised.[8] God wants us to love others, not just for their benefit, but for ours as well.

4. We unleash the power of God. Part of the reason humility works is because it opens the door for God's power to work in the situation. It is not our job to convict others of their sin or wrong doing. That is the job of the Holy Spirit.[9] When we try to force things to work our way we become an obstruction to God working in the situation. When we humble ourselves and submit to God's authority and will, we free Him to work, not only in our life, but in the lives of those around us as well.

Digging Deeper

Let us now take a more specific look at God's will for some of the different relationships in our life. We will start by looking at the husband and wife relationship. But a word of caution before we start. This instruction is not for your spouse, it is for you. If you read this thinking about how your spouse should change it will do more harm than good. God's Word is directed towards us. Let Him deal with your spouse.

1. What does Genesis 2:24 reveal about God's will for a marriage relationship?

A marriage is not just two individuals living together for their own benefit. Marriage was designed by God for the man and wife to become one. This is not just speaking of the physical relationship. It is speaking of the spiritual and emotional as well. Now it is true that the emotional, physical and even spiritual make-up of the man and woman are very different. This is not a mistake God did it on purpose so the two would complement each other. These differences make us stronger, but they also make it more of a challenge for the two to become one.

Becoming one does not mean we become the same. Not only is this impossible, but it would also mean we would lose the strength that our differences bring to the marriage. Becoming one means that our life is no longer about what is best for me, but rather it is about what is best for us. We naturally think of what is best for me, so in order for the marriage to prosper, we must work at thinking about what is best for our spouse.

2. Who is responsible for meeting the needs of the wife, and who is responsible for meeting the needs of the husband? (1 Cor. 7:3-4)

If the focus of husband and wife is to have their own needs met then the result will be that neither will be satisfied. In focusing on their own needs they will draw apart, weakening the bonds of the marriage, until in the end there is nothing left. But if the husband and wife are both seeking to meet each other's needs, then they draw together, building the bond of marriage, and in the end both feel fulfilled. God knows what He is doing. It really does work!

To fulfill one's duty toward one's spouse is not just talking about physical needs. It is talking about what that person needs to feel whole and loved. This is not the same for each person, and is usually different between a man and a woman. If the man is trying to reach out to the woman by meeting the kind of needs he feels, he will probably completely miss fulfilling the needs she feels, and vice-versa. This will leave both sides feeling neglected and confused, even though they both may have been trying to reach out to the other. This is why communication is so important. We are not mind-readers. In order for our spouses to understand what we need, and for us to understand what they need, both sides must be willing to work at communicating with each other. This means sharing and listening. Paul helps us get a picture of what some of these needs are in Ephesians chapter 5.

Read Ephesians 5:21-33

3. Who are we to be subject to? (Eph. 5:21)

4. What does it mean to be subject to each other?

Just as Paul told us in 1 Corinthians, the husband's life belongs to the wife, and the wife's life belongs to the husband. We are to meet each other's needs.

5. What is the primary reason for submitting to another? (Eph. 5:21)

Meeting the needs of our spouse is not just a good idea it is something God will hold us accountable for.

6. What is the basic need of husbands that Paul tells wives to meet? (Eph. 5:33)

For a husband to feel like a man, he needs to feel the respect of his wife. The foundation of the husband's identity is found in the respect of his wife. If he feels she respects him he can take on a load of weight. But if he does not feel the respect of his wife, then he becomes weaker and less sure of himself. This is why nagging is counter-productive. The wife may feel she is trying to help her husband improve, but what she is doing is tearing him down. She may succeed in changing a behavior, but she will make him less of a man, and weaken her marriage. If a wife points to the weakness of her husband, she will have a weaker husband. If she points to his strengths, she will have a stronger husband. It is not enough that she respect her husband. He must feel her respect.

7. How does Paul say she should show her respect? (Eph. 5:22-24; Col. 3:18)

8. What does it mean to submit to someone else? (John 10:17-18; 15:12-13)

Christ is the example of submitting. He laid down His life, not because he was forced to but because He chose to out of love. It was His choice to submit His life to the Father, and because of it the Father loved Him. God has called wives to submit to their husbands, not because they do not have a right to their own life, but out of love. It is not God's intention that a wife must always agree with her husband, or that she cannot share her opinions or concerns. Rather, she is to be willing to recognize that God established the husband to be the head of the household, and even though she may not agree, she will submit to his authority. This is an act of faith. It says, "God, I will be obedient to You and trust that You can deal with the situation."

9. Why would God ask a wife to respect, or submit, to a husband who is ungodly?
(1 Peter 3:1-2)

It is very hard for a wife to respect or submit to a husband whose faults are so apparent, but when she chooses to do so because of her commitment to the Lord, it can be the best tool she has to reach him for the Lord. But her focus must still be to please the Lord.

10. What is the basic need of wives that Paul tells husbands to meet? (Eph. 5:33; Col. 3:19)

It is not enough for a husband to feel love for his wife. She needs to feel loved by her husband. This is not the same thing. Men and women think differently and a husband must learn what it is that makes his wife feel loved. He needs to find out what things that make her feel special and cared for. The truth is that most husbands get lazy in this area. It is a lot easier to just assume that what is important for him is also important for her. This is easier, but it is not love.

11. What is the role the husband is to play in the household? (Eph. 5:23)

12. What example of being "the head" does Paul give, and how should that affect how husbands should treat their wives?

The husband is to be the leader of the family. Christ is our example of what a leader is supposed to look like. Christ's example was of a servant-leader, one who sacrificed Himself for the sake of His bride.

13. We may think we would be willing to die for our families, but what does it mean to be a living sacrifice?

14. If a husband's relationship with his wife is not as it should be, what other relationship will that effect? (1 Peter 3:7)

When we fail to treat our spouses in the manner God has directed, we have sinned against them and against God. That sin, like any other, will stand in the way of our relationship with God until we are willing to surrender it and work at dealing with it. And like any other sin, we need God's help to be able to deal with it. Walking by faith in a marriage means we commit to be the kind of spouse God has directed us to be before we have the ability to do so. Then we put our trust in God as we try to be obedient to His will. It asks more of us, but in the end we receive far more.

We now turn to relationships in regard to children. We started with the husband and wife because the most important thing you can do for your children is to work on your relationship with your spouse. In the family, the priority of relationships should be; God first, your spouse second, and your children third. To get these priorities mixed up will not only hurt us, but it will end up hurting the children as well.

15. What directions does God give for dealing with children?

      Deut. 11:18-21

      Prov. 22:6

      Prov. 13:24; 29:15-17

      Eph. 6:4; Col. 3:21

      1 Tim. 5:8

16. What is involved in providing for one's household?

While the world's primary focus on providing has to do with physical, social, and emotional needs, God's primary focus is on spiritual and character development. Now all of these areas are important, but parents have a tendency to neglect the spiritual and character needs of the child in favor of the physical, social and emotional needs because it is easier. We think, "If I give the kid what he wants and maybe he will give me rest." Issues of right and wrong, or being obedient to God, often get pushed aside for the sake of convenience. This is easier, but not only will we end up paying for it later, so will our children.

17. What is God's promise in regard to the well being of our children? (Deut. 4:39-40)

Training up a child by God's direction does not guarantee that they will always be happy and healthy. Nor does it guarantee they will not make wrong choices. But God knows what He is talking about. Not only is His direction what is best for our children, but when we put our faith in God and act out of obedience to His will, we free God's power to work in the lives of our children. None of us are perfect parents, and we never will be. Parenting by faith means we commit to doing it God's way and pray that He will overcome our weaknesses and failures.

18. What is God's direction for dealing with parents?

       Ex. 20:12

       Col. 3:20

19. What does it mean to honor your parents?

Jesus made it clear that honoring our parents is not to stop after we leave home.[10] It pleases God when we honor those He has placed in authority over us, even when they may be wrong or unfair. Honoring your parents does not necessarily mean agreeing with them, or always do what they say. It means that we demonstrate that they, their feelings and opinions, are important to us. It means we show them the respect due their position. They may or may not deserve the respect, but God does deserve our obedience, and honoring them is better for us as well. Resentment held against our parents can and does have a negative impact on other relationships in our life. It can affect relationships at work, in the church and with our own family. Surrendering the past to God and striving to be obedient to His commands is the key to bringing healing to our lives.

20. What is the benefit God said would come from honoring our parents? (Ex. 20:12)

It is not just with family relationships that we must walk by faith. There are people all around us with whom we share relationships.

21. What do you think it means to "love your neighbor as yourself? (Matt. 22:39)

22. What does Paul mean that our love should be without hypocrisy? (Rom. 12:9-10)

The word we translate as "hypocrisy" means to pretend, or to playact. It was what actors did up on stage. Paul is saying that our love for each other must be more than an act, our love must be genuine. We cannot make ourselves feel love for someone, but we can strive to reach out to each other with the genuine commitment of love.

23. Keeping in mind what we have learned in this lesson, how you would deal with the following scenarios?

A. You want to serve God, but you have a spouse who does not. To ignore God is dangerous to your soul, but to be active in service to Him at times brings stress to your marriage. What should you do?

B. You live in a society that tells you that being a good parent means you have your kids involved in five activities at once, provide them with the latest toys and fashions, and provide them with a college education so they can get good paying jobs. What does God say they need and what does He expect you to focus on?

24. What does will it mean for you to walk by faith in regard to you relationships?

25. What is one area you can work on to show love to your spouse, children, or neighbor?

Life Examples
CaroLynn[11]

For a long time I wrestled with anger and a sense of betrayal. I felt I had followed God's direction for courtship and marriage. I had prayed and sought God's will, and had been sure Steve was the man God had chosen for me. I envisioned us serving in ministry together, serving the Lord as a team. Then the unthinkable happened. Three years into our marriage, Steve walked away from the Lord. I was shocked and very angry, not only with Steve, but with God as well. How could He have let this happen to me? In my heart I battled with pride, self-pity and self-righteousness.

From examples in scripture, I knew that one could be open and honest with God without fear of His rejection, if one did so with humility and respect. I must admit I didn't always go to God with respect. There were moments when I didn't care how God felt - since He didn't seem to care how I felt. Even with my poor attitude He didn't reject me, but He would let me know that it wasn't His job to cater to my demands. Usually His correction came through scripture, such as Job 40:8 - "Will you really annul My judgment? Will you condemn Me that you may be justified?" I am grateful that He always has found a way to humble me gently.

I found I was struggling a great deal with idolatry. I wanted the ideal marriage - one that was led and centered on Christ. I asked God, "Why should this be such a problem? Isn't this what You want as well? If You are not able to make it happen, then what good is my faith in You? How can I trust You, and believe in Your Word, if you can't help us to live up to it?" God showed me that while my ideals may be scriptural, they, in themselves, were not to become my "God." He showed me that there were many choices of scenarios in how to live a godly marriage. I had allowed my expectations of Steve, and my own desires, to become "have to have's" in order to be happy. The things I thought I had to have were my ideas, not God's, and He would not be bound to them. I had judged my plans to be the "right" ones and had tried to usurp my will over God's. My ideals had become idols.

I also struggled with an ungrateful and condemning heart, both towards God and towards Steve. I was seeing the glass as half empty rather than half full, although, in actuality, it was more like 9/10th full. I almost destroyed my marriage by focusing on the 1/10 which I felt was missing. The Lord taught me to value and respect Steve as the Lord sees him.

In the midst of my pain, I struggled with my understanding of what "Truth" was. What was it? Where was it? Was Jesus truly able to do "abundantly beyond all that I could ask or think?" Was there really "nothing too difficult for Him?" How was I to pray? What was I to believe? I wanted to please my Lord, and I knew that "without faith it is impossible to please Him," but all I could see was the inconsistencies between what He said and what I saw playing out in my life.

God eventually helped me to see that my understanding and focus of "Truth" was too narrow and small. There is still much about truth I have yet to learn, but God began to open my eyes to the truth about me. I was just as big of a sinner as Steve or anyone else. He showed my own rebellion, envy, distrust, self-centeredness, and self-righteousness. He showed me that "being right" is not near as important as being submitted and obedient. The "Truth" was, I don't need to understand all that He is doing to have confidence in it. It's okay if what He is doing doesn't make sense to me because my perspective is so limited. I came to choose to hold on to the truth that I knew, and to thank Him for that. I chose to hold on to His Word and to the many times He did show me His love and favor. I chose to hold on to these even tighter when I could not see or feel Him near. I released Jesus from my understanding and expectations, and proclaimed His Word and His sovereignty over my life and my home.

Another area I struggled in was in my attempts to manipulate God. I had interpreted scripture to say, "that if I lived as a godly woman, and treated my husband and God just right, that I would win Steve without a word." If I prayed just right, fasted and was in His Word enough, then God's power would be released and Steve would be won back to the Lord. I thought if I did all the right things then I would get what I desired. But as the years went on and Steve continued to battle against God, I felt as if I must have failed. Satan and my own pride threw guilt upon me, making me feel that I was a complete failure.

God finally broke through that with the huge revelation that I didn't have to always be doing the "right' thing to meet God's approval. I didn't have to earn His love. God chose to give it to me as a gift, and wouldn't let me pay for it. My job is only to do my part in being "in relationship" with Him. I needed not only to accept God as He was, but I also needed to accept me as I was. The one thing that really mattered about who I was, was that I belonged to Him, and in Him, I found grace. He knows my heart's desire to honor Him, even when I blow it.

God also helped me to understand that my failures were not responsible for Steve's continuing struggle. That was largely between God and himself. I just need to pray and focus on my own personal relationship with the Lord. I must let God be God, and leave Steve's heart to Jesus, knowing that He was doing everything in His power to convict Steve, because He loved him so. It was not easy to leave Steve to the Holy Spirit. The deeper my relationship grew with the Lord the more I wanted to share it with Steve. But God convicted me to talk less about Him and learn to live more like Him instead. This was not only for Steve's sake but for my own as well to protect me from further pain in receiving Steve's critical and cutting remarks.

Jesus helped me to know that He understood my pain. Family and friends often conveyed the message that I was over-reacting, and made me feel foolish for feeling such hurt. Jesus, on the other hand, let me know that He hurt over Steve even more than I did. I saw in scripture the depth of God's love for us, and realized that He hurt not only for Steve, but for my sin as well. He helped me to understand that pain was nothing to be ashamed of, that it was a privilege to stand in "the Fellowship of Suffering," for this is a part of what it means to "take up the cross, and follow Me."

About three years after Steve denied his faith, I found out that he was having an affair, an affair largely due to my sin of disrespect towards him. There was a three day stretch of major crisis of faith that I had to wrestle through. I spent most of those days in my room, huddled in a corner, numb, weeping, and in a fog. I was full of fear that my marriage was ending, that I had failed, and God had failed me. If I could not count on Him, what was the point of even believing in Him? I did not eat and I do not remember sleeping. I did not care about anything. Everything about my life seemed futile. If I had failed as a wife, surely I had failed as a mother as well. So what was the point to living?

I briefly wrestled with the notion of suicide, but that would leave my children without a mother. They would never get over the emotional trauma of that, even if they were better off without me. I was selfish, but not that selfish. So I concluded that suicide was not the answer. I decided that if I chose to believe that neither God nor His love for me was real, then it would mean my life was purposeless and hopeless. I realized that in day to day living I put faith in many things I didn't really understand. If I was willing to put faith in them, then why couldn't I hold onto faith in the One who created me and knew me best of all? Was He not worthy of my faith, even if I didn't understand Him or what He was doing?

So as I curled in a ball on the floor of my bedroom, I told God that I was not happy with Him, and did not know how I would ever fully trust Him. But I was choosing to believe that He knew more than I did. I was going to continue to seek Him and His purpose for my life. I would hold on to His Word and believe it to be true. If He would still have me, I would be His. It was gut-honest, and excruciatingly painful, but I did feel a sense of peace and relief once I made that decision.

God did not do any amazing miracle for me right then, nor did I feel Him close to me. But I knew He was there and trusted He would prove it to me in His time. That day I let go of my demanding heart and never again have I seriously considered walking away from my faith. I have had many questions and have challenged the Lord many times. Sometimes He answered me, and other times He didn't. I have found no formula in how to make Him answer. Nearly each time He did answer, it was unique. But through the process of it all I have come to know Him, and He to know me. He often reminded me of Romans 4:24-5:11, 1 Peter 1:1-11, and Galatians 6:9. These passages spoke of God promise - that there is a meaning to our trials and that, if we do not give up, we will see the benefit. Jesus helped me to hold on to this promise. I was too weak to do so on my own. But I had to keep making the choice to take His hand and believe He knew what He was doing, even if I did not.

Steve did return to the Lord nearly four years ago now, after twenty-one years of running away. We are still in the process of working on our marriage. We found we have a great deal of learning to do in how to re-relate to each other. We both have much to do and undo. When I asked Steve about the question my brother Bob posed (What has it meant to walk by faith through the difficulties of my relationship?), Steve responded, "You persevered in submitting to God and then to me, even when it didn't make any sense. It was the key to my return to faith in a loving and gracious God." Praise the Lord! He is for real, and so is His Word! He truly is able to do abundantly beyond all I could ask or think, but in His time and in His way.

Chapter 6
FAITH IN DEALING WITH OUR RESOURCES
"For where your treasure is, there your heart will be also." (Matt. 6:21)

The Question of Faith
The widow of Sidon - 1 Kings 17:8-16

"So much for the God of Israel," I thought, as I bent down to pick up another stick. At least there was plenty of dead firewood around, although that was about all there was in abundance. Ever since the beginning of the drought, everything else had become increasingly hard to come by. Most people were managing to get along, but then we were not like most people. We were alone, my son, Joetha and I. There was no one else. My husband had died a couple of years ago. I stopped for a moment and thought, "Could it have been so long as that?" In one respect it seemed like just a short time ago that life had looked so promising.

My husband, Ahmed, had been a farm laborer, working for a wealthy land owner. We did not make much money, but we had enough to get by. We had our small home, a donkey, and we had our dreams. We always thought that some day we would save up enough to buy some land of our own. Then we would become the wealthy land owners, we would laugh. We laughed because we knew we would never become wealthy, but it didn't matter. We had our dreams and we had each other.

When our son came it seemed that the gods were truly smiling upon us. He brought so much joy into our life. Ahmed would pick him up and toss him into the air and they would both laugh with delight. I loved to listen to the sound of Ahmed's laugher. It was full of so much joy and warmth. But now that laugh, as well as our dreams, are only a fading memory.

I remember the day they brought the news of Ahmed's death. I had been gathering sticks for the fire, just like I'm doing now, when they arrived with the news. There had been an accident at work, and Ahmed had been killed. They were so sorry, they said, so sorry. The land owner had come and given his condolences, but nothing else. There had been little time to mourn. After all, there was Joetha to think of, and it took all I could do just for us to survive.

At first, I admit, I had been too proud to ask for help. I had no family and I had never been close to Ahmed's relatives. Instead, I had gone to the fields where I could glean what there was to find. To that I added the small amount I could make doing cleaning and odd jobs. Life became hard. Laughter no longer filled our home. There was too much emptiness there, too many memories. But still we managed to survive. I had thought that we had experienced the worst life could give us, and that now things would get better. But I had been wrong, for it was then that the drought came.

The rainy season came, but it came without clouds or rain. What water there was began to dry up, and the crops with it. The sun beat down, and ground turned to dust, which then settled down upon everything. The whole world appeared to turn brownish gray. There was no longer any food to glean from the fields. What harvest there was,

was stringently hoarded by the landowners. They would not even allow us on their land, for fear we might find something that had been missed. My odd jobs, along with the land, seemed to dry up and blow away. No longer could people afford to pay. Everyone was cutting back for fear of what may lie ahead.

It was then that I began to ask for help. If I had been on my own I might have chosen to starve first, but there was Joetha to think of. For him I would ask, beg, or steal, if need be. But it had done no good. All those I asked either did not have the means or the inclination to help. They told me to seek the gods for help. Pray to Baal or to Asherah. They would help me. But I had enough of Baal and the other gods. I had prayed and sacrificed and had got less help than I did from Ahmed's relatives.

I even tried turning to the God of Israel. After all, it was said that it was He who had brought the drought in the first place. If He was able to overcome our gods, then He must be powerful indeed. Somewhere I had heard that the God of Israel was called Yahweh, but I had no idea how to talk to Him or what to say, so I just fell to my knees, and cried out, "Oh Yahweh, God of Israel, please hear my prayer! I am a nobody. I am unworthy of Your concern, but I ask Your forgiveness and plead for Your mercy. I ask You, God, for the life of my son. You can take my life and do with it as You please. I have nothing, but what I have I give to You if You would just please spare my child! Please, Yahweh, help us!"

I'm not sure what I was expecting to happen, but what I got was nothing, at least as far as I could see. There was no sign from above, no voice from heaven, just silence as I knelt there in our house. And yet it had seemed that there was something different, as if an ember of hope had begun to burn within the cold ashes of my soul. With all the disappointments that had come my way, I dared not hope, and yet it was there all the same. But as one day turned into another, and I still got no response, I realized I must have been mistaken. Yahweh had not heard me, or if He had, He had not seen me as being worthy to help.

I had rationed out our food as tightly as I could, hoping against the inevitable, but now there was no more hiding from the fact that we were going to die. There was barely enough flour and oil for one more meal, and then it would be gone, with no hope for more. I thought of holding the food back one more day, but as I had looked at Joetha playing by the tree, I decided, what is the point? He looks so thin and has barely enough energy even to play. He might as well eat today, and we won't think about tomorrow. How, I wondered, am I supposed to watch my little boy die?

I brushed back the tears and bent to gather sticks for our last meal's fire. When I stood up I noticed a stranger walking up to the gates. From his dress, he looked to be an Israelite. Generally, Israelites have little time for strangers, but to my surprise he looked directly at me and came my direction.

"Please," he said, "get me a little water in a jar that I might drink."

I looked at him for a moment in surprise, and then nodded and turned to go get the jar. I was perplexed by his behavior. It is not that the request in and of itself was so uncommon. In a land where water supplies had become few and far between, travelers often stopped and requested water. Even with the town's water supply growing low, the codes of hospitality required that a travelers request for water not be denied. It was not the request that seemed strange, but that he would single me out among all the people to ask. It had been clear by the way he approached the city gate that he had been looking for someone, and when he had seen me, he had smiled as if he had known me. But I certainly didn't know him.

I had only gone a few steps when he called to me again, "Please," I turned to look at him and he was looking at me with a strange expression in his eyes. It seemed to be a mixture of amusement and anticipation, as if he had a secret to share, but instead he made another request. "Please bring me a piece of bread in your hand." I nearly laughed at him. It was not that his request was so outlandish it was just that he should make it of someone who had so little to give.

I said to him, "As Yahweh your God lives, I have no bread, only a handful of flour in the bowl and a little oil in the jar; and behold, I am gathering a few sticks that I may go in and prepare for me and my son which we may eat it and die."

I expected him to seek out someone else when he saw how little help I could be to him, but instead he smiled, and said, "Do not fear; go, do as you have said, but make me a little bread cake from it first and bring it out to me, and afterward you may make one for yourself and for your son. For thus says Yahweh, God of Israel, 'The bowl of flour shall not be exhausted, nor shall the jar of oil be empty, until the day that Yahweh sends rain on the face of the earth.'"

For a moment I just stood there. This man must be mad, I thought, how could he ask me for our last bit of food? Did he expect me to take the food from the mouth of my own child? Giving him water was one thing. Giving him all I had to live on was quite another. I had to admit that the bit about Yahweh making the flour and oil never run out was creative, but a bit far fetched. Yet, What if it was true? What if this man was from Yahweh? He was, after all, an Israelite, and I had asked Yahweh for help. What if this was His answer? But this was not the kind of answer I had been looking for. I had asked for Yahweh to send help, and it was just my luck that instead He had sent a request for the little bit I had left. Was this the way a loving God worked? Was it a joke, or was He wanting to make us suffer even more?

Although in truth, I guess, it didn't really matter that much. What food we had couldn't save us. If I refused him and kept the food for ourselves, it might feed us one more day, but what then? Without help, we would still be lost. I suppose it wasn't much to hold on to, it's just that it was all we had. True, I had told Yahweh that I would give Him all I had, but I hadn't expected that He would actually take it.

I stood there for a moment, torn in indecision. Then I thought, What do I have to lose? My life is a mess anyway. Everything else I've tried has failed what other hope do I have? What other hope is there for my son? If Yahweh is really reaching out to me, then maybe there is hope yet. I don't see how this will work, but I guess I'll just have to trust that He knows what He is doing. With that, I turned and went to prepare the bread.

As she prepared the meal for Elijah, the woman found that the prophet's words were true. Beyond all reason, no matter how much she used of the flour and oil, they did not run out. Elijah continued to stay with the woman and her son until the drought was over. While she provided for Elijah's physical needs, God provided for hers. The woman surrendered to God the last of what she had, but through her sacrifice she found more than just flour and oil. She found God.

A Closer Look

When we look at what it means to walk by faith in dealing with our resources, we are not just talking about tithing. We are talking about how we view the material things of life. It has been said, that all we need is love. But the truth is that there are material things we need as well. Jesus Himself said that God knows that we need these things.[1] Money and possessions, in and of themselves, are, for the most part, not evil. Paul did not say "money is the root of all evil." Rather he said, "the love of money is a root of all sorts of evil." In the Old Testament we see God blessing many of those who were faithful to Him with material blessings. There are enough passages in scripture that portray a positive view of wealth to allow us to justify living the life-style we would like. However, walking by faith is not about justifying what we do. It is about seeking God's perspective and trying to match our life to His will. As much as we might prefer the question, "What can we get away with?" The real question is, "What does God desire?"

We have a tendency to avoid asking, "What does God desire?" We are afraid we will not like the answer. With finances we are afraid that God's desire may be that we are dirt poor and live in poverty. The truth is that nowhere in scripture does God require us to live in poverty. He does ask us to give up all we have and put His priorities first, but this is not the same thing as living in poverty. In fact, it is the key to living in blessing. The blessings of the Lord are far greater than the riches we can achieve on our own. We have nothing to fear from a life provided for by the blessings of the Lord. But for us to experience those blessings there are some lessons we must first learn and apply to our lives.

1. We are stewards, not owners. What is a steward? Some would describe a "Good Steward," as being someone who makes wise use of that which God has given them. The problem with this definition is not so much with what is said as with how we usually interpret it. We have a tendency to look at this from the position of an owner rather than a steward.

A steward understands that what they have does not belong to them. It belongs to the Master. God has entrusted it into their hands for a short time. While they are allowed to derive their living from what the Master has entrusted to them, it is still to be used under His direction and primarily for His benefit. A steward's goal is the benefit and pleasure of his master.

An owner thinks in terms of what is best for him. He sees the things in his possession as belonging to him, and therefore to be used for his benefit. The thinking runs something like, "I worked for it, I earned it, and it's mine, so I can do with it as I please." This person may give some his resources to God because he thinks it is a good idea, but it is still his to do with as he see fit. The problem with this is that if Christ is Lord, then He is master of all - our work, our abilities, our resources - all. This is what I believe Jesus is talking about when He tells us that we must be willing to give up all of our possessions if we are to be His disciples.[2]

None of us are perfect stewards or servants. We begin by giving our heart to the Lord, and from there He helps us to understand what it means to live for Him. Even when we truly try to live for Christ, we all have a tendency to hold things back. The more we hold back, the more that gets in the way of our relationship with the Lord. Generally Christ will not forcefully take from us that which we refuse to let go of, at least not right away. Rather He invites us to surrender it into His care. When we surrender it into His care, it does not mean we no longer have any use of it. It means His priorities become our primary concern.

It also means that He now has the primary responsibility. We are responsible to be obedient to His direction, but the responsibility for the outcome belongs to Him. God takes care of that which He owns, and He does a far better job than we can do. The blessings of God fall upon that which is given into His care. Many times we may have asked for God's blessing or help in a situation and have not received it because we have not let go of control. Our lack of faith stands in the way of what God wants to do for us.

Even a faithful steward or servant may forget from time to time who really owns what he has, but the real problem comes when we willfully choose to ignore the fact that we are stewards and not owners. In the parable of the talents[3] Jesus tells of a master and three of His servants. The master entrusted to each of the servants a treasure. A talent was about a year's salary. While Jesus used money for the illustration, you could use any of the other many things God has entrusted to us, even life itself. They were each entrusted with a different gift, and it is clear that the important part was not what they were given, but what they did with what they were given.

Two of the servants went out and used what they had been given to gain profit for the master. Now keep in mind that what *we* often consider as profit is not necessarily profit to God. What benefit is there for God in our bank accounts or portfolios? Often what we see as being a good steward is more like what the unfaithful servant did. He buried what he had been given in his own backyard. Now mind you, he did not squander it in loose living, or throw it away on foolish ventures. He just decided that the Master was asking too much to expect him to take what he had been given and use it for the benefit of the Master. After all, the servant had his own life to live. So while the other two are out laboring for the master, he focused on his own needs.

This appears to work well until it comes time to settle up accounts. Then we find that the lazy or selfish servant's approach cost him a number of things. 1. It cost him the blessing. While the other servants' gifts grew, his remained the same. 2. It cost him the gift itself. God expects servants to use what they have been given for the benefit of the master. If they do not, they will end up losing it. 3. He lost his position as a servant. A servant uses what he has in the service of the master. If he does not, he is not really a servant. Not only did the selfish servant not receive a reward, he was also cast out of the household. While his arguments may have sounded convincing to himself, they did not convince the master. He knew what was expected of him and he just chose not to do it.

2. God's wisdom is not our wisdom. When we think of making wise use of our resources, we are usually thinking of the wisdom of the world. We tend to think of saving, investing, and getting good paying jobs. This sounds wise to us, but Paul lets us know that our wisdom is not God's wisdom.[4] How we use our resources is one of the areas in which this is most evident.

We say it is better to be rich than poor. Jesus says it is better to be poor than rich.[5] Why should it be better to be poor than to be rich? A poor man is more likely to rely upon God for His needs, and to seek his reward in the life to come. A rich man is more likely to look to himself for his needs, and to seek his reward in this life. Scripture is full of warnings of the dangers of pursuing, or even having, wealth. Jesus warns us that it is nearly impossible for a rich man to go to heaven.[6] Thankfully He also lets us know that things impossible with man are possible with God.[7] But we must not take His warning lightly, for it is directed at us.

Whether we like to admit it or not, we are the wealthy of this world. Even those of a lower income here in this country live in a style that the vast majority of people in this world would see as extremely wealthy. Much of our life is consumed with either the pursuit or the enjoyment of wealth or pleasure, often leaving little time for the things of God. This pursuit of wealth is greed. We may not see it as greed or being evil, because we are not doing anything bad to gain it, but Jesus warns us against any form of greed.

> "Then He said to them, "Beware, and be on your guard against every form of greed; for not even when one has an abundance does his life consist of his possessions." (Luke 12:15)

Jesus goes on to tell the parable of a farmer who had a good year. He built barns to store his wealth, and thought that now he was set. Only then he died and found out that he had been a fool. He had wasted his life pursuing things that would end up being of no value to him.[8] Jesus tells us rather than seeking to be rich we should have the attitude, or spirit, of the poor. We should put our faith not in the things of this world, but in God, and seek our reward in the things of heaven rather than in the things of this world.

Now in all honesty, many of us try to have it both ways. We may say that our faith is in God, while at the same time seeking the things of this world. But Jesus warns us that we cannot serve two masters. Keep in mind, faith involves commitment and faithfulness. Either our loyalty is to God, and we seek a heavenly reward by using our earthly resources according to God's priorities, or our loyalty is to the things of this world, and we seek earthly reward and try to use God to achieve our priorities. In which category would your life fit?

Another area our wisdom differs from God's is in the idea of preparing for the future. Our wisdom says, take some of what we earn and put it away because we may need it sometime in the future. God says, do not store up for yourselves the things of this earth that fade away and end up being of no use to you.[9] Rather, use what I entrust to you for my priorities, and store up for yourself true wealth that lasts forever. It is not that God does not want us to prepare for the future. He does. But instead of wasting our lives preparing for that which only lasts for a short time, He wants us to work at preparing for a future that lasts for an eternity.

Having a nest egg seems like wisdom to us. But does this wisdom come from God, or does it come from the world? Scripture tells us that the world's wisdom is foolishness to God and God's wisdom appears foolish to the world.[10] Now it is true there maybe times when God may direct us to put some money aside to meet a need that is coming, but much of the time, our storing of wealth is more like the man who built the barns. We call it wisdom, but Jesus calls it greed, and He says to avoid any form of it.

You probably do not like this section very much (I know I do not), but that does not make it any less scriptural or any less true. This type of teaching does not go well in America, because we are the rich. We tend to trust our money rather than our God. We cannot have it both ways. God may direct us to put away money for the future,[11] but if He does, it will be for a purpose, not just so we can have wealth. We are supposed to provide for our families, but if our example teaches our children to be materialistic and to put their trust in the wealth of this world then we are doing more harm to them than good.

Putting money away for the future is not evil. But unless it is done in accordance with God's will, it is not faith either. All too often, our saving, are in reality a refusal to use what God has entrusted to us for His purposes because we do not really think He will be able to take care of our needs in the future. It is not that we should go out and spend foolishly, but we need to understand that God gives us resources for a reason. The question is, "Are we seeking His priorities or ours?" Preparing for the future is a wise thing to do. God just warns us not to waste our life preparing for the wrong one.

3. God's blessings are true blessings. I saved this for last because, while the first two points are definitely scriptural, they are not very comfortable or easy to accept. They are like getting medicine from a doctor. We know it must be good for us, but that does not make it any easier to swallow. It may seem up to this point, that God wants us all to be dirt poor and miserable, but this is not true. Our Father wants to bless His children. He wants to give us the truly good things in life.[12] He knows our needs and He wants to take care of them.

God does not require that we have nothing, He requires that He owns all that we have. It is not that He does not want us to have what we need, or to ever enjoy some of the pleasures of the world. What He wants is for us to put His priorities first so that He can bless us with all we need, and more. One does not have to be poor to be godly. I know of godly people whom God has blessed with wealth, but they do not live in wealth. They live in moderation so they can use what has been entrusted to them for the glory of God. As we saw in the parable of the talents, it is not about how much you have. It is what you do with what you have. It is our faithfulness that God seeks. If we are faithful with what He has entrusted to us, God has said that He will entrust more to us. If we are not faithful with what we have, whether it is little or much, then God is not going to bless us with more.

When we put our trust in God, He shows himself faithful. We cannot, however, try to use this to manipulate God into giving us what we want. God will bless those who put their faith in Him, but God's blessings are not always what we expect, or even desire. God knows that our spiritual and character growth is far more important to our happiness and well-being than our financial growth. There are some things that can only be learned the hard way. They may not be pleasant, but they still may be a blessing. The truth is, God knows that some of us cannot handle wealth. If we had it, we would fall away from the Lord. Having wealth can lead us away from God, which would be the worst thing that could happen to us. The temptation to take our eyes off of God must be continually guarded against.

Not all "blessings" come from God. Some come as temptations or tests. If the blessing brings with it guilt for us or pain for others, then it is probably not from God. Sometimes we even take a blessing that is from God, and turn it into a curse by letting it distract us from our commitment to our Lord. I have seen this when people have received jobs, money and even children and then shifted their focus onto those things rather than God. What a tragedy for us to use a blessing from God as an excuse to be unfaithful to Him. For not only do we displease God and harm our relationship with Him, but we also cut off God protection and future blessing on the gift He has entrusted to us.

If our desire is to please the Lord, and we show that through a willingness to sacrifice, God will bless us. That blessing may come in a financial form. If it does we may enjoy it without guilt, but God will still want us to be faithful with that blessing. If our desire is for the blessing itself, or the wealth, then even if we manage to succeed in achieving our goal, it will not bring us the happiness we desire.

> "A faithful man will abound with blessings, But he who makes haste to be rich will not go unpunished." (Prov. 28:20)

> "But those who want to get rich fall into temptation and a snare and many foolish and harmful desires which plunge men into ruin and destruction. For the love of money is a root of all sorts of evil, and some by longing for it have wandered away from the faith and pierced themselves with many griefs." (1 Tim. 6:9-10)

We can only have one master. We cannot serve both God and wealth. We must choose to serve one and to disdain the other. If we serve God and disdain wealth, we will at the very least have our needs provided for. Added to that will be God's blessing, and even more important, we will have His presence and His pleasure. If we serve wealth then we will disdain God, and in the end we will have neither.

> "For what will it profit a man if he gains the whole world and forfeits his soul? Or what will a man give in exchange for his soul?" (Matt. 16:26)

Digging Deeper

While walking by faith in dealing with our resources is not just about tithing, it probably is the best place to start. We do not see Jesus talking very much about tithing in the New Testament because He is trying to push us beyond the minimal requirement to a life that is completely dedicated to God. This is the goal, but we have to start somewhere. Tithing is a good place to start.

1. Why did Jacob tithe to God? (Gen. 28:20-22)

There are a number of reasons for tithing, but the main one is to acknowledge that the Lord is our God. In this way, we demonstrate our allegiance to Him. Tithing to the Lord was a part of the commands God gave to His people.

2. Why do you think God picked this as a symbol of His authority? (Matt. 6:21)

What we do with our money is a good indication of what is truly important to us. It also shows where we put our faith.

3. Why do you think so many Christians neglect to tithe?

Tithing, in and of itself, does not earn us anything. God does not need our money, but He does require our loyalty.

4. How does God view the issue of tithing? (Mal. 3:8-9)

The reason the people's efforts were being cursed instead of being blessed was because they decided it was not that important to honor God first with what they had.

5. What does God invite them to do? (Mal. 3:10-12)

It was not so much the gift itself that God desired as the sincerity of heart that the gift demonstrated. Without the obedience or humility of heart, the tithes and offerings meant very little.

6. What are some directions God gives us about giving?

    Matt. 6:1-4

    2 Cor. 9:6-7

In both the Old Testament and the New, what we do with that which we consider of value still indicates where our heart is. And our attitude in giving is still more important than what we give. Money, in and of itself, is neither bad nor good. When dedicated to the Lord, it can be used for good, and be pleasing to God.

7. What is the promise Paul made to the Philippian Christians? (Philip. 4:19)

We need to keep in mind that Paul makes this statement after discussing the gifts the Philippian Christians had given for his ministry. In Second Corinthians, Paul speaks of the Philippian Christians' sacrificial giving, and says that they gave "beyond their ability."[13] This is why Paul can assure them that God will provide for their needs.

8. What are the provisions Jesus puts on His statements about God providing for us?

    Matt. 6:31-33

    Matt. 19:29

9. God may choose to bless us with wealth, but for what reason? (2 Cor. 9:8-11)

Wealth can be used for God's glory, this does not, however, negate the dangers connected with wealth.

---

10. What are some of the problems associated with wealth?

     Deut. 8:10-20

     Prov. 23:3-6

     Matt. 13:22

     1 Tim. 6:10

     Eccl. 5:10-11

One of the problems of wealth is that there is never enough. The more we have, the more we feel we need. This is why even people who make plenty of money often find themselves in debt.

11. What is God's view of debt? (Rom. 13:8)

12. Why do you think God does not want us to be in debt?

     Prov. 22:7

     Matt. 6:24

Being in debt is actually a form of bondage or slavery. While we are in debt, we are not free to do as the Lord may direct us. Paul reminds us that we have been bought with a price. We do not belong to ourselves, so we are not to enslave ourselves to men.[14] Now, it is true that there is some debt we may not be able to avoid; but in truth, most debt is incurred because of either our lack of contentment in God, a lack of trust or patience in God, or because of our lack of faithfulness to God. We rob ourselves of many of God's blessings because we do not act in faith.

There probably should be some distinction between investing and going in debt. In order for some people to have a home, or have a business, they may have to borrow. When you can get your money back out of something you buy, then it may be seen as an investment.

But even here we must be very careful. There may be times when God may lead us to take out a loan for some reason but all too often this is done more because of the world's wisdom than God's. While these things may not be bad, their requirements upon us may still keep us from following God's will in our life. Seeking God's will for our life may include having a home or a business, then again it may not. We have to decide what is going to be our main priority, what God says we need or what the world says we need.

Avoiding debt is something God wants us to do, but what about the millions of people who already find themselves in debt? Wither they should or they should not be in debt, is not near as important as what they do now.

13. What is Paul's advice to Christians who lived in bondage? (1 Cor. 7:21-23)

We see a couple of things here. First off, if you are not in bondage (or debt for our discussion) do not get into it. Your life does not belong to you. It belongs to Christ. You are not free to mortgage it just to gain something you desire. Secondly, if you are in debt, do not let it overwhelm you. Give the situation over to Christ. Some debt may be unavoidable, some come from bad choices, but in Christ there is freedom for all. Take your eyes off of your debt and put them on Christ. We need to try to deal with our debt, but it does not have to control who we are. Debt may keep us from being free to do as we would like, but it cannot keep us from walking with Christ. Even in dept we can live in the freedom of Christ. Our hope and happiness is found in Him, not in our financial situation.

Paul says, ". . . if you are able also to become free, rather do that."[15] This means if you are in debt, then by all means try to get out. How do you do that? I do not profess to be a financial expert, but there are some things I have learned the hard way.

1. Stop doing whatever it was that got you into debt in the First place. Again some debt may be unavoidable, but most of it comes because we are living beyond our means. If you are ever going to get out of debt then you have to make some changes. You may need to get a smaller house, or a cheaper car. You will probably need to change some of your eating or shopping practices, and by all means get rid of the credit cards! There maybe situations where credit cards are beneficial but for most of us they only become a trap. If you have any trouble with keeping your credit card balance paid off you then you need to get rid of your cards. I do not suggest this will be easy. But if you belong to Christ, it means sacrifice. You can not be pleasing to Christ and be walking in the pattern of the world.

2. Work on a plan to get out. This means developing a real budget and sticking with it. If you cannot do it on your own, ask for help, there are lots of groups that can help you. Work with your creditors, develop a payment plan. Getting out of debt is neither fun nor easy, and it takes time (avoid the quick fixes, they usually just make things worse). But it is the only way you are going to be free to follow God where He leads. Make a plan, but put your trust in Christ. Getting out of debt is a good thing, but it is not the most important thing. If you face a choice between following your plan to get out of debt, and faithfully walking with Christ, stick with Jesus.

3. Once you get out, stay out. It is foolish to go back to the same patterns that got you into debt in the first place.

14. What does Proverbs 26:11 say about this?

Paul's advice to Timothy in regards to the temptations of money was to flee from it. Do not hang around the edge, thinking you can handle it this time. Run from it and seek God's priorities instead.[16] Being in debt may not be a sin, but ignoring God's priorities and doing things just because you want to is.

15. What are some directions scripture gives to those with wealth?

    Matt. 6:19-21

    1 Tim. 6:17-18

    James 1:9-11

Jesus said that the kingdom of heaven belongs to those who are poor in spirit.[17] Being poor in spirit is the same as glorying in our humiliation. It is understanding that we have nothing without God, and only the things of God will have any lasting value. The things of this earth hold little true value. If we spend our lives seeking them or trusting in them, we will end up with nothing. Our only hope is in God. If we are not rich in the Lord, then we are truly destitute.

16. What advice does Jesus give the Christians in Laodicea? (Rev. 3:17-18)

We may not think of ourselves as being rich, but the real point is not so much what you have, as what you do with what you have. God expects us to be faithful with what He has entrusted to us, small or large. Jesus tells us that if we are not willing to be faithful with a little amount, we will not be faithful with a larger amount. He goes on to say that if we are not faithful with the things of this earth, then why would God entrust to us things of heaven?[18] It really comes down to how you view the things you have. Do they belong to you, or do they belong to God? If they belong to you, then putting God's priorities first would be a huge sacrifice, and may seem like asking too much. If they belong to God, then putting His priorities first is the least we can do, if we are going to be faithful.

17. Keeping in mind what we have learned in this lesson, how you would deal with the following scenarios?

      A. You've been tithing to your church, but your spouse just lost their job. Looking at the bills, you do not know how you can make ends meet. Your friend tells you they think you should hold off on your tithing for a while. What should do you do?

      B. Your family has a single income with the wife staying at home raising the young children because you believe that would be God's preference for your family. You are trying to tithe, but you find you are having a hard time keeping up with the bills, and now your car broke down and you would like to get a new one. What should you do?

18. What will it mean for you to walk by faith in regard to your resources?

19. What is one area with your resources that you can work on walking by faith?

LIFE EXAMPLES
JERRY[19]

For me, living by faith in regard to our resources, began when I was almost thirty. Before that I knew about faith and belief in God and Christ, but it was not a personal relationship. I grew up in a church that did not really teach that I was the sinner who needed to be saved. I knew that Christ died for the world, but felt I was a pretty good person so God would accept me. As a soldier in Vietnam, I prayed to God, and felt that He was there for me. But it would have made such a difference if I had known Him then like I do now.

When I was twenty-eight, living in Montana, I started going to a church with a pastor who was not afraid to proclaim all of the truth of God's Word. It was there I accepted that I was the sinner deserving God's judgment but that Jesus died to pay the price for me. He became my living Savior and started me on the road to letting Him become the Lord and controller of my life. As He became the Lord of my life I slowly learned that this meant all of my resources as well. My wife, Cindy, grew up believing in the importance of tithing, but this was something I had to learn. I learned that tithing was the minimum a Christian should give. It is just returning the portion due God. Giving more to God is a way of expressing our love and gratefulness to Him. Our church often had missionaries come and share, and I learned the joy of helping to support God's work. I also learned that when we step out in faith, God is faithful as well.

At this time I was working as a timber faller and was making a good wage. Our income fluctuated with the jobs and we learned to watch in amazement at how God always took care of our needs. Seeing this, we were encouraged to reach out and support missionaries more. When logging jobs disappeared I got a job in a mine working with explosives. I had no experience and the mine was being flooded with job applications but God opened the doors for me to get on. Working in the mines is not the best work for your health, but God used this time to give me an opportunity to share the Gospel there. I am not a public speaker, but the working conditions gave me the opportunity to reach into the lives of several men I would not have met otherwise. He gave me the privilege to be involved with helping some of them come to accept Christ as their personal Savior.

It was also during this time that I learned that God was interested in more than just how I spent my money. He was also interested in how I spent my time. I was an avid hunter. I would spend at least six months a year focused on hunting. It was a consuming passion with me. Because of this passion, I was unwittingly sacrificing many of the things of true importance, including my family and my relationship with God. I rationalized that if I didn't hunt during church time on Sundays, then my hunting was not interfering with my relationship with God. But God showed me that hunting had become a god to me. He finally made me understand the fact that an idol is anything I sacrifice to. My hunting was controlling me, my family and almost every area in my life.

At first I tried to just to cut back, but found myself falling into the same old patterns by the end of the season. God finally had to prevent me from getting all the game I was used to. He used my failure to break the hold hunting had on me so I could truly turn it over to Him. My obsession for hunting was one of the reasons I would never leave Montana. Letting go was not easy, but once I could let go of it I was amazed at the freedom it gave me. I still hunt occasionally but it just isn't that important any more. God had a different plan for my life.

I really enjoyed our life in Montana, but God began working to move us to Oregon. There were changes at work that affected my responsibilities and my opportunities to share the gospel. The weather and other factors were limiting our ability to get to church. God used these challenges to prepare us for a new life. A friend was moving to Oregon with a new job and he wanted us to go with him. God had already prepared our hearts to go so we were ready to agree but first we went home and prayed about it. Soon we became sure that God wanted us to go. We watched in amazement as God opened the way. In five days our home was sold for cash. We left Montana with nothing to go back to or hold us from what was ahead. It wasn't easy to leave everything and start a new life. It meant leaving friends, relatives, a good paying job and a lifestyle we had enjoyed for 24 years. Yet we went with confidence that this was what God wanted. We had learned from past experience that He could do amazing things for us when we were in His will and it is better to be in His will in new areas than out of it in the same old comfortable style.

With the new job I was promised a good wage that would provide us a good living and allow us to continue to support the missionaries like we enjoyed as well. Only things don't always work out as we think they will. The business ran into problems not long after we got there and lower wages caused things to become financially tight for us. I became very frustrated when we would get mail telling of financial needs of missionaries but had no extra funds for which to help. We began praying about our desire to support missions more and looking for other ways to earn more money.

Through my daughter we became acquainted with an opportunity to get involved with an automotive glass business. I knew nothing about running a business or working with auto glass. We did a lot of praying and despite the obstacles we felt it was the opportunity God intended to use to change our finances so we could be able to give more. Up to this time with God's provision we had been living free from debt. But in order to go into the business we would have to mortgage our home to get the finances to buy and build the business as well as to live on until the profits came. It was no small decision to jump into a different world and risk that which we already had, but we felt it was the answer God had given our prayer to serve Him. Therefore, no matter how it turned out it would be His will.

At first the business built slowly. After a few months we started making enough to pay our bills but there still was only a very limited amount of extra for giving over our tithes. We continued to pray and felt God wanted us to move to a more rural area and to expand. Once again we stepped out feeling it was God's directing. We had two years of learning experience and believed God was going to increase our business. We took on two franchises 400 miles away. After we moved, God was kind and sold our house. The new area was a real blessing. We found a strong church and a lot of support for our kids. In the meantime, God kept our business growing at a steady pace. It was exciting to see

His hand working through the jobs and timing. There was no question He was involved. I do not claim to be a gifted businessman, but God seemed to open the doors for me and bless the decisions we made.

As God blessed our business we were excited to increase our giving, and the more we gave, the more He blessed. The first full year in the new area we made $100,000. This continued to increase each year. By the fifth year the business made almost $500,000. God had answered our prayers beyond our dreams. But then things began to change. As I learned more about our business I began to get more and more uneasy with some of the practices of the company we were involved in. I began to feel God was warning us that it was time to sell out, but I was reluctant. We enjoyed the business and besides, we had family and missionaries depending on our support.

When we were slow in responding to the various warnings God was giving us, He put more direct pressure on us. Cindy was a major part of the workings of the business. By March she began to develop serious health complications which we knew were magnified by the stress involved in running the business. I felt God had given us a choice before, but since we had not responded willingly, He was now leaving us no choice. We began to seriously pray for a buyer for the businesses and to know God's new direction for our lives.

In the meantime we were worried about the missionaries we were major supporters for. God taught us that was His business not ours. Three of the families we were most concerned about had changes in their financial needs that very spring that made our donations no longer necessary.

It was fascinating to see the different maneuvers God did to get a cash buyer lined up for our major franchise. It sold fast, for cash and a very good price which is quite a challenge when selling a mobile business like ours.

In the meantime God was planning our next work. I had wanted to work at camps for many years but didn't see how I could and have the support we would need. I am not one for speaking in front of people. How could I raise the needed support? An opportunity to serve at a camp came up. After strong prayer I finally felt God was going to allow us to do it. It was so exciting to be allowed to work full-time for Him. We thought we would be able to do it if we supported ourselves by selling both franchises and our house. We would simply live on the money until it was gone and let God take care of it from there. God found the Bible camp he wanted us at and sold the main franchise so that we were able to turn it over by the first of July, the exact date we would need to be at camp if we wanted the job.

Our new life has been full of surprises. We thought we were just coming to give some trail rides and help with camp work in general, but soon we found ourselves asked to be in charge of a Bible horse camp for kids. While we have been involved with horses most of our lives, we knew nothing about running a camp of this kind. It is a special ministry because of the large number of unsaved kids that will come for the horses that wouldn't come to a Bible camp otherwise. The blessings we have received being here have been amazing. We have been privileged to see kids saved, kids baptized and lives changed. It has really been a special blessing to see how many wonderful youth and adults God uses at our camp to meet the needs here. More and more we are aware of how much running our automotive glass business, which we thought was for the money for missionaries, was also God's training ground for many of the skills we would need for our work here at camp. We see the miracles of small things God makes work and in the big miracles as well.

God has had a lot of lessons for us here, too. One is the reminder that He is still the one who supplies our needs, not us. Since we came here five years ago we have had the loss of the sale of one of the franchises, problems with our house we were selling, five operations, one heart attack and two other emergency runs to the hospital. These have made a major change in our finances. We have learned even more not to trust our plans but God's. It is all His anyway, our time, our energy, our health and the money. He will do what He knows is best. While our income in now very limited, God has provided for us in other ways instead, including gifts of support from others.

We don't know what the future holds for us. We just know that the joy of serving Him is better than any of the riches and lifestyles the world has to offer. God's plans are always best. God has blessed us with His love and care for our lives and our children, including a missionary son. All we can say is "thank You" and praise Him for His love and care.

Chapter 7
FAITH IN THE SILENCE
". . . I will never desert you, nor will I ever forsake you,"(Heb. 13:5)

The Question of Faith
Joseph - Gen 39-40

The early morning light filtered down through the bars of the high set window, and shone palely on the wall of my prison cell. I knew that it was time for me to get up and begin my morning ritual, but right at the moment I was having difficulty finding the motivation to get out of bed. If you would call a thin blanket draped over a stone shelf a bed. Years ago I would not have even considered stepping foot into this stinking, depressing hole. Now it was the place where I lived, or should I say - existed.

I think it rather ironic how my perspective of what "low" is has changed over the years. When I was back with my family, I had thought then that it was at its lowest point. I saw it as drab and boring. I was so eager to get out and experience the world. I felt trapped in the confinement of my little world. I had no idea, back then, of what confinement really was.

When I was sold into slavery by my brothers (Even now I can't think of them without feeling that strange mixture of pain, anger, and longing) I had thought that my life had reached its low point. I was sure that life couldn't get any worse. I was wrong. At least when I was serving Potiphar, there was some freedom of movement, and the food, while not being the best, had at least some variety. Life as a slave in Potiphar's household had not been enjoyable, but at least I had a purpose. Now my life consisted of meaningless days, punctuated by times of unbearable misery and unending loneliness.

I still find it hard to understand how my life has gotten to this point. Thinking back, I can see that when I was younger I was spoiled and arrogant. I knew I was my father's favorite and I took it for granted. Somehow I thought I deserved it. I saw the privileges I enjoyed as being mine by right. I not only thought they belonged to me, I assumed that I would always have them. Now I realize that life makes no promises. The things we take for granted are not rights but gifts that can be lost in the blink of an eye.

Perhaps it is true that I brought some of my problems down upon myself. I had flaunted my father's favor in front of my brothers. I thought they would not dare to touch me. I had been wrong about that as well. It seems I was wrong about a lot of things. Back then I thought God had special plans for me. I had dreams of me being someone great. One of the dreams involved my brothers bowing to me. I shared this with them, which in retrospect seems like rather a foolish thing to do. I guess I thought it would impress them with my importance. All it did was make them hate me even more. Another dream was of the sun, moon, and stars bowing to me. Oh, how lofty I was in my dreams. Now even the rats paid me no heed. Although I may have brought some of my brothers' animosity on myself, I still cannot find it within myself to forgive them for what they did. Nor can I understand why God has allowed all this to happen. I admit I wasn't perfect, but did I really deserve being sold into slavery, and then to be locked away in a dungeon?

When I first became a slave, I was angry with God. But as time went on I realized that God was still God, and fighting against Him would do me no good. I decided to put my trust in Him in spite of my circumstances. It appeared at first that this pleased God, for He blessed everything I did. When the animals were put in my care, they flourished. When the crops were in my care, we had a bumper year. Potiphar took notice of me and ended up making me his personal servant, putting me over his entire house. I thought, "Finally things are going well." But then there was Potiphar's wife. She would not leave me alone. She was continually trying to entice me to sleep with her. Sure, it was tempting. She was attractive enough, but I knew I would be a fool to get involved with the master's wife. More than that, I wanted to obey God. I still was not perfect, but I was truly trying to do what was right. But that doesn't seem to have benefitted me much.

The mistress made up some lie about me. Potiphar believed her and had me thrown into this pit. Once again I was betrayed only this time I had done nothing to deserve it. Not that it made it any better. In fact, it made it worse. I shouldn't be here, but here I was, none-the-less. And here I had been for ten long years, or something like that anyway. In truth, after five years I stopped counting the days. All I knew was that I had been here for a very long time, and I didn't know why. Why had God forsaken me?

Even as I asked that question, I knew it wasn't really true. It was just my depression talking. I could not deny that, even in this prison, God's hand was with me. Once again, He blessed whatever I did. He gave me favor in the sight of the chief jailer, and it wasn't long before I was in charge of all the other prisoners. Even here, God was taking care of my needs. If the bed was hard, at least it was clean. If the food was monotonous, at least it was edible. Because of my position, I had more freedoms than the other prisoners, and the guards treated me well enough.

Things, I knew, could be far worse. In truth, I could deal with life in this prison, if I just had some answers. If I just knew why, if I just knew how long, if I just had a glimpse of what God had planned, then I could deal with the present drudgery. It is true that at different times and in different ways, God has let me know that He is still with me, and yes, I am thankful for that, but how long?! How long, oh God, do I have to wait? How long before You bring me up from this darkness? How long before I see Your will? How long?! Over and again I ask these questions, but still I get no reply.

A year or two ago, I thought maybe things were about to change. We had received two new prisoners. One was Pharaoh's chief cupbearer, and the other was his chief baker. The chief jailer had put them under my charge. I tried to make them as comfortable as possible. After all, as I well knew, one never knew how long one might have to stay here. Then one night, both men had disturbing dreams. They felt sure their dreams had some meaning, but they were unable to understand them. God had often used dreams to speak to me, so I asked the men to share their dreams and maybe God would reveal to me their meaning.

The dreams were indeed messages from God. The chief cupbearer's dream revealed that in three days he would once again be restored to his office. The man was overjoyed. He thanked me again and again. When the chief baker heard the favorable news, he was eager to share his dream as well. His, though, wasn't so favorable. His dream revealed that in three days he would be killed. He didn't thank me for my interpretation. In fact he told me I was crazy. He said, I was a mad man and didn't know what I was talking about. I couldn't blame him. It was not news I would have appreciated either. I guess there are some things worse than sitting in prison.

I turned to the chief cupbearer and asked him, "Please, when you are released, mention me to Pharaoh. I have done nothing wrong and I do not belong here."

"If things go as you say," he said, "you can count on me."

Things had indeed gone just as God had foretold. You can rely on what God says, even if you can't rely on what people say. The chief baker was killed and the chief cupbearer was restored. For a time I waited in hope that the chief cupbearer would come through for me and I would be released, or at least would have some inquiry into my case. But as time went by, I realized that he, too, must have forgotten me. Sometimes I wondered if there was anyone out there who knew of my plight? Did anyone cared? Did anyone even remember my name? Would I die here, forgotten? It seemed cruelly ironic that God would reveal to me the future of others, but would be silent about my own.

As I lay on my stone bed, I suddenly thought of my father, and of the night he spoke of sleeping with his head upon a rock. It had been there that God had revealed Himself to my father, and had made him a promise that father had spoken of so often. God had said, "Behold, I am with you and will keep you wherever you go, and will bring you back to this land; for I will not leave you until I have done what I have promised you."[1] I remembered my grandfather Isaac telling me of God's promise to bless him and his descendants, "Sojourn in this land and I will be with you and bless you, for to you and to your descendants I will give all these lands, and I will establish the oath which I swore to your father Abraham."[2]

Grandfather Isaac told me, "This promise Joseph, is for you as well." I wonder now, how long I will have to wait to see the benefit of that promise. Then my thoughts shift to my great-grandfather Abraham, and how he had waited for twenty-five years for God to fulfill His promise of a son through my great-grandmother Sarah. I thought of all the stories my father had told me about how Abraham had trusted God, even through all that time, and how God had blessed him, time and again.

With my eyes closed, I once again hear the promises of God, only this time it was to me. "Behold, I am with you and will keep you wherever you go. I will be with you and bless you." As I open my eyes, tears began to run down the sides of my face. Sitting up I look around my cell. Taking a deep breath, I say out loud, "Okay Lord, let's start again." Kneeling down beside my bed I began to pray. "Dear God, help me one more day to walk with You."

Joseph's time as either a slave or a prisoner lasted about fourteen years. These years were not time wasted. God used this time to prepare Joseph to become the man he would need to be to fill the position of leadership God had planned for him. At the right time God had Joseph delivered from prison and established as second in command of all of Egypt. From this position he was able to save his family from starvation and extinction. It may have appeared at times that God had forgotten Joseph, but the truth was, God was working all the time. It was just that before God would work on Joseph's circumstances, He first had to do a work in Joseph.

A Closer Look

"How long, O LORD? Will You forget me forever? How long will You
hide Your face from me?" (Ps. 13:1)

There are few people that are very good at waiting, and probably none who enjoy it. Yet this is a part of every Christian's life. Numerous times scripture tells us to wait on the Lord.[3] God Himself tells us, "Wait for Me."[4] Often our response is either, "Why? Why must I wait?" or, "How long, O Lord?[5] How long will You look on?[6] How long will You hide Yourself?[7] How long will You keep us in suspense?"[8] If you have trouble with waiting for God, you are not alone. Throughout scripture we find people struggling with this very same thing. Sometimes it is connected with hardship or suffering. Other times, the circumstance itself wouldn't be so hard to deal with if it was not for the waiting, if it was not for the silence.

We pray and we pray, and we do not seem to get any response. This not only wears on our patience, it can make us wonder if God is listening, or if He even cares.

"How long, O Lord, will I call for help, and you will not hear? I cry out to
You, 'Violence!' Yet You do not save." (Hab. 1:2)

Sometimes in our struggles one of the hardest things we have to deal with is the feeling that God seems so distant. We pray, but nothing seems to happen. We wonder, "Why won't He answer me? What is He waiting for?" The truth is, He may be waiting on us. Sometimes God chooses to wait to act for reasons which He may or may not let us know. Other times God is ready to act. It is we who stand in the way. Sometimes it is God who asks, "How long? How long will you refuse to humble yourself?[9] How long do you refuse to keep my instructions?[10] How long will you remain unclean?"[11] God desires to help us, but we must first turn to Him.

"Therefore the Lord longs to be gracious to you, And therefore He waits
on high to have compassion on you. For the LORD is a God of justice;
How blessed are all those who long for Him." (Is. 30:18)

Turning to the Lord is not just asking for help, it is also submitting to His authority. God's promises of responding to our prayers are directly connected to our submission to Him.

"Yield now and be at peace with Him; Thereby good will come to you. Please receive instruction from His mouth And establish His words in your heart. If you return to the Almighty, you will be restored; If you remove unrighteousness far from your tent . . . For then you will delight in the Almighty and lift up your face to God. You will pray to Him, and He will hear you." (Job 22:21-23, 26-27)

"Then you will call upon Me and come and pray to Me, and I will listen to you. You will seek Me and find Me when you search for Me with all your heart." (Jer. 29:12-13)

To find help from God, we do not have to be sinless, but we do have to be sincere in our submission to Him. We do not have to fix our lives before we can come to Him. God loves us even at our worst, but for God to work in our life, we must be willing to surrender it to Him, and surrender it completely. A half-hearted commitment is not going to work. This is one reason why we sometimes pray to God for help, but see no result. We seek God's help, but are unwilling to give full control over to Him. Even when we truly give our life to the Lord, there are still times that we either refuse to let go, or try to take back control over certain areas of our life. We pray to Him, wondering what is taking Him so long, while all the time He is waiting for us to finally surrender the matter into His hands.

The first step, then, in receiving help from the Lord is to surrender our situation and ourselves to His authority. This does not mean we are required to fix the situation. That is God's job. Our job is to hand it over to His care and do our best to follow His lead. Our best is seldom, if ever, perfect. Then again, if we could be perfect we would not have needed God in the first place. God can deal with our weaknesses, if we will sincerely seek Him with all our heart.

The second step is to wait. Even when our heart is right with the Lord, we may still need to wait upon God to receive the help that we seek. God's ways are not our ways and God's timing is seldom our timing. But God's timing is always the best timing. Henry Blackaby in his book "Experiencing God" tells a story of a time he was serving in a church in Saskatoon. They felt God was leading them to start a building program, even though they no money to do so. They decided to trust God to provide. Through different means God began providing the money, but still they were $60,000 dollars short, and they were facing a deadline. They were expecting some money from a Texas foundation, but the money was continually delayed. They prayed, but still the money did not come. They could not understand why God was not answering their prayers.

During this time of waiting, the exchange rate for the Canadian dollar hit its lowest point in history. This fluctuation only lasted for two hour, but during that two hours the money from Texas was transferred, and because of the fluctuation, the church received $60,000 more than they would have otherwise.[12] God's timing is not only about what is best for us, but is also about what will help us to come to know Him more. While the people thought they needed the money, God knew that what they really needed was to experience His provision in a way that would affect them for the rest of their lives. God met their need for the money, but He did it His way and not theirs. Because of this, not only did they receive a blessing that had temporary benefits, but one that had eternal benefits as well.

We often get so caught up in the situation that we think things have to happen a certain way or all will be lost. We put our trust in the result we desire, rather than in God. We forget that the key to our future and our happiness is not in getting what we want, but is in walking with the Lord. If we do not wait upon the Lord and follow His leading, then even should we be able to achieve the results we want, they will not bring us the happiness we desire.

> "Bread obtained by falsehood is sweet to a man, but afterward his mouth
> will be filled with gravel." (Prov. 20:17)

This is true with obtaining our desires through falsehood. It is also true when we obtain our desires by refusing to wait upon the Lord and take matters into our own hands. Refusing to wait upon the Lord puts a lie to our faith. When we say we trust in the Lord but do things our way, we are living a lie. Living this way may enable us to gain the things we want, but eventually they will turn sour.

Take Sarah, for example. In Genesis 15, God promises Abraham that he would have many descendants. The only problem was that Sarai (Sarah) was childless. Sarah desperately wanted a child. If only she could have a son, she would be happy. She must have been excited when Abraham told her of God's promise. But as time went by, she must have begun to doubt whether God could really give them a son. After all, she was barren and now she was getting on in years. Why God delayed in fulfilling His promise we are never told, but Sarah decides she has waited long enough. She determines that if she is ever going to have a son, she is going to have to make it happen herself.

Sarah talks Abraham into taking her maid Hagar as a second wife. Her thinking is, if Hagar has a son, then he will be like a son to me. Sarah thinks that by this means, she can make God's promise come true and gain what she feels she needs to be happy. At first, things seem to work out. Hagar conceives and has a son named Ishmael. The problem is, this does not end up bringing Sarah happiness. In fact, it brings the opposite. Hagar's success only heightens Sarah's failure. Sarah's victory in doing things her way only ended up bringing her defeat. By doing things according to her plans she ended up making things worse. Sarah's solution, Ishmael, brought her only grief. God's solution, Isaac, brought her laughter and joy.

Digging Deeper

Why God makes us wait is not always clear. In fact, we may never know. But it is not necessary for us to understand God. What is important is that we understand what He desires of us. How can we expect to understand a God who could speak the universe into being? God's wisdom is beyond our comprehension, but He has explained the things we need to know. The question is, how do we respond to the things He has already told us?

1. When God seems to be silent and distant, where is a good place to start? (Ps. 139:23-24)

God wants us to know Him and His will. There may be times when He holds back from communicating with us for a particular reason, but usually it is things in our life that stand in the way.

2. What are some things that God may be waiting for us to deal with before He can answer our prayers?

Ex. 10:3

Num. 14:11

Josh. 18:3

1 Kings 18:21

Ps. 4:2; James 4:3-4

Jer. 13:27; Is. 59:2

James 1:6-7

We may not be able to remove the things that interfere with our communication with God, but God can. He does not ask us to fix our life. He asks us to surrender it. If we are willing to give the situation over to the Lord, and try to walk in faith, He can give us the strength we need. His grace can cover our weakness when we fail, and help us to start again.

3. After surrendering whatever it is that is standing in the way, what is the next step? (Ps. 25:4-5)

If we are unclear as to what God is doing in our life, the best thing we can do is ask. God wants us to ask Him what we should do, rather than just assume that we know what is best. When the Israelites were moving into the Promised Land, they got into trouble were when they moved forward by their own thinking rather than seeking God's counsel.

4. What should be our primary motivation for seeking God's will? (Ps. 143:10)

Following the leading of God will be best for us, but our primary motivation should be, because He is Lord. There is nothing wrong with wanting to know God's will, but if our motivation is for our own sense of security, or benefit, we are missing the point. The point is so that we might please God. A selfish desire, God may not answer, but if our desire is just to please Him, He will let us know what we need to know, when we need to know it. We do not have to be afraid of missing it, because God wants to let us know.

In the Bible, God used different means to let people know His will. Sometimes He used signs and wonders.[13] Other times He used angels,[14] visions,[15] or dreams,[16] as well as other means. The important thing was not the means by which God spoke, but the attitude of the one listening. Pharaoh saw God's signs, but his heart kept him from understanding them. God gave a dream to King Nebuchadnezzar, but only Daniel could understand what it meant.[17] When God spoke from the mountain, the Israelites heard only thunder, while Moses heard the voice of God.[18] In the same way, when God spoke to Jesus from the heavens, the people heard only the sound of thunder. How God spoke was not nearly as important as the heart of the hearer, and their relationship with God.

Today we do not have a cloud to show us where to go, as Moses did, but this does not mean God has left us without a guide. He has given us His Spirit and His Word to guide and direct us. How do we use them to tell us what we want to know? We do not. We let God use them to tell us what He wants us to hear. Today people are continually looking for signs to tell them what God's will is. This was true in Jesus' time as well. They were continually asking Him for signs,[19] but Jesus never gave into their demands. He would use signs from time to time, but He never did them on demand.

5. What was Jesus' attitude towards those who sought for signs? (Luke 11:29)

Jonah came preaching repentance, and the people of Nineveh listened and did what God told them to do. Rather than seeking for signs, the people should have been responding to what they already knew they should be doing. God may use signs from time to time to help us to know His will. But rather than seeking signs, God desires that we seek Him and be obedient to what we already know we should do.

6. What are some of the things God wants us to do? (Ps. 37:3-7)

God wants us to trust in Him and be satisfied with where we are at. Rather than worrying so much about what we do not know, He wants us to work at being faithful in what we do know. When our desire is centered on pleasing Him, then He will grant us what we need to know to do that.

Read Luke 18:1-7.

7. What is the point of this parable?

God is not bothered by the fact that we do not understand what He is doing. Nor is He annoyed by our continual seeking His help. In fact He desires that we be persistent.

Read Daniel 10:2-5, 12-14

8. Daniel was seeking to hear from the Lord but for three weeks he heard nothing, why?

9. If Daniel had given up after one week, what do you think would have happened?

10. God will be faithful. He will not abandon us, but what is He looking for from us? (Luke 18:8)

It is very frustrating for us to be facing a decision and not know what God would have us to do.

11. What is it that allows us to hear the voice of Christ? (John 10:14, 27)

Our relationship with God is still the key to our hearing His voice. If we want to know God's will, what we should seek is not signs but to deepen our relationship with the Lord. If our relationship with the Lord is right, then we will know when He speaks. We will not have to wonder if this is God speaking to us or not. If we are not sure what His direction is, then the best thing we can do is wait. Be content to "dwell in the land and cultivate faithfulness," and trust God will make Himself plain when we need to know.

12. Keeping in mind what we have learned in this lesson, how you would deal with the following scenarios?

A. You have been seeking God's will about making a change in the direction in your life, but do not seem to be getting any answers. What should you do?

B. You are going through an especially difficult period in you life. You pray to God but He feels so distant. Others say to have faith, but faith does not seem to be working. How do you break through the wall of silence?

13. What does will it mean for you to walk by faith in silence?

14. What is one area where you are struggling with not hearing God that you can work on walking by faith in?

Life Examples
Stan[20]

It was 1980 and my family and I lived in the heart of the Maasai territory in the Great River Valley of Kenya E. Africa. We were serving with Christian Missionary Fellowship. It was our job and calling to work with the Maasai people and learned to love them. They are a nomadic people who raise cattle, sheep and goats. They are also a very proud people and thought anyone who would stoop so low as to scratch the earth to make a garden, was unfit to live with. The Maasai live in cow dung huts and surrounded their Boma's, (villages) with a thorn tree fence to keep the unwanted visitors, like Lions and Hyena's, out. It was my job to learn the Maasai language and to go out to the villages to get to know them and to share the gospel of Jesus Christ with them.

This was not an easy task. Hours were spent each visit just listening and practicing the language. I would sit under a tree with the elders listening to them chew the news or squeeze into a small hut for tea with a family. They really had very little but what they had they were always willing to share. I had a language helper who would accompany me anywhere I went to try and teach me and keep me out of trouble. William became one of my best friends and kept me from making some major mistakes as a rookie missionary.

After a year and a half of going to a small village that was located about one half hour south of our home, I had finally gotten to the place where I had earned the right to talk to the people about Jesus. Up until this point I had read them Old Testament Bible stories about people who lived much like they did. The Old Testament stories of famine and wars kept them riveted and provided time to build relationships and gain creditability. It also gave me time to talk about a God who not only judges people but loves them and does not give up on them.

When I introduced the son of God into the story it made sense for I had been telling them all along, about the prophesies and one who would come to save all mankind. The Maasai people already believed in one God who created everything and gave it all to them. He was a god who demanded animal sacrifice to pay for the sins of the people. Enkai (their name for their God) was distant and was feared, not worshiped. Introducing Jesus to them added a completely new dimension to their God picture but they listened and eventually a group of about thirty said they wanted to start a church. All our hard work at last seemed to be paying off.

One day traveling to the village I picked up a man walking down the side of the road dressed not in traditional garb but in a suit. It happened that he was an evangelist for the Anglican Church in Kajiado, the town where we lived. I told him what I was doing and he invited himself along. That began a six month adventure where he came and helped me teach and prepare for a grand church opening.

As the day came closer for the first church plant to actually take place, I could hardly contain my excitement. I had arranged for communion to be available and for one of the local bore- holes (wells) to be working so we could baptize the new believers. Marcus, the young evangelist who had been accompanying me, and I had talked about what would take place and how it would all transpire so we could really have a great beginning. As you may or may not know, in Africa time is meaningless as far as the clock is concerned. Meetings rarely started on time and usually they happened at least three hours late. The timing all depended on when everyone got there.

On the Sunday we were to start I thought we should get there just a little early so we could make sure everything was in order. As we arrived at the tree where we had decided to set up some benches for the first service, I noticed that there was already a large crowd gathered and that they were singing. We got out and started over to the gathering only to be cut off by Marcus, who had a big smile on his face. He explained to me that the people had gathered early due to their excitement and that he had gone ahead and they had done everything they needed to do and that they were just getting ready to close and would I like to give the closing prayer.

He said the bore-hole did not work so he had sprinkled the ones who could be baptized and that they decided communion wasn't needed. Needless to say, I was floored. In a little over one hour all my plans and dreams had been turned around. Instead of fighting about the day or causing a problem that could affect the church from then on, I told Marcus that he had just planted an Anglican church and that he would now be responsible for it. He grinned with delight and I do not even think he realized the dilemma he had put me in.

Years of work and now I had to step away. I could not understand how God could have let such a thing happen. How was I going to legitimize my efforts and all the money that had been spent on us so we could plant Christian Church Churches? I had no pictures of baptisms, no snap shots of me preaching under a tree to adoring new Christians, no evidence that I had done anything at all with my time and effort. Depression set in and a sense of failure overwhelmed me. Why would God let this happen? Hadn't we sacrificed enough? Couldn't we just have a moment in the Missionary sunlight? I must admit now that it was a hard pill to swallow and self pity ran wild for a short time. Nor was this the only difficulty we were dealing with. There were health issues as well. To get a clear understanding of this, let me go back a few months.

I had gone down to Oletaukitauk on the foot hill of Kilimanjaro. Ronnie Briggs (a fellow missionary) and I were teaching in a course for Maasai evangelists. It was about a four hour drive from where we lived in Kajiado. After a week of teaching Cheryl decided she wanted to pack up the kids and come down to be with us. She and Ronnie's wife Maggie packed up the kids and headed down. The road was rough and had two foot potholes most of the way which were covered with dust so you couldn't see them. Needless to say it was a very rough ride. Did I fail to mention that Cheryl was five months pregnant at the time?

After they arrived we had a great reunion and as it was late we all went to bed. About two in the morning Cheryl woke up with terrible pain. I sat up with her for about an hour before she miscarried. As morning broke we knew we were in trouble as she continued to bleed badly. I arranged to trade rigs with Ronnie as we had a big land cruiser and he has a Toyota pickup. He would bring everyone back in my rig and I would take his with Cheryl and head for Nairobi, about five hours drive away. We headed out at first light and made it about two hours down the road when the pickup suddenly gave a shudder and stopped dead in its tracks.

We were on a sand road as flat as a pancake. I got out and tried pushing it to no avail. I took out the fuel filter and tried cleaning that. I checked all fuel lines and the fuel pump. I am no mechanic but I tried everything I knew and still nothing. Again I tried pushing it while Cheryl popped the clutch. Cheryl was getting weaker by the minute and looked a ghostly grey. I pushed until I could push no more. It was about 90 degrees out and my hands were burnt just resting them on the metal of the rig. Cheryl began to pass out due to the loss of blood and I was beginning to think that we would not make it.

There was no traffic on this road and as far as the eye could see there was no relief or shade. I fell on my knees and did what I should have done from the very beginning. I prayed like I had never prayed before. I admitted to God that I was at the end of myself and could go no further. I asked Him for a miracle and for my wife's life. I told Cheryl that we were going to try one more time and not to pop that clutch until I yelled at her. I knew I couldn't do this by myself and that the only reason this peace of junk might start was because God had stepped in.

With every ounce of energy I had left I pushed the truck until I thought my lungs and legs would burst and then yelled to drop it now. She did and as it gave its last cough and sputter it started. I ran up and jumped into the bed of the truck and then managed to climb in the window as Cheryl kept her foot on the gas. When we got to Nairobi the Doctors said if we had not gotten there in the next hour or so it would have been too late.

Now, months later, Cheryl was pregnant again. This was a great joy to us but also a concern, for the pregnancy was not going well. Cheryl was weak and ill. The doctors determined that she needed complete bed rest or she could lose the child. Not only did my concern for my wife and child weigh upon me but this also limited my ability to go out to the bush and do the work I had come to do. After much prayer and thought we decided that we should go back to the states. This was not an easy decision and left us with many questions as to why things should happen as they did. We had many questions but few answers.

Looking back now I can see God's wisdom. It was a blessing that Marcus had taken leadership of the church, for in just four months my family and I were headed back to the states. If we had been in charge of the church we would have left a baby cognation sitting out on the valley floor of Kenya with no support and no leadership. Five years later we would return for a visit and find the church still thriving and spreading the influence and message of Christianity to the other nearby villages.

Our time in Africa did not turn out as we had expected and there are some questions for which we may never know the answers. But God used that time to bless us in many ways. From that pregnancy God blessed us with a wonderful baby girl. Some of the friends we made there continue to be relationships we cherish today. And while we had to leave our work there in Kenya, God has blessed our ministry here in the states. But perhaps some of the biggest blessings came in the form of the lessons God taught us through the difficulties we faced.

I really learned to know God rather than just know about God. I have been a Christian most of my life, but in all truthfulness, I can't say that I have always walked in faith in regard to how I lived that life. I did not doubt that God existed or that He had a plan for my life. I had faith and believed in God and claimed Jesus as Lord and Savior. But my Christian walk involved me walking, hoping I was going God's way. I had never been stretched, and did quite well talking care of myself. I heard people talking about their faith, but what I mostly saw was people living just like me- by their abilities. That worked for me until my abilities ran out and life's chalenges didn't. It was then that I truly learned to walk by faith. God taught me that success in ministry isn't so much about the perceived results as it is about being faithful in our walk with Him.

I learned that not only could God take care of me better than I could, but He was just waiting to prove it. If I could only get out of the way, He was more than willing to show me on a day-to-day, moment-to-moment basis, what to do. I wish I could say that once I learned this important lesson, I never struggled again. I, however, seem to be a slow learner. And lessons learned are easily forgotten when habit and impatience get in the way. I continually ask God for guidance, only to then turn around and tell Him what that guidance should look like. I do spend a good deal of time seeking to walk by faith, because I know how important it is to wait on God's timing.

Chapter 8
FAITH IN SURRENDERING OUR PAST

. . . "forgetting what lies behind and reaching forward to what lies ahead, I press on toward the goal for the prize of the upward call of God in Christ Jesus. (Philip. 3:13-14)

The Question of Faith
Joseph - Genesis 42-45

The heat waves shimmered and danced as I gazed out across the parched, dry land. It wasn't even mid-day yet and already the sun was hot enough to boil your blood if you stayed out in it too long. One more day of cloudless skies and endless drought. Indeed, to many of the people gathered here it must seem as though the famine must go on forever. I knew that it would not go on forever, but I also knew it wasn't going to end anytime soon. Egypt was in the second year of a seven year drought. I knew how long it would last because God had given Pharaoh a dream predicting it. The dream had foretold seven years of bumper crops to be followed by seven years of drought. The dream had not only forewarned us of disaster, they had also turned out to be my deliverance from prison.

A small smile played at the corner of my mouth as I thought of the way dreams had affected my life. Long ago, my dreams of grandeur had infuriated my half brothers. Their jealousy and hatred for me had moved them to sell me to slave traders. Like some kind of animal, I was sold off for twenty shekels of silver. The traders brought me to Egypt where I spent some time as a servant before being unjustly accused of a crime against my master and thrown into prison. There I spent the following years feeling abandoned and forgotten. But God had neither forgotten nor abandoned me. Even there in prison He had blessed me. Through His power, I gained a reputation for interpreting dreams. It was this reputation that eventually led to my freedom.

The dream God gave Pharaoh was powerful and unnerving. He knew it must be important but he didn't know what it meant. Nor could his wise men give him the answer. When Pharaoh learned of my reputation, he brought me out of jail to see if I could discern the meaning of his dream. In truth, my freedom came not from Pharaoh's dream, or my reputation. It was the hand of God that delivered me. It was God who gave Pharaoh the dream, and it was God who gave me its meanings. Pharaoh was so impressed that he made me second in command of all Egypt. It was my job to prepare the nation to deal with the coming drought.

"Three bushels, Your Excellency." The words brought me out of my memories and back to my present task. "Three bushel is acceptable, I hope," said the man standing before me. He had taken my brooding silence as disapproval, and was now clearly frightened that I would deny his request and send him away empty handed.

"Yes, yes," I said, giving him a smile, "three bushels will be fine."

The man was clearly relieved. His very survival depended on whether or not I would sell him grain. He was no different than the thousands of others who had come before him, or who would be coming after. The years of plenty had come and gone.

During that time, in Pharaoh's name, I had gathered all the grain I could lay my hands on. I had vast storage bins constructed and filled all over Egypt to prepare for when the food ran out. Many doubted my predictions and thought me a fool. Food was so plentiful they couldn't imagine any danger of starvation.

Even during the first year of drought many had thought it wouldn't last. Few came to buy food, for even though the harvest was a total loss, most of them had enough surplus from the last year to get by. The second year of drought brought an end to the people's surpluses and their doubts.

"Next," I called, as I worked my way through the throng before me. The line of people stretched out for a great distance. It made me weary just looking at it. I was hot and tired, but I knew these people were suffering even worse. I tried to show kindness to those who came before me seeking aid. It was not that long ago that I had been one who faced hunger and starvation.

I smiled at the next person in line, and was about to ask him how much he wanted, when I saw something over his shoulder that made everything around me seem to fade. A short distance down the line, I saw a group of men. From their dress and beards, I recognized them as being nomads from up north. But more than that, I knew them. It had been 21 years since I had last seen them, but I knew them just the same. They were my half-brothers. A flood of conflicting emotions rose up within me. Anger, regret, curiosity, anticipation, fear, and even hope, all seemed to jumble together. These men were my flesh and blood, but they were also the ones who had betrayed me. They were my family, but they had treated me as filth, and now they were coming to me for help. With the famine, I had thought that one day I might see them again, but now that they were here I wasn't sure what to do.

I decided to keep my identity hidden for the time being. I wanted to see what kind of men my brothers had become. Being clean shaven and in Egyptian dress, I didn't think they would recognize me, but just to make sure I put on my headdress that would cover part of my face. I was hardly aware of what I was doing as I dealt with the next few buyers. Then it was their turn. They couldn't speak Egyptian, and I wasn't about to let them know I could speak Hebrew, so I called for an interpreter.

"Where have you come from?" I demanded. The compassion I had shown the others was now nowhere in sight. They could tell by my voice and the look on my face that their hopes of buying food were for some reason in jeopardy. One of them, whom I recognized to be Reuben, gave the others a signal and they all knelt before me. Then he went on to speak.

"We have come from the land of Canaan," he said, "to buy food."

As I looked at them bowing before me, suddenly a dream from many years ago flashed into my mind. In that dream my brothers' wheat stocks had all bowed before me. They had laughed at my dream then, but now here they were. Other memories came to mind as well, and few of them were pleasant. Reuben had not been there when they sold me to the slave traders, but he had been there when they threw me into the pit, so I was not inclined to make things easy for him, or any of the others for that matter.

"You are all spies," I snarled at them. "You have come to spy on our land. When my words were translated, the blood drained from their faces, leaving them pale and shaken. They realized that they were in danger of not only losing their food, but their lives as well.

"No, no," they all began to protest, shaking their heads and wringing their hands.

"We are your servants, my lord," Reuben cried out, "We have only come to buy food. We are not spies. We are honest men, all sons of one father."

"Lies!" I insisted, "You have come to spy on us."

This time Judah spoke up. "Your servants are only twelve bothers, sons of one man living in the land of Canaan. The youngest is back with our father, and one other is no longer alive."

So they no longer thought of me as being alive. Well, they had a surprise coming. "I still say you are spies," I said, "but by this you can prove yourselves. You must bring your youngest brother to me. One of you will be sent to bring him while the rest of you remain in prison. We will see if what you say is true, or if you are spies as I believe. Take them away," I commanded.

For three days I let them sit in prison. For three days I let them have a small taste of what I had experienced for years because of their treachery. I doubt they got much sleep, and surprisingly, neither did I. The revenge I had sought so long was not bringing me any satisfaction. God began to speak to my conscience. He convicted me of all the times I had failed, and how He had forgiven me. I tried to rationalize my anger, but it did little good. Still, I was not ready just to let them off the hook. First, I wanted to see if they had changed, or if they were still as hard as they had been when they laughed at me as I pleaded to them for help.

On the third day I brought them out. "Do this and you may live," I said, "for I fear God. If you are truly honest men, then let one of you remain here in confinement, and the rest of you can go and carry food back for your families. But when you come back, make sure you bring your youngest brother, if you want to live." I wasn't sure if just keeping one of them would ensure their return. After all, they had sold my life cheaply enough. But I knew the famine was only beginning, so I knew they would be back. They agreed to my command. I dismissed the interpreter and my brothers began speaking together, having no idea I could understand what they were saying.

"Truly," Naphtali said, "we are now paying for our guilt, because we ignored the distress of our brother's soul when he pleaded with us. We wouldn't listen to his distress so now it has come upon us."

"Did I not tell you," said Reuben, "do not sin against the boy? But you wouldn't listen? Now we face the reckoning for his blood."

So, I thought, they did feel some remorse for what they had done. And they hand not forgotten me after all. Conflicting emotions surged within me. The feelings were so strong that I had to turn away so they would not see my tears. When I turned back I was once more in control of myself. I looked them over. Simeon had always been the hardest of my brothers, and as I listened to their talk, it didn't seem that he had changed much. A little time in a dungeon might do him some good. I pointed him out to be bound and taken away. The rest I gave permission to buy some grain and leave. I wasn't about to take my father's money for the food, so I secretly had the money put back in their sacks. As I watched them go, I wondered when I would see them again.

They didn't return right away. It fact, months went by and there was still no sign of them. I wondered what Simeon must be thinking. Had they abandoned him? Was he to be left to die in that stinking cell? Was he going through the same fears and emotions I had faced for so long? Sometimes was would go by and look in on him, but I never let him know I was there. I had thought that watching his misery would bring me pleasure, and at first the revenge had tasted sweet, a dirty pleasure. But as I watched my brother sink into despair, the pleasure faded and all I felt was dirty. The anger that I had clung to for so long, left me feeling empty and cheated.

It was during this time that God began to soften my heart towards my brothers. I realized that God had been a part of all that had happened to me. It was not out of kindness that my brothers sold me into slavery, but God had used the situation for my good, in fact, for all our good. If I had not been taken to Egypt, if I had not been there in jail at the right time to hear Pharaoh's cup bearer's dream, then I never would have had the opportunity to interpret Pharaoh's dream. I wouldn't be in the position I am now, and I wouldn't be able to save my family from starvation.

At that time I had not been able to see what God was doing. For years it seemed like I was forgotten, but God had been there working all the time. I had learned much during those years of hardship, and one thing I had learned was the importance of compassion. People who lost their compassion became little more than animals. Their hearts became as cold as a serpent's embrace. Although they may hold power over others, in truth they lowered themselves beneath those they despised. I had determined not to become like that. Now God was putting that determination to the test. It is easy to speak of compassion when you don't have to share it with someone who has hurt you. Still, I didn't want to become cold and hard. "Lord," I prayed, "I will give you my pain and my anger. I surrender my right to revenge. Please, help me to forgive."

Eventually my brothers did return. When I saw Benjamin with them, my heart seemed to swell to the point of bursting. My brother, he looked so much like our mother. I wanted to throw my arms around him, but I held back. This was a day for celebration, but I wasn't yet willing to reveal myself. I gave instructions to have Simeon released and to have my brothers brought into my house. I ordered a feast to be made ready. I wanted to see how they would act when they were more at ease, and I was especially interested in how they would treat Benjamin.

I asked of "their" father's welfare. (How I longed to see him again.) When I heard he was doing well, my emotions threatened to overwhelm me. I stepped out of the room for a moment to take a few deep breaths, splash some water on my face and regain my composure. When I returned I called for the dinner to be served. I purposely lavished more food and honor on Benjamin. I did this not only because he was my full brother, but also to see if they would become jealous of him as they had been of me. As I watched them eat and talk, I saw no animosity towards him. In fact, they seem to be protective of him. Still I was not convinced. I had one more test for them.

I gave them permission to buy more grain and to leave. Then I gave instructions to my steward to put their money back in their sacks. In the sack of Benjamin he was to hide my silver cup. Then he was to follow them and when they had left the city he was to stop them and accuse them of stealing the cup. They were then to be brought back to me.

When they next appeared before me, my brothers all fell at my feet. With my face hard set against them I demanded, "What is this you have done? Do you not know that I have the power to discern the truth?"

"What can we say, my lord?" Judah responded. "There is no way we can justify ourselves. God knows our guilt. We are all your slaves to do with as you please."

"No," I told him, "only the one who took the cup (pointing at Benjamin) shall become my slave. The rest of you are free to go." I wondered, would they sacrifice Benjamin to save themselves, or had they changed over the years?

"Please, my Lord," said Judah, prostrating himself before me, "hear me speak. You asked us of our father and if we had another brother. We told you of our younger brother and how dear he was to our father. His older brother was killed, and our father dearly loves this lad. If anything should happen to him our father would surly die. But you told us that we had to bring our younger brother or we could not come back. Our father was very reluctant to let him come, and if he doesn't return, then our father will surely go to his grave. Please, let me take his place. I will be your slave, only I beg you let the lad go back with his brothers."

Here at last was what I was hoping for. God had indeed changed their hearts. Judah was willing to offer himself up to save his half-brother. Still I hesitated to open myself up to them. To do so would make me vulnerable. What if they rejected me again? If I revealed myself to them I would lose my advantage over them. But I realized that holding on to my advantage was bringing me no happiness. It was only separating me from the peace for which I longed. "Lord," I silently prayed, "I surrender all into Your hands." With that I dismissed the servants and turned to my brothers. "I am Joseph," I said, speaking in Hebrew. "I am your brother!"

It took a while for Joseph's brothers to realize that this was indeed their brother, and even longer to believe that he was not going to take revenge for what they had done to him. In fact, even years later on they were still afraid that Joseph would strike back at them. Joseph's forgiveness allowed him to be reunited with his family. While his brothers lived with guilt and doubt, Joseph lived in freedom for he had surrendered the past into the hands of God. Joseph's forgiveness was a benefit to his brothers, but the one who benefitted most from it was Joseph.

A Closer Look

Surrender is one of the most powerful things a Christian can do. When we completely give something over to God then not only does this please God, but it also opens up the situation to the power of God. When we stop trying to dictate how things are to work, God is free to act. Unfortunately, surrendering is not something we are very good at, or enjoy.

We are often hesitant to surrender complete control to God because we are afraid of what that might mean. We are afraid He might ask of us something we do not want to do, or take something away that we do not want to lose. The more we grow in our relationship with the Lord, the more we find we can trust Him. We experience His love and care and come to realize that we have nothing to fear from trusting in the Lord. While we may realize this with our mind, it does not necessarily mean we will always feel this way. Even when we learn to surrender one area of our life, we often have to go through much struggle before we learn to surrender other areas of our life as well.

In "The Pineapple Story"[1] Otto Koning tells of how his life and ministry were in a shambles until he finally learned the power of surrender. When he surrendered his rights of ownership, not only did it bring peace within his life, but it was then that God stepped into the situation. It took some time, but God used the situation to begin reaching the hearts of the people that Otto had failed to reach on his own, and to bring blessing to Otto far beyond what he could have managed while holding on to control. This lesson was something Otto had to learn many times. Not just in the area of rights of ownership, but also in the areas of health, family, reputation, and others. Each time Otto was brought to the point of losing what he had before he was willing to surrender it to God.

Surrender is a key component to walking by faith. It plays a part in every chapter of this study, and is something we will have to learn over and over again. In this chapter we will look at surrender as it connects with forgiveness and letting go of the past. Over and over again in the New Testament we are told that we are to forgive others.[2] Why are we told so often? Because the truth is, we are not very good at it. Now to be fair, it is not very easy. It is our nature to think of ourselves first and to strike back when others hurt us. We reason that they deserve it, or that if we do not they will just keep on hurting us or others. The idea of just letting someone get away with doing wrong (especially against us) goes against our passion for justice.

We need to understand that forgiveness is not about ignoring justice, or saying that what someone else did is okay. Forgiveness is about surrendering the situation into the hands of God, and trusting that He will take care of it. God says, "VENGEANCE IS MINE, I WILL REPAY."[3] Forgiving someone does not necessarily mean there will not be consequences for their actions. God is willing to forgive us for our sins, but sometimes we still have to deal with consequences. We may forgive our children for their wrongdoing, but we may still need to discipline them. To forgive someone means we let go of anger and the need for vengeance. Why should we do this? First, because God has told us to. Secondly, because anger and vengeance often lead us to do things that not only hurt others, but usually end up hurting us as well.

God has told us to let go of anger, vengeance and bitterness. This is for our benefit more than anyone else's. The more we hang onto anger and bitterness, the more they warp our entire being. It affects our relationship with others. Have you ever been around an angry, bitter person? If you have, you know how little you enjoy their company. Their anger often does more damage to their life than the original offense.

When we look in the news we see places in this world where people's lives seem dominated by the need for vengeance. They sacrifice lives, the well being of their country, and the future of their own families, all out of anger. Their thirst for vengeance is destroying them, while forgiveness could bring peace and prosperity. We can see the foolishness of their actions, but we often miss how foolish we are when we are the ones holding on to anger. We may feel we have the right to anger or bitterness. But if we have given our lives to the Lord then we have also surrendered the right to respond as we choose. Our anger, indeed, the entire situation belongs to the Lord. We are to seek His will not ours. Our bitterness grieves Him[4] and puts a wall up between us and Him. When we hold on to bitterness it is we who sin against God, no matter what someone else may have done. Becoming angry is not sin.[5] There are some things we should be angry about. But we must deal with our anger in a manner our God would have us to.

We are not to strike out in our anger, nor are we to just bury it. Sometimes people feel the need to get on with life, but they do not want to let go of their anger, so they just push it to the back of their mind and go on. This may work for a while. It may fool those around us, and we may even think we are beyond it. But anger and bitterness that is not dealt with will continue to fester. It will affect our lives and rob us of our joy. We may not even be aware of the source of the problem. Unresolved anger can lay hidden for years, and then begin to show itself in ways we would not expect. It may appear as a numbness of spirit, or in flashes of irrational anger against people who do not deserve it. It may appear as self-loathing or depression. Unresolved anger may be at the root of many of these problems. To be free of them the anger must be dealt with. God's way of dealing with anger is to forgive, to surrender into His hands and seek His will. The sooner we do that, the better it is for us.

Letting go of anger can be easier said than done. We may want to be free of anger, and yet still find ourselves coming back to it time and again. I believe this is part of the reason why God has called us to go beyond letting go of anger and to reach out with love.

> "But I say to you who hear, love your enemies, do good to those who hate
> you, bless those who curse you, pray for those who mistreat you."
> (Luke 6:27-28)

Loving our enemies may seem to be more than we can handle. But the love God requires of us is not about feeling love towards our enemies, but that we treat them in a loving manner. This is both to help our witness, and to help us.

If we want God to forgive our sins, then the bare minimum that is required of us is that we are willing to forgive others.[6] But when we go beyond that, and actually reach out in kindness to those who have harmed us, not only will we mystify them, but we open ourselves up to receive God's blessing. One of the biggest blessings of going the extra mile[7] is that it frees us from the evil of anger and bitterness. Even when we try to forgive someone, we may still, at times, feel overwhelmed by resentment. When we choose to act in kindness towards them, it breaks resentment's hold upon us. This does not mean that what they did, or are doing, does not bother us. It just means it does not control us. We are free because we have surrendered the matter into the hands of God and we choose to walk by faith, trusting that He can deal with the situation.

Walking by faith in forgiveness is not easy. It means letting go of fears and anger. It means turning the other cheek, and going the extra mile. Why should we do it? First, because God told us to and our goal is to please Him. Secondly, because in the end it really is what is best for us and those around us. Walking by faith is not about convincing others to change their ways. That is God's job, not ours. Walking by faith is doing our best to be obedient to God's will for our life, and trusting the rest into the hands of God.

Not only do we need to learn to forgive others, we also need to learn to forgive ourselves. Sometimes it is our sins we have the most difficultly forgiving. When we give our lives to the Lord, He owns our sins. They are no longer ours to hold on to. Christ has already paid the price for those sins on the cross.[8] Satan may tell us that our sins are too much to be forgiven. We must continue to pay for them. But Satan is a liar. It is true that there may be earthly consequences for our sins that we may have to live with, but as far as God is concerned, when we give our life to Christ our sins are removed, all of them. There is no more price that needs to be paid.[9] Should we sin again, all we need to do is confess that before God, and He will cleans us from that sin.[10] God not only can forgive our sins, He wants to forgive our sins. This subject will be discussed in more depth in a later chapter.

Another area of the past that we need to be willing to surrender is our past experiences, whether they be disappointments or successes. The past is good to learn from, and even build upon, but if we cling to the past it will keep us from experiencing what God has for us in the present and future. When Miriam and Aaron thought their past successes entitled them to positions of honor[11] they soon found out that God is not impressed with our accomplishments, especially since He was the one truly responsible for them in the first place. What God is looking for in His servants is humility. When we become impressed with our successes we diminish our usefulness to God.

Holding on to past disappointments can also diminish our usefulness to God. When the People of Israel were defeated by the people of Ai,[12] Joshua tore his cloths and fell on the earth before the Lord. He thought God had abandoned the people, and all was lost. God basically told Joshua to get up and quit whining. The reason they had failed was because they had not been obedient to what He had told them to do. What they needed to do was not to focus on the failure, but to repent, or change what was wrong, rededicate themselves to the Lord, and go forward.

When Saul turned out to be a failure as a godly king, we are told that Samuel grieved over him.[13] Then God spoke to Samuel.

"Now the LORD said to Samuel, "How long will you grieve over Saul, since I have rejected him from being king over Israel? Fill your horn with oil and go; I will send you to Jesse the Bethlehemite, for I have selected a king for Myself among his sons." (1 Sam. 16:1)

We have a tendency to hold onto past disappointments, but God wants us to look forward. This does not mean that we forget the past or just give up on those who have disappointed us. It means we surrender the people or the situation into the hands of God, and we seek His will for the present.

If Christ is Lord, then he is Lord of all. This includes our successes, our disappointments, our hurts, and our sins. We have held on to some of these things so long that they seem to be a part of who we are. We may be afraid that if we let go of them we will loose a part of ourselves. But that which we cannot surrender becomes an idol in our lives. It stands in the way of our relationship with Christ. Surrendering something to God does not mean that we necessarily lose it. If it is causing us harm God may remove it from us, or He may change it into something beautiful. God loves us more than we can ever know. He wants to help us, not harm us. We can trust Him with our present, our future, and our past. It is not easy to surrender that which we have held onto for so long, but it is a part of what it means to walk by faith.

Digging Deeper

Surrendering is one of the hardest things for us to do, but it is also one of the most powerful and freeing things for us to do.

1. We often connect surrendering something with losing it, but what does Jesus connect surrendering to? (Luke 17:33)

2. One of the hardest areas we have to deal with is the area of forgiveness. What does Jesus say about forgiveness? (Matt. 18:21-22)

We sometimes struggle with whether or not someone deserves to be forgiven when they continue to do the same thing over and over. We may not feel like forgiving someone time and again. In Luke 17, when Jesus told this to His disciples, they asked Him to increase their faith. They must not have felt up to the task either. Jesus then goes on to speak of how a servant is expected to do the work he has been given. For a Christian, forgiveness is not about whether or not the person deserves it, but the fact that God has commanded it.

3. Forgiveness doesn't come naturally. What may help to motivate us to forgive others?

     Matt. 6:14-15

     1 Peter 3:8-9

4. If we choose to forgive someone, does that mean they are free from the consequences of their act? (Rom. 12:17-19)

5. What are some of the benefits of going beyond forgiveness and choosing to reach out in love? (Rom. 12:20-21)

6. What is the example of what forgiveness is to look like? (Eph. 4:29-32; Col. 3:12-13)

Christ is our example of forgiveness. This makes the standard pretty high, but it can also be encouraging, for He will not ask us to forgive others any more than He is willing to forgive us.

7. How often are we to forgive others? (Luke 17:3-4)

Seven is seen as the perfect number. It represents completeness. In other words, we are to forgive others as often as they repent and ask for forgiveness,.

8. How often then will God forgive us?

9. How much of our sin is God willing to forgive? (Col. 2:12-14; 1 John 1:9)

10. When we bring our sins to God, how long does He hold them against us, and what will we need to do to pay for them? (Heb. 10:17-18)

Continuing to punish ourselves for past sins is not a godly thing to do. It goes against God's will. If we hear a voice bringing up past failures, it is not God speaking but Satan. We must remind ourselves that we have already surrendered those sins to God. They are no longer attached to us. Christ has already paid for them, and they no longer exist in the eyes of God.

11. Our past success or failures will have their own rewards or consequences, but what is God most interested in? (Ez. 33:12-15)

12. The churches at Ephesus and Sardis had in their past been very faithful, but then had grown lax in their faithfulness. What was Christ's message to them? (Rev. 2:5; 3:2-3)

13. How important did Paul regard the things of his past? (Philip. 3:7-8)

Paul had many disappointments in his life, betrayals, imprisonments, and calamities. He could have dwelt on what could have been, but he did not.

14. Where did Paul keep his focus? (Philip. 3:12-14)

15. Keeping in mind what we have learned in this lesson, how you would deal with the following scenarios?

      A. Someone at work who is harboring a grudge against you has been spreading false rumors about you. Now you find you have been assigned to work on a committee with him/her. How will you deal with him/her?

      B. You have been in charge of a ministry at church for a number of years. Now the leadership has decided to have someone else be in charge of the ministry. How do you respond?

16. What will it mean for you to walk by faith in surrendering the past?

17. What is one area you need to work at letting go of?

Life Examples
Sue[14]

      A few years ago I experienced an incident in my life that helped me understand the power of prayer and the strength found in faith. The focus of the incident was a clarinet which I loaned to my sister for her daughter to use. In order to fully understand what was involved in the situation, I will need to go back a few years. I have a grandson named Joey, who is very dear to my heart. In fact, I raised Joey myself for ten years. His first few years before he came to me had been very unsettled. I poured myself into him, and did my best to provide a loving and stable home for Joey. He meant the world to me. At one point, Joey wanted to learn to play the clarinet. I thought learning to play an instrument would be good for Joey, so even though it was rather expensive, I bought him one. It was a gift of love. His interest in the clarinet eventually waned, but the instrument still held sentimental value to me.

      When Joey reached high school age, his mother took him out of my home. I had legal custody, and could have fought to force him to come back with me. But I thought that would only put Joey in the middle of a mess and would do him more harm than good. I loved Joey, but I decided that he was old enough to choose for himself where he wanted to live. My rules were more strict than Joey wanted, and so in the end he decided to leave. It broke my heart to lose this boy who meant so much to me. When he left, he took most all of his things, but one thing he left behind was the clarinet.

Later on, my niece also expressed an interest in learning to play the clarinet. I was reluctant to loan out Joey's clarinet because it was one of the few things I had that belonged to him. But I also knew that it would be foolish to have her buy a clarinet when this one was just sitting unused. I loaned them the clarinet but I made sure they understood that I wanted it back when she was done with it.

The years went by and my niece graduated from high school, so I decided to ask for the return of the clarinet. I was assured they would get it back to me, but time went on and still they didn't return it. I inquired again and was told that they weren't sure where it was located, but they were sure they could find it and would send it to me. But again nothing happened. The fact that I was dealing with family only made things harder. If I was dealing with someone else, I would have been more forceful, and demanded its immediate return, but I didn't feel that I could do this with family. I also felt that as family they should have been more sensitive to my wishes. Their continual inaction made me feel as if they had little concern for me and the things that were dear to me.

As it turned out, it was a good thing they hadn't returned the clarinet sooner, because I had a house fire and all that I owned was destroyed, including the few things I had to remind me of Joey. If I had his clarinet it would have been destroyed as well. This, however, only made me more concerned with getting it back. Now it was the only thing of Joey's I had left. After the fire I decided to move to another area. Once again I asked for the return of the clarinet, and I was promised that they would get it to me before I moved. But that promise proved to be false as well. It felt that I was leaving behind my past, and Joey along with it.

My new home turned out to be a blessing from God. I found a church body to be involved in, and God blessed my life. I was thankful for all God was doing, but still Joey's clarinet seemed to haunt me. In fact, it became almost an obsession. The frustration over not receiving it was causing me to feel anger and resentment against my family. This anger was robbing me of peace, and I knew this is not what God would want, but I couldn't seem to put it behind me.

One day I was talking to my pastor and I confessed to him my anger over the situation, and asked him how I could be free of it. He asked if I would be willing to give the clarinet to God. He said that my anger was connected to my ownership of the clarinet. If I wanted to be free of the anger I would need to surrender the clarinet, and indeed the entire situation, over to God. "The Lord," he said, "takes far better care of the things He owns, than we ever can. You may never get your clarinet, but at least it would lose its hold on you." He asked me to write, "my clarinet" down on a piece of paper, and to put it in the offering tray next Sunday.

I told my pastor that I would do this, but after he was gone I began to have second thoughts. I wasn't sure I wanted to let go of the clarinet. I never have worried about things that much, and have always been willing to share what I had. But I was afraid that surrendering the clarinet would mean that I would lose my last piece of Joey. I got down on my knees at the end of my bed, and I prayed for God's strength. Then I surrendered the clarinet over to Him. I told Him that I would be thankful for its return, but if He wanted to use the clarinet for some other use that would be fine with me. Whatever God wanted, that was fine with me.

As I knelt there praying, it was as if there was a tremendous load removed from me. My head felt clearer and my body felt stronger than it had for a long time. My heart felt free, and it beat with joy. As I knelt there, I felt something I had never felt before. It was as if there was an angel standing there beside me with his arm around me, telling me it was going to be okay. That Sunday I wrote, "my clarinet" on a piece of paper and put it in the offering tray. In truth I had already surrendered the clarinet earlier at the foot of my bed, but this was a confirmation of the transfer of ownership. The clarinet wasn't mine any more. It belonged to God. After I put the piece of paper in the tray, I didn't even think about it anymore. I was free.

A few days later I got in the mail a package. It had no return address, and I didn't have a clue as to what it might be. When I opened the package, there I found my clarinet. It must have been mailed shortly after I had surrendered it to God. What I had been trying to do on my own, for years was accomplished by the power of prayer and surrender in such a short time. I try to remember this incident whenever I face other challenges in my life. It comes down to the simple fact: if we continue to serve God and have faith in Him, we will get answers.

Chapter 9
FAITH IN FACING THE FUTURE

"'For I know the plans that I have for you,' declares the LORD, 'plans for welfare and not for calamity to give you a future and a hope.'" (Jer. 29:11)

The Question of Faith
Abraham - Genesis 22:1-19

He was getting so tall, this son of mine. Walking beside him, I was made to realize that he wasn't a little boy any more. Isaac wasn't yet a man, but already I could see within him the man he would become. He was thin and a bit gangly, but I could tell by the way he handled his load of wood that he had a strength about him that his thinness belied. He is a son of whom any father would be proud. For me he was even more than a child to love, he was my hope for the future, and a symbol of God's love, faithfulness, and awesome power. For this son of mine was truly a walking miracle.

For years Sarah and I had tried to have children, but we had been unable to gain the child we desired. What seemed to be so easy for others, proved to be impossible for us. We prayed for God to give us a child, and couldn't understand why He refused to answer our prayers. Eventually, I became resigned to the fact that I would never have a son. How could I hold on to resentment against God when He had done so much for us? He brought us up to this land of plenty, and blessed us in so many ways. Even when I failed Him, He was still willing to forgive me and to continue to watch over me. If it was His will that we should be childless, then so be it. He was God and I would serve Him.

Then one day the Lord appeared to me in a vision. He told me that He was going to reward me. I could think of nothing I desired except a son, but at my age I knew that was impossible. I assumed that my nephew would become my heir, but the Lord told me that I was to have a son of my own. He showed me the stars and said, "Thus will your descendants be." It all seemed too good to be true, but in spite of what reason seemed to dictate, I chose to believe that God would do just what He said. I chose to believe in God's faithfulness.

God did indeed show Himself to be faithful. My son here beside me was a testimony to that faithfulness. It didn't happen exactly as we had expected. God's timing isn't our timing, and at first, nothing changed. Months drifted into years, and still no child came. In some ways, this was even harder to deal with after we had received God's promise. Had I been mistaken? Had God changed His mind? We got impatient and tried to help things along, and as usual, only made things worse. Finally I just had to stop worrying about it and trust God would do as He said, and sure enough, God showed Himself to be true.

At the age of 90, Sarah became a first-time mother. Isaac came into our lives bringing joy and laughter. He has been such a blessing to our lives in so many ways. It's hard to conceive of life without him, which makes this present journey all the more difficult. For though he doesn't know it yet, Isaac walks this path to die. And I, his father, am to be the one who kills him.

Three days ago God spoke to me once again. I heard His voice call out to me, "Abraham."

"Here I am," I replied. I was surprised and excited to hear His voice, and I was eager to discover what He had to say to me. My excitement soon turned to shock and dismay when He continued on.

"Take now your son," the Lord said, "your only son, whom you love, Isaac, and go to the land of Moriah, and offer him there as a burnt offering on one of the mountains of which I will tell you."

For a while I just sat there, stunned. I was sure that there must be something more, something that would change the message and bring some sanity to the situation. But that was all there was to the message. I was to offer Isaac as a sacrifice. I wanted to believe that there must be some mistake, that I heard wrong, or that the message had just been my imagination. But I knew the voice to be God's, for I had come to know it over the years, and the message had been too clear to interpret any other way.

In the past I might have tried to change the message or make a partial attempt at obedience. But after being around for over 100 years, you eventually learn a thing or two. One thing I learned was that partial obedience doesn't work. Numerous times I have tried that game, being obedient up to a point but then changing things to fit what made sense to me. Each time that I tried to help God by changing the plan, not only did I displease God, but I ended up making a mess of things for myself as well. Eventually God helped me to see that selective obedience was disobedience. I was left with only two choices. I could ignore what God told me and do things my way, or I could be obedient and do things His way.

"My father," Isaac said, snapping me out of my thoughts and bringing me back to the present.

"Here I am, my son." I said, as I turned and looked at him with a smile.

"Behold, the fire and the wood," he said, looking about questioningly, "but where is the lamb for the burnt offering?"

The smile melted off my face, and I took a moment looking off over the horizon before I responded, "God will provide the lamb." I turned and looked at Isaac once again and said with more conviction this time, "He will provide the lamb for the burnt offering, my son." And as I said it, I believed it to be true. Somehow, someway, God would provide.

I know this may sound like wishful thinking, but it is the conclusion I came to that evening three days ago when God had given me the direction. My first inclination had been to say, "No, this is asking too much." But as I thought about it, I began to feel that God must have a plan for all this. After all, had He not promised that I would become the father of many nations, and that they would come through Isaac? I knew that God didn't lie, and that His promises are true. If we believe and obey Him, God always comes through. From experience, I knew that God's ways are not our ways, but He is faithful. Somehow, God would provide.

In the back of my mind, a persistent voice kept asking, "But what if He doesn't? What if He takes Isaac away and leaves you with nothing? Are you willing to sacrifice your only son?" Was I really willing to sacrifice my son? I believed that God would provide, but if He didn't, would I still obey? I realized, then, that I must. Not out of fear of what He might do if I didn't, but because the Lord is my God. He is my all and all and my very life belonged to Him. It was He who had given us Isaac in the first place. If it's He who gives, then can I deny Him the right to take way? Even should He take my son, would He still not be God?

"But how could He ask of you such a thing?" the voice questioned again. "What kind of God would take away your son? He doesn't care for you. He is merely playing with you."

"No," I said to myself. "My God loves me. He has shown me that time and again, and I will not doubt Him." To doubt Him would be like doubting that my heart would continue to beat. It would be like doubting that the sun would rise in the morning. It was true that all seemed dark at the moment, and I couldn't understand what God was doing, but I believed that God held my future and the future of my son in His hand, and He would not fail us. Not now, not ever. I would believe. I had to, for it was life itself.

That night had been a long one, but in the morning I arose with a confidence and a determination. It took us three days to journey to Moriah. There Isaac and I had left the servants and begun the climb to the top of the mountain. He carried the wood, and I carried the coals for the fire and the knife for the sacrifice.

As we reached the top I felt a dread begin to creep over me. I had hoped that somehow God would have intervened before we got here, but here we were. "How can you take the life of you own son?" The inner voice cried out once more. I sat down, feeling very old indeed. Isaac dropped his bundle and rushed to my side.

"Father," he said with concern showing in his face, "are you alright?"

"Yes, my son," I replied, patting his arm, "I'm just not as young as I used to be. Go gather the stones for the altar, and let me rest a bit. I will be fine soon."

Isaac moved away hesitatingly, still concerned about me, but obedient to my wishes. I watched him as he moved the stones and built the altar. He stopped a couple of times and looked around. I suppose he was still wondering about the sacrifice. I didn't know how I was supposed to tell him. "Lord, please," I prayed, "if it be Your will, may you remove this from me." But no answer came, no matter how many times I made the request.

When Isaac was done, he looked over at me and said, "It is ready, my father."

I could put it off no longer. I got up and walked over to him. Those few steps were the hardest I have ever walked.

"Stretch out your hands," I told Him. Isaac looked at me with surprise and confusion written across his face, but he did as he was told. In our culture children are taught not to question their fathers, but as I lashed his wrists with a leather strap, Isaac could restrain his question no longer.

"Father," he said, "I don't understand. What are you doing?"

I looked into my child's eyes, and could not stop the tears which ran from my own. "I'm not sure I understand either, my son, but I need you to trust me." He nodded, and at my urging, sat down, allowing me to tie up his ankles.

"Trust you," that inner voice cried out in accusation, "trust you when you are about to take his life? What kind of father are you? How can you do this?"

As I knelt there binding him, a tremendous weight seemed to press down upon my shoulders. I stopped for a moment and closed my eyes. "Lord," I prayed, "I don't think I can do this. Help me, please!"

From deeper within, a different voice spoke, or maybe it was just an echo of my own. It required of me the same thing I had asked of my son. "I need you to trust me."

I thought again of the many times God had provided for me. I thought of the promises He had made, and how He had fulfilled them, time and again, when I trusted in Him. I thought of the night the Lord had shown me the stars in the heavens above. I remembered the day Isaac born, holding him in my arms. I remembered the night I took him out and showed him those same stars. "He must have a plan," I told myself. The only way I could ask Isaac to trust me was if I was willing to trust God. My God is a loving god. He is all powerful and faithful. He wouldn't ask this of me if He didn't have a reason and if He didn't have a plan. I knew that He could protect Isaac from death, or even bring him back to life if need be. "He must have a plan," I told myself again.

I gathered Isaac up into my arms, and for a moment just held him against my breast. Then, with tears steaming down my face, I looked to the heavens and prayed, "Lord, I lift up to You my son, my future, my hope, and my life. I will trust in You, for You are my God." I laid Isaac upon the altar, and stooped to pick up the knife.

"Father?" Isaac's voice quavered, "Father?!"

I could not look into his frightened eyes, and I shut my ears to his questioning voice. I took hold of the knife that would pierce my son, as well as my heart, with the same blow. With a trembling hand, I lifted it above my head, and cried out once again, "He must have a plan!"

Abraham didn't have to use the knife on his son. God intervened and provided a ram to be used as a substitute. But because of Abrahams faith, God promised to bless Abraham and his descendants. This blessing included Isaac. What looked at first to be a sacrifice of his son, turned out to be a blessing upon him instead.

A Closer Look

I think most of us have looked at this story and wondered, "How could Abraham have done this? How could he have been willing to kill his son? Well, one thing we have to keep in mind is that Abraham lived in a far different culture than we do today. In Abraham's time, child sacrifice was a custom carried out by the people living in the area.[1] Abraham's neighbors may very well have carried out this custom. The practice continued on even to the time of the exile in Babylon.[2] Nor was it only done by foreigners, some of people of Israel fell into this practice as well.[3] The practice was done in connection with fertility gods. The idea was that if they sacrificed their first child, then this would ensure prosperity and fertility in the years ahead.

Abraham may not have been as surprised as we may think when God made this request, but it would not have made it any easier. Isaac brought so many things to Abraham's life. He brought laughter, joy, new life and a hope for the future. Through Isaac his line would be carried on. Through Isaac, God's promise would be fulfilled. But God wanted Abraham to know that the key to the future was not in Isaac, but in his faith in the Lord.

Child sacrifice was never something acceptable to God. It was an abomination to Him, and expressly forbidden by Him in the law of Moses.[4] Even here God did not tell Abraham to kill his son. He told him to offer him up as a sacrifice. Now Abraham would have understood this to be the same thing. But what God wanted was not Isaac's death, but Abraham's willingness to surrender to the Lord even that which he treasured the most. It is not that God originally intended for Abraham to kill Isaac, and then later changed His mind. God had it planed this way from the beginning. The question was whether or not Abraham was willing to trust God.

While God did not require child sacrifice, He did want His people to know that the first of everything, including their children, belonged to Him.[5] Unlike with other religions, God allowed a substitute to take the place of the child. By this God not only showed His mercy but also that it was not the death of the child that would ensure the well being of the family, but the faith and obedience of the parent.

God asked a lot of Abraham, but no more than He was willing to do Himself. In the story of Abraham and Isaac we see many similarities to what God did for us through His Son Jesus Christ. He too was a beloved only son who was willing to be obedient to His Father. Jesus left His servants behind, walking the path up a hill with His Father. He, too, carried the wood for the sacrifice upon His back. However, God did not use a substitute to take Christ's place. Rather, He became the substitute to take our place. Once again, God provided the lamb.

Today the idea of child sacrifice seems barbaric to us, and yet in many ways it continues to be the way we try to deal with the future. Abortion, primarily, is a parent's attempt to ensure the well-being of their future by sacrificing the life of the child. Rather than to the god of fertility, the child may be sacrificed to the god of pleasure or of convenience, but it is no less an abomination to God. Nor is abortion the only way children are sacrificed.

All too often, with our eyes on our "future," we sacrifice the well-being of those who need us most. Whether it is because of a career, a relationship, or some other driving force, our children are either left behind or are conditioned by our example to ignore God's directions. The irony is that often it is in our pursuit of securing a good future that we end up making a mess of the present, and then of the future as well. Sometimes the focus is on our happiness. We feel if we just had certain things or had a different relationship, then we would be happy. Other times our concern is for the happiness of our family. The problem is that we mistake what it is that is required for us to secure the future that we need.

The Bible does not talk a lot about what we are to do about the future. Its focus is more on what we are to do about today. This does not mean God does not want us to prepare for the future. He does. Scripture tells us that one of the reasons the nation of Israel got into trouble is because it did not consider its future.[6] In Deuteronomy, Moses is giving his farewell speech to the people of Israel as they prepare to head into the Promised Land. Over and over he tells them what they need to do to ensure the well-being and prosperity for themselves and for their families in the days ahead.

> "So you shall keep His statutes and His commandments which I am giving you today, that it may go well with you and with your children after you, and that you may live long on the land which the LORD your God is giving you for all time." (Deut. 4:40)

> "Be careful to listen to all these words which I command you, so that it may be well with you and your sons after you forever, for you will be doing what is good and right in the sight of the LORD your God." (Deut. 12:28)

When we think of preparing for the future, we often think of savings, education, getting a good job. We think of these things because we know there are going to be situations and responsibilities that we are going to need to take care of. Most of us realize that not all of the things we want are true necessities, but we would like them anyway. Other things are true needs. God knows this. He does not tell us, "Do not be concerned with the future, for you do not really need anything." God knows we have needs and He wants to provide for them. He wants us to prepare for the future, but the best way we can prepare for the future is by focusing on walking with Christ today.

> "Do not worry then, saying, 'What will we eat?' or 'What will we drink?' or 'What will we wear for clothing?'. . . for your heavenly Father knows that you need all these things. But seek first His kingdom and His righteousness, and all these things will be added to you." (Matt. 6:31-33)

If God knows that we need these things, how can He expect us to put His priorities first? There are a number of reasons.

1. God knows that many of the things we think we need really will not provide for us the future we desire. The things of the world do not satisfy. They never have and they never will. For a time they may give us pleasure, but they will always leave us wanting more.

> "He who loves money will not be satisfied with money, nor he who loves abundance with its income. This too is vanity." (Eccl. 5:10)

"Do not weary yourself to gain wealth, Cease from your consideration of it. When you set your eyes on it, it is gone. For wealth certainly makes itself wings like an eagle that flies toward the heavens." (Prov. 23:4-5)

2. God knows that when we focus on earthly things, we neglect the things we need most. We were created for an eternal purpose. Our life has eternal meaning, and our choices have eternal consequences, whether we want to think of them or not. If we focus on earthly things, not only will they not bring us lasting happiness, but we will end up forfeiting the things that do. We will have squandered our life on things that have no lasting meaning, and we will end up with nothing.

"Do not store up for yourselves treasures on earth, where moth and rust destroy, and where thieves break in and steal. But store up for yourselves treasures in heaven, where neither moth nor rust destroys, and where thieves do not break in or steal; for where your treasure is, there your heart will be also." (Matt. 6:19-21)

"For what does it profit a man to gain the whole world, and forfeit his soul?" (Mark 8:36)

3. God wants to provide for His children. He wants to bless us, but blessing comes through faith and obedience. There are many times God wants to provide for us but we are so busy worrying about ourselves that we get in His way. Our lack of faith robs us of the blessings God desires to share. The true benefit of the blessings God desires to share with us are not in the things themselves but in the way they can point us to God, and can help us experience the reality of God's presence.

"But seek first His kingdom and His righteousness, and all these things will be added to you." (Matt. 6:33)

"'Bring the whole tithe into the storehouse, so that there may be food in My house, and test Me now in this,' says the LORD of hosts, 'if I will not open for you the windows of heaven and pour out for you a blessing until it overflows.'" (Mal. 3:10)

4. God is to be first. It is not our benefit that is to be most important. It is not even our families that are to be most important. God's priorities are to be first in our life. Abraham is not the only one God has called to sacrifice his family. We, too, are called to put our families on the altar, or to surrender them under the authority of God.[7] This does not mean that He wants them dead any more than He wanted Isaac dead. We are called to place all we have, including ourselves, and our family upon the altar of God.

"So then, none of you can be My disciple who does not give up all his own possessions." (Luke 14:33)

"Therefore I urge you, brethren, by the mercies of God, to present your bodies a living and holy sacrifice, acceptable to God, which is your spiritual service of worship." (Rom. 12:1)

This is not the forfeiture of our family's future. This is what guarantees our family's future. Whatever is surrendered to God belongs to Him, and He is the one responsible for its well-being. God can do a far better job in taking care of our future than we can. That which we forfeit for the sake of Christ, He has promised to give back in abundance.[8] Because Abraham was willing to forfeit his son, God promised to greatly bless Isaac and his descendants after him. Many of the blessings and second chances that the people of Israel received were because Abraham was willing to entrust his future into the hands of God.

But we must keep in mind that sometimes forfeiting something may actually mean we lose it. When we put something on the altar, it means we give God the right to take it. Usually, surrendering something to God will work out to our benefit, but sometimes it does not, at least not in this life. Sometimes the loved one dies. Sometimes the dream falls apart. In those times when the future looks so dark, all we can do is hold on to the promise of God's love and believe that He must have a plan.

Digging Deeper

In some ways, this chapter is a continuation of the one dealing with the silence of God. We are a people who what to know what the future holds. We have the idea that the best way to prepare for the future is to know what is coming. We can get rather frustrated with God because He seldom gives us information about what is to come. Even in the rare occurrences when God does give information about what is to come, it is almost never in the detail we would like.

When God revealed to Joseph that he would become a great leader.[9] He did not mention that it would only come after years of slavery and imprisonment. When God told the Hebrew people that He would lead them to the promised land,[10] He did not mention the hardships they would face along the way. When God revealed to David that he would be the next king of Israel,[11] He did not mention that it would only come after years of running for his life.

1. Why do you think God seldom gives us details about what is ahead?

It is probably true that if we knew what following God would cost us, we may not choose to go. But I think there is even a bigger reason for God's silence. We think that reaching the goal is what is important, but God knows that what we learn along the way is far more important than reaching a goal we desire. It is because of the lessons Joseph learned along the way that he became the leader God intended. It is because of the lessons David learned on the way that he became a king after God's own heart. God is more concerned with the change within us than He is in a change in our circumstances. The change that God is seeking in us and that most of us desire as well, usually only comes through trials. If we knew beforehand what those trials involved or when they would end, they would not be near as effective.

2. What difference do you think it would have made if God had told Abraham beforehand that he was not going to have to actually kill Isaac?

What God desires from us is faith, a faith which we are willing to demonstrate before we know what the outcome will be. When we refuse to act in faithfulness until we can understand what God is doing, this is not faith at all. The key for our future is not knowing what is ahead, but in faithfulness in what we face now. It is not the difficulties themselves that please God or that bring about the change within us. It's in our willingness to show faithfulness in the difficulties. The trials the Hebrew people faced on the road from Egypt to Canaan were to prepare them to enter into the Promised Land. But when they refused to face their difficulties with faithfulness, they forfeited the future that had been prepared for them. It was left to their children to learn the importance of obedience and faith so that they could receive the reward.

3. What are some of the things the world tells us are important to secure the well-being of our future?

4. What are some things scripture tells us are important for securing the well-being of our future?

Deut. 5:33

Ps. 112:5

Ps. 128:1

Jer. 7:23

1 Tim. 6:17-19

The first key to securing our future is to walk in faithfulness in regard to the things we already know we should be doing. But how do we deal with those situations in which we do not know what we should do? There are a lot of challenges or questions that we face that scripture may not give us any clear direction on. How then, are we to know what we should do? We first must realize that it is more important for us to do God's will than to just fix the situation. This is what Sarah found out when she tried to fix the situation of wanting a child by having Abraham take Hagar as a second wife. She got what she thought she wanted only to find out it was not what she really needed. What she needed was to wait upon God's will. But how do we know what God's will is?

If our desire to know God's will is so that we can know what is going to happen in the future, God is not likely to let us know. Our goal needs to be that we can know His will for us now, so that we may please Him. We, like Sarah, can get so caught up in the situation that we may think that what we need most is an answer to our problem, when what we truly need most is to walk with the Lord.

5. How did the Israelites know where they should travel, how long they should stay and when they should go? (Num. 9:17-20)

6. What was the most important factor in the people's well-being?
    A. The situation they were in.
    B. Where they were headed.
    C. The problems that they faced.
    D. Staying in the presence of God.

As long as the people stayed with God, their needs were always met and the future was always secure. Sometimes God took the people to places of difficulty so that they might be reminded of their reliance on Him, and so that He might show Himself to them in a new way. Other times, God would stay put when the people wanted to move on, so they would learn patience and the importance of waiting on the Lord.

The way we learn God's will about a situation isn't to seek the answer to the situation, but to seek God.

7. Who are those who will find God? (Jer. 29:13)

8. What are some things that keep us from finding God's will even when we seek it? (Prov. 1:28-30; Is. 58:2-11)

The more we come to know God, the clearer we will be able to discern His will for us.

9. How do we get to know God more? (1 John 2:3-5)

When we read the Bible to get to know God and to seek his will for our lives (not just the situation we are interested in but what God wants of us) He will reveal His will to us. How we then respond to it is crucial. If we ignore God's direction because it does not fit with what we desire or because it is in an area we do not want to deal with, then our disobedience will keep us from hearing Him in the other areas as well.

As we look into His Word, even if it does not speak directly to our situation, we will find principles that will help guide us. The more we act in obedience, the more we act in faithfulness to His teaching, the more God's Spirit will become apart of us and will be able to direct us. As we walk in faithfulness, we will find that the trials we face are not something we must escape or even solve. Rather, we can see them as an opportunity to please our God and to get to know Him. The more we get to know God the less we have to fear about what we may have to face.

10. What are some promises God has given us regarding the future?

     Ps. 37:4-5

     Ps. 55:22

     Is. 41:10

Rom. 8:28

1 Cor. 10:13

Jer. 29:11

The Jeremiah passage encourages us by letting us know that God is working and is preparing our future. But it is important that we understand the context of Jeremiah 29. Jeremiah is speaking to the captives who have been taken to Babylon. For obvious reasons they are not happy about their situation. They were crying out to God to deliver them from their problems, and there were "prophets" there who were telling the people that God would soon answer their prayers and they would be able to go home. This was what the people wanted to hear, but it was not what God had in mind.

11. What was God's message to the people? (Jer. 29:4-10)

God told them not to listen to those who were saying that their problems will soon go away. Rather He told them to learn to get on with life where they are at, for they will be there for the next 70 years. They were there as a consequence of their sin, and they had some lessons to learn before they would be free. The fact of their continual exile did not negate God's promise for a good future. What they needed to understand was that the goodness of their future was not based on their being able to get to where they wanted to be. It was not based on their circumstances at all. It was based upon their willingness to be content in the Lord whatever their circumstances were.

The more we seek God, the less we will need to know what the future is, for we will find that our happiness and contentment are not found in our ability to control the future, but in our willingness to be controlled by the One who holds our future, and who holds us.

12. Keeping in mind what we have learned in this lesson, how you would deal with the following scenarios?

A. You are thinking about making a change in your career, but are not sure what to do. You want to be faithful to God, but are not sure how that should affect the choices you face. What should you do?

B. You are trying to plan ahead for the future of your family. There are all kinds of needs you need to prepare for: financial needs, educational needs, physical needs, and so forth. What will you family need most for its welfare, and where do you start?

13. What does will it mean for you to walk by faith in facing the future?

14. What is one challenge of the future that you can work on walking by faith in?

Life Examples
Michelle[12]

It's funny how differently things sometimes turn out from what we expect. Somehow as I grew up, I always assumed that I would be married and well on my way to child-rearing by the time I turned 21. Reality for me, though, meant marriage at 24 and the first child at 32. In looking back, I can see so much of God's wisdom and guidance intertwined in all of it, but there were definitely times when it wasn't so easy. The uncertainty of the future often worried me, but it was reliance upon God's promises which pulled me through.

As a young adult, it wasn't until I surrendered my boy-girl relationships totally to Him that I was able to finally discover self-worth through His eyes. Then and only then I began to be truly content in Him, and also later a friendship formed which blossomed into a marriage relationship. I finally learned for the first time what it meant to "let go and let God." I know from personal experience that it is when we surrender ourselves to Him that He will work wonders in our lives. I cannot imagine now life with any other man but my husband, Bob.

It was Proverbs 3:5-6 which carried me through those college years.

> "Trust in the Lord with all your heart; Lean not on your own
> understanding. In all your ways acknowledge Him and He will make your
> paths straight."

After being married several years, I once again found myself expecting life to be very different from what reality dealt me. In 1991, my husband had gotten a steady job while attending seminary and we moved into a rather large parsonage with four bedrooms and three bathrooms. I just knew God had provided this house for us to fill it with children. After all, the time was right, in my eyes. But God had other ideas. It never occurred to me that once we decided to have children that they wouldn't just come. So as our desire to have children turned into an ache to have even just one child, the months and then years began to inch by.

At first I read books that offered all kinds of advice. Nothing. Then we went to a doctor for answers and even underwent laparoscopic surgery. Still no answers. We were two healthy individuals with no known cause for infertility. The third approach involved taking fertility pills. After a couple months of this, both my husband and I were convinced that we were attempting to manipulate God by taking the pills. It was as if we were telling God, "Okay, God. If You won't (or can't) get me pregnant, then we'll make it happen ourselves." So, once again, we were at a dead end. A couple more years had gone by and still I was not pregnant.

It was here though that we were finally able to surrender even this to God. The honest truth of realizing that I was really trying to manipulate God into doing what I wanted Him to do caused me to stop and cry out to Him in prayer. I remember acknowledging that my ability to have children was in His hands (as it always had been) and that even in this, I would obey Him. I would no longer continue to manipulate Him in this area of my life. After a while, we even began paperwork towards a home study and explored the options of adoption. We were finally at His feet where He wanted us all along. Whatever His will for us, we were willing to follow.

I'd like to say that the deep ache for a child disappeared. It didn't. I'd like to say that folk's flippant comments about getting pregnant stopped hurting me inside. They didn't. But one thing I can say for certain is that I clung to Him in a new way. Jeremiah 29:11-13 took on new meaning for me personally as I digested His words.

> "For I know the plans I have for you," declared the Lord, "plans to prosper
> you and not to harm you, plans to give you hope and a future. Then you
> will call upon me and come and pray to me, and I will listen to you. You
> will seek me and find me when you seek me with all your heart."

Somehow amidst the heartache, God worked in me and drew me closer to Him.

It was in June 1996 that one of the busiest and most stressful weeks in our lives occurred. My husband graduated from seminary, was ordained officially, family and friends arrived to visit, and we went on vacation to the nation's capitol together. I know in my heart that it was during this week that I became pregnant with our first child, Janae. (She is truly a "gift from God," for which she is named.) The conditions of the time went against every book's and every person's advice for things one needed to do to get pregnant. Yet I did. And God's kindness and mercy poured out on me, His miracle of a baby beginning in my womb.

I must admit I took three at-home pregnancy tests before I was willing to believe it. Even then, I was afraid it wasn't true. I had surrendered my ability to even be pregnant up to Him and yet I still longed for it to be true. This time it was.

Now I am the mother of four wonderful children, and I still marvel at His works and wisdom of it all. I can look back and see how I was so not ready to marry until I was 24 because of immaturity in my walk with Him. I also see the wisdom in beginning a family when we (He) did as well. I still have hopes and dreams for my future but have relaxed on the exact details of it all. The future is still unclear in many ways but one thing I know. God is faithful to keep His promises and as long as I continue to seek Him with all my heart, I can cling to Romans 8:28 as well.

> "And we know that in all things God works for the good of those who love
> Him, who have been called according to His purpose."

I know that even if my future dreams never do come true the way I had hoped for, I can rest in the truth that He will work it out for my good. That is definitely something I can cling to, no matter what happens to come my way.

Chapter 10
FAITH IN OUR SERVICE

"If anyone serves Me, he must follow Me; and where I am, there My servant will be also; if anyone serves Me, the Father will honor him." (John 12:26)

The Question of Faith

A lad with nothing of importance to give - John 6:1-14

I looked at the crowds milling around me and thought, "I really ought to be getting home. Mother will be wondering where I am." And yet something was holding me back. I had this feeling that I should be doing something, but I wasn't sure what it was supposed to be. By the looks of it, most the other people gathered here were feeling much the same. Dusk was only an hour or so away, and yet few people seemed inclined to want to go home. Thousands of people were out here gathered in the middle of nowhere, with no food or shelter, but still they stayed. The entire hillside was covered with them. Most were talking together in small groups. Some of the groups quietly discussed the events of the day. Others could be heard arguing loudly over something the Rabbi had said or done. Here and there, scattered amongst the groups, people sat alone, lost in thought over the things they had seen and heard. And indeed there was much to think about.

The day had started normally enough. I went to the potter's shop where I served as an apprentice. Master Able was beginning his instructions as usual, when someone came running in with news that the Rabbi, Jesus of Nazareth, had been seen heading over to a deserted part of the countryside a few miles south of town. We had all heard much about this Jesus whom some said was like the prophets of old. Master Able was as eager to see Him as we were, so he declared in his booming voice, "Lessons are done for today. You are all dismissed." With that, he took off his apron, grabbed his cloak off the peg and headed out the door.

The other apprentices and I lost no time in following his lead. A day off of work is always appreciated, but this was something special. I had heard my parents talking about this Jesus, and I wanted to see Him for myself. I started down the road, but then stopped when I realized I was still wearing my apron. I might have just kept going, but I knew my mother would tan my hide if I forgot my cloak and the lunch she made me. I turned around and hurried back to the shop. There I threw off my apron, grabbed my things, and then turned to race after the others.

Watching and listening to Jesus was even more amazing than I had expected. When we got there, a crowd had already formed, even though Jesus and His disciples had just arrived in their boat. Jesus smiled and greeted us as He walked over to a rock outcrop where He turned and sat down. He motioned for us to be quiet, and then He began to speak. The place He had chosen was like a natural amphitheater. His voice seemed to reach for miles. He began telling us about the kingdom of God.

"The kingdom of heaven is open to all," Jesus said, "to the small as well as the great. In fact, the kingdom of heaven belongs to the poor and the weak.[1] It is the strong and the wealthy who will have a difficult time getting into it.[2] I could tell by the looks on the faces of the scribes and Pharisees who were standing nearby that they were shocked and angered by what Jesus said. But most of the crowd was intrigued. Here was good news that seemed to be directed to them.

"How do we become a part of this kingdom?" someone asked, "What do we need to do?"

"You become a part of the kingdom of God," Jesus answered, "by turning away from your sins and believing."[3]

"Believing what?" someone else asked.

"I'll believe in anything that will get me a kingdom," another shouted. "Sign me up!"

Many of the people laughed, and even Jesus smiled as He replied, "That's not quite the kind of belief I'm talking about. If you want the kingdom of God you must believe in Me, and that won't be easy. You will need faith, the faith of a child,[4] the faith to trust, the faith to act. The good news I bring you is that the kingdom of God isn't just for the righteous. It is for sinners, but you must be willing to repent of your sins. And it's not enough just to say you repent. You will need to bear fruit of it as well."[5]

"The kingdom of God," He said, "is like a treasure hidden in the field, which a man found and hid again; and from joy over it he goes and sells all that he has and buys that field. It is like a merchant seeking fine pearls, and upon finding one pearl of great value, he went and sold all that he had and bought it."[6]

Jesus went on talking about the kingdom of God. He told many parables, and to be honest, most of them I didn't really understand. But as He spoke, my heart seemed to catch on fire. I wasn't sure I really understood what the kingdom of God was, but I knew I wanted to be a part of it. Jesus spoke through the morning and on into the afternoon. It took so long because He was continually being interrupted by people asking questions, or seeking help.

Jesus never seemed to get annoyed with the delays. He just stopped what he was saying, and turn to the person in need. He gave them his full attention as He listened to their complaint. Then He would smile, and say a few words as he reached out to touch them. At His touch they would suddenly be made well. I've never seen anything like it. People who had to be carried to Him jumped up and started dancing. Blind people walked away staring around in amazement, and those who had been mute suddenly couldn't stop talking. He cast demons out and healed every disease that was brought to Him. Every time it happened, we would all cheer and praise God. But Jesus just seemed to take it in stride. He would raise His hand to quiet us, and then go on with His teaching.

It was an incredible day, and no one wanted it to end. But as the day drew to a close, Jesus finally lifted up His hands and said, "My friends, the time has come for some rest. Go, and may you go with God." With that, He turned and moved further up the hill and sat down. At first some of the people called out to Him to come back, but He didn't answer. Others tried to follow Him, but His disciples kept them back. Eventually the crowd seemed to accept that it was over, but still nobody wanted to leave.

As I looked around me, I could see within many of the people a lingering sense of anticipation, as if there might still be more to come. They had never seen anything like this, and they were reluctant to let it go. I had never seen anything like it either, but it was something different that held me here. Jesus' words about faith and the need to act and to serve God kept running through my mind. It was as if He had been speaking directly to me. I felt within me a desire to do something, but what? I wanted to help, to give, to do something important, but I was just a kid. I was no one of importance. What could I do?

I wasn't rich. I had no special ability. I wasn't dumb, but I knew I wasn't exactly brilliant either. I had learned a little bit about how to make pots, but what good was that? I was no one of importance, and yet Jesus had said that the kingdom of God wasn't just for the important people. In fact, He seemed to indicate that it was more designed for people like me. But what was I supposed to do? He had told a story of a man who gave up all he had to gain a great treasure. I wanted this treasure as well, and I was willing to sacrifice to get it. I had a picture in my mind of me walking up to Jesus with some gift of great value. The disciples were all looking impressed, and Jesus, Himself was thanking me for my great gift. The image faded as I came back to reality. Though I might want to give Jesus something special, the truth was that I had nothing to give. I looked around me as if some hidden treasure might suddenly appear, but all I saw was a bag containing my lunch. I had been so enthralled with Jesus, I had forgotten all about it.

My stomach growled to remind me that I hadn't eaten since breakfast. I took out some bread and was about to eat it when Jesus' words seemed to speak to me, "He gave up all he had."

I sat there looking at the bread in my hand and thought, "This is ridiculous. What would Jesus want with my lunch?"

But the words came back again, "He gave up all he had."

"Surely Jesus couldn't have meant something like this. Besides," I thought, "I'm really hungry." I wasn't sure I wanted to give up my lunch.

A flood of excuses flowed through my mind. "He is bound to have His own food. With His power, He could just call food down from heaven or something. The food I've got wouldn't be nearly fancy enough." But the more I thought about it, the more I realized that unless I am willing to give to Jesus whatever it is I had, no matter how unimportant, I probably wouldn't end up giving Him anything.

Another picture popped into my mind. I was walking up to Jesus again, only this time all I had was my lunch, and everyone was laughing at me, and Jesus was looking offended. "No," I thought, "this is not a good idea. I have nothing Jesus would want. If I walked up to Him with my lunch, I would just end up looking like a fool." But then I remembered how Jesus looked at those who came up to Him. He always seemed so interested in whatever it was they had to ask or say. I felt again within me the desire to do something for Jesus. So before I could talk myself out of it, I got to my feet and, with my lunch in hand, I started walking up the hill.

My heart was pounding in my ears, and I had to fight back the urge to turn and run. The thought kept running through my mind, "This is not a good idea. This is not a good idea." But I was determined not to quit, so I kept going. I saw ahead of me one of

Jesus' disciples (Andrew, I think was his name). I bit my lip, and summoning up all the courage I had, I walked up to him.

"Excuse me, Sir," I said, "but I don't suppose that Jesus could have any use for five loaves of bread and two fish?"

Such a small gift and yet it was used in such a powerful way. With that lunch Jesus fed thousands, and even more important, He displayed the power and glory of God. We don't know anything else about the lad except his willingness to give. What he gave may not seem like much, but through that gift he had a part in one of the greatest miracles known to man.

A Closer Look

In service we see the importance of both aspects of faith - belief and faithfulness. We will first look at belief. There are a lot of people out there who would like to be active in service to God, but do not feel they have much to offer. Maybe it is because they do not see themselves as being very gifted, or maybe it is because they have made a mess of their life and do not see how God could use them now. In either case, the problem is that we are focused on the same thing - who I am. In service, the importance is not on who I am, but on who God is.

When we look at the people whom God used in scripture, what we find is that few of them would have topped our lists of "Most Likely to Succeed." Moses was a failure from Egypt with a speech problem. David was the runt of his family. When we look at the disciples, the men Jesus picked to be the foundation of the church, whom does he choose? Does He pick the learned and the gifted? No, he picks common laborers and a political traitor. Paul was the only one we know of that had much education, and when Jesus picked him, he was championing the opposing side. Even after his conversion, it was a long time before anyone was willing to believe that Saul/Paul could be used by God. Paul reminds us that few of those called by God would be considered wise, mighty, or noble.[7] God does not call the qualified to do His work. He qualifies those who are willing to answer the call.

How do we know if God wants us to serve Him? That is easy. If there is breath in our body, God expects us to be serving Him. This does not mean that everyone should quit their jobs and seek to become a missionary or minister. There are many different ways to serve God, and each is just as valid as another. What is important is not what you do for God, but that you do what God calls you to do. We were all created to serve God, and to do good works.[8] This is the reason for our existence. Each of us has been gifted in different ways, and the reason God gave us those gifts is so we might build up the body of Christ, and bring glory to God.[9]

Like the lad in the story, we might not feel that we have much of value to offer, but when we are willing to surrender what we have into the hands of God we will find He can do some amazing things. In truth, the real point is not what God does with our gifts, but our willingness to please Him by being obedient to His call. Others may never notice what we do, but this makes it no less important in the sight of God.

Now let us look at the faithfulness side of service. Not only does scripture tell us that we are made to serve God, but it also lets us know that we will be held accountable for our faithfulness in that service. A number of Jesus' parables[10] deal with the consequences of our faithfulness, or lack-there-of, in regard to service. In Revelation, the church of Sardis received a very severe warning because Jesus found their service to be lacking.[11] Service is important to the Lord. It is true that in the book of Ephesians Paul lets us know that our salvation is not based on our works.

"For by grace you have been saved through faith; and that not of yourselves, it is the gift of God; not as a result of works, so that no one may boast." (Eph. 2:8-9)

But he continues on to let us know that God does expect us to be involved in service.

"For we are His workmanship, created in Christ Jesus for good works, which God prepared beforehand so that we would walk in them." (Eph. 2:10)

The service which we do for Christ is nothing to boast about. It does not make us better than anyone else. It does not earn us a ticket to heaven. It is merely what a servant is expected to do.

"So you too, when you do all the things which are commanded you, say, 'We are unworthy slaves; we have done only that which we ought to have done.' " (Luke 17:10)

There are many different ways to serve, and we are only required to serve as we are able. But if we are Christians, then Christ is Lord, and we are expected to serve our Master. Faith without works is dead.[12] A servant who refuses to serve is not really a servant at all.

Most of us, if we are honest, would probably have to admit that we do not serve as much as we should. Some, while seeing themselves as committed to Christ, do not really serve much at all. Why? The parable of the soils gives us some insight into the reasons for unfruitfulness.

"Listen to this! Behold, the sower went out to sow; as he was sowing, some seed fell beside the road, and the birds came and ate it up. Other seed fell on the rocky ground where it did not have much soil; and immediately it sprang up because it had no depth of soil. And after the sun had risen, it was scorched; and because it had no root, it withered away. Other seed fell among the thorns, and the thorns came up and choked it, and it yielded no crop. Other seeds fell into the good soil, and as they grew up and increased, they yielded a crop and produced thirty, sixty, and a hundredfold." (Mark 4:3-8)

The seed, Jesus explains, is God's Word.[13] The soil along the road, or the hard soil, represents someone who hears God's Word but does not receive it or act upon it because their heart has become hard. They have resisted God's conviction so many times that they no longer hear Him speaking to them, or if they do, they assume He is speaking to someone else. Their heart has become hard, and their neck has become stiff (this was a description of an ox that no longer responds to the tugging of the reins, but instead goes just where it wants to go). Satan has an easy time keeping this kind of person from being affected by God's Word, because they start off assuming they do not need to be affected. They feel they are fine as they are.

This kind of person does not serve because they do not think they need to, or if they do serve they do so based on their own motives and with their own agenda. Service of this type may make the person feel good but gives no pleasure to God. This is a dangerous situation to be in because often these people are blinded to their problem. The only way hard soil can be used is for it to be broken. The only way hard hearted people can be reached is for God to break them so they might see their need and respond to His conviction. If they continue to ignore God, their future is not good.

> "Therefore, just as the Holy Spirit says, 'Today if you hear His voice, do not harden your hearts as when they provoked me, as in the day of trial in the wilderness, where your fathers tried Me by testing Me, and saw my works for forty years. Therefore I was angry with this generation, and said, They always go astray in their heart, and they did not know My ways'; As I swore in My wrath, 'They shall not enter My rest.' " (Heb. 3:7-11)

The rocky soil represents those whose faith is shallow. These people receive the message of the gospel gladly and may want to serve the Lord right away. The problem is that they do not put enough effort into working on their relationship with Christ. This may be because their commitment was low in the first place or because they did not understand the importance of deepening their relationship or walk with Christ.

Sometimes a person wants to jump right into serving the Lord. This is not bad, but when someone begins serving the Lord, they become a target for Satan. He will use all kinds of ways to put pressure on them to weaken their commitment. If their relationship with the Lord is not strong enough, they will not have the strength needed to resist the attack, and they will wither. Service is important, but relationship is vital. God gave us the Sabbath to remind us that, while doing things is important, it is vital that we spend time being with the Lord. The service God is looking for from us is that which comes out of our relationship with Christ, not that which is a substitute for the relationship.

> "Abide in Me, and I in you. As the branch cannot bear fruit of itself unless it abides in the vine, so neither can you unless you abide in Me. I am the vine, you are the branches; he who abides in Me and I in him, he bears much fruit, for apart from Me you can do nothing." (John 15:4-5)

This does not mean that one has to be a mature Christian before they can serve God. New Christians can serve as well, but they must also focus on walking with the Lord. Even mature Christians can get caught up in doing for the Lord and forget to be with the Lord. When they do this, they become weak and vulnerable to Satan's attacks. This is why we find even ministers and church leaders who fall to things they know they should not do.

To build our relationship with Christ we need to start off by being honest with ourselves and with Him. We must be willing humble ourselves before the Lord so that He might speak to our hearts. But if we want to bear fruit, we can not stop there. We need to continue in a walk with Him, spending time with Him in prayer, worship and study. As we walk with Him we must be careful not to slip into the mind-set of just going though the motions. Instead, we should continue to be faithful out of a desire to be with Christ, to know Him and to please Him. The only way a crop in rocky soil can produce fruit is if the roots work at digging deeper. This does not guarantee that things will go easy for us, or that we will not stumble, but it does provide us with the strength and grace we need to continue on.

The weedy soil represents those who want to serve God, but find the demands and enticements of this world to be too much of a distraction. Jesus warned us long ago that we can not seek the things of this world and the things of God at the same time.

> "No one can serve two masters; for either he will hate the one and love the other, or he will be devoted to one and despise the other. You cannot serve God and wealth." (Matt. 6:24)

James repeats the warning.

> "You adulteresses, do you not know that friendship with the world is hostility toward God? Therefore whoever wishes to be a friend of the world makes himself an enemy of God." (James 4:4)

Somehow we either ignore this or choose to think it can not really mean what it says. So we go right on chasing all the things the people around us chase, and find our life is just too full or too demanding for us to be able to serve God. We think, "God understands." And in truth He does, more than we may wish.

> "Do not be deceived, God is not mocked; for whatever a man sows, this he will also reap. For the one who sows to his own flesh will from the flesh

reap corruption, but the one who sows to the Spirit will from the Spirit
reap eternal life." (Gal. 6:7-8)

When a plant is surrounded by weeds, the weeds drain all the resources, leaving the plant too weak to produce any fruit. The only way for the plant to produce is for the weeds to be removed. The farmer may never remove them all, but he must continue to cut them back if he wants any results. The truth is that we may not be strong enough to remove all the things that drain our life and keep us from serving God as we know we should. That is okay, because weeding is more the job of the farmer than the plant. It would be better for us if we could learn to let go on our own, but God knows our frailty and He will help us by do what weeding or the pruning we are too weak to do. We just need to be willing to surrender it into His hands and learn to let go of that which we find ourselves clinging to. It many not feel like help when God begins to prune the things that stand in the way of our growth, but without it we soon become barren of fruit and end up sharing the fate of the thistles that surround us.

"I am the true vine, and My Father is the vinedresser. Every branch in Me
that does not bear fruit, He takes away; and every branch that bears fruit,
He prunes it so that it may bear more fruit." (John 15:1-2)

It is no fun to be weeded or pruned; in fact it can hurt quite a bit. We would be far better off giving these things up on our own. But if we do not, God will sometimes do the pruning for us (Ouch). If we refuse to be pruned, and choose to cling to the things of the world, then we will share the world's fate. God does not enjoy our suffering, but He would rather cause us to suffer for a time than lose us forever.

The fourth soil is the good or productive soil. But no field starts this way. The productive soil is merely hard, shallow, weedy soil that has been broken, worked and weeded, so that it can produce the desired fruit. Few of us see ourselves as "good soil." What we see is our pride, our shallowness, and our worldliness. It is God who works within us when we surrender ourselves (weeds, rocks, and all) to Him. He is the patient farmer who continues to work with us, and to help us to become the type of people through whom He can bring a bountiful harvest. This is God's desire for us, and hopefully it is our desire as well. So that one day we might hear from the Master, "Well done, good and faithful servant. Enter into the joy of your Master."[14]

Digging Deeper

Within most congregations, much of the ministry or service is carried out by a minority of the people.

1. Whose job is it to carry out the ministry or service of the church? (Eph. 4:11-12; 1 Cor. 12:7)

Ministry and service mean the same thing, and it is something we all are to be involved in.

2. What are some reasons for us to be involved in service?

> Eph. 2:10

> Mark 10:43-45; John 13:14-17

> Luke 12:37

> 1 Tim. 6:18-19

If you belong to Christ, then you are to be His servant. But getting involved in service can be easier said than done. There are a lot of people who may want to be involved in service but do not know what to do, or do not feel they can.

There are many different ways of being involved in ministry.

3. What are three different areas we can direct our service?

> Ps. 100:2

> Heb. 6:10

> Matt. 5:13-16

4. What are some of the different ways we can serve the Lord?

5. What are some of the different ways we can serve other Christians?

6. What are some of the different ways we can serve the world around us?

There are endless opportunities to serve, but not all service is the same. We could spend our whole life helping out in various ways, but as Christians, we are not just to spend our life, we are to use it in a way that pleases God.

7. What is the primary consideration for determining what areas we should be involved in? (Ps. 143:10; Matt. 7:21)

There are many things we can be involved in, and most of them are good, but our primary goal is to please God. Therefore, our primary question needs to be, "Lord, what is Your will?" There is nothing necessarily wrong with being involved in secular activities such as sports or hobbies; and in fact, it may be God's will that we are. But when those activities keep us from serving in obedience to God, then they become a problem. This is not just with secular activities. We can be very active in service in the church, and still not be obedient to God's will.

The place to start is to ask God to reveal His will. This, however, may not give us the clear answer we are seeking, and that is okay. As long as we are seeking to please our Lord, we can be assured that even if we have not understood or followed God's will perfectly, His grace covers us. However, there are some things we can keep in mind that can help us get a better idea of what we should or should not be involved in.

8. What are some things that can help us know what areas God would like us to serve in? (1 Cor. 7:7, 12:5-7)

Here we find that there are a variety of ministries we may be involved in, but God has gifted us in regard to certain ones. It is not necessarily wrong to try to serve in an area that you are not gifted in, but it will usually be frustrating and unproductive. There are different ways to try to learn the areas in which you are gifted. You can ask those whom you respect for their opinion. You can experiment and see what areas others seem to benefit from. The reason for our gifts is not for our own benefit or to build up our ego. It is for the building up of the body. If our efforts are not acknowledged by others as a benefit, then maybe we should try something else.

9. What is another indication of where God may have us serve? (Philip. 2:13)

Another way to find where God desires us to serve is to look at the passion or heart[15] He has put within us. If God has put within us a passion for kids or for music, then that can give us an indication of the area He wants us to serve in. Sometimes our passion does not match our gifts. Someone may have a passion for music, but can't hold a tune. In this case, the person may look for some type of supporting role to play - helping out with the sound system or something like that. This way they can be involved with their passion, but still be doing something that is a help and benefit to others.

10. What is one good reason we may serve in an area we are not gifted in? (1 John 3:17)

There will be times when others will need our help even though it may not be an area we are gifted in. Such service is done out of love, and it is pleasing to our God. But we will probably want to shift to another area as soon as the opportunity allows.

11. What is another good reason we may serve in an area we do not feel gifted in?
(2 Tim. 1:9)

Our areas of giftedness may give us an indication of where God desires us to serve, but often we will not even know what God has gifted us in until we step out in faith and obedience to His call. More often than not, our response to God's call is, "Who, Me?!" We may feel anything but gifted in the area God calls us to. Keep in mind, spiritual gifts and natural abilities are not the same thing. Abilities are what we can do. Spiritual gifts are what God does through us. Some of our greatest leaders in scripture felt anything but gifted when God called them. When they heard God's call they did what we often do - the made excuses.

12. What was Moses' excuse when God called Him? (Ex. 3:11; 4:10)

13. What was God's response? (Ex. 3:12; 4:11-12)

14. What was Gideon's excuse when God called Him? (Judg. 6:15)

15. What was God's response? (Judg. 6:16)

16. What was Peters excuse? (Luke 5:8)

17. What was Jesus' response? (Matt. 4:19)

It is not who we are, but what Christ makes of us that will really matter. Where He calls us to serve, He will enable us to serve.

Not all areas of service are going to be directly connected to the church. Christ has called us to reach out to the world, and that generally is going to involve service. With so many opportunities for service, how do we decide which one or ones to be involved in?

18. What is one very important consideration to keep in mind when we are looking at serving in the community? (Matt. 5:16)

Everything that we do is to give glory to God.[16] This does not mean we will always be outwardly proclaiming Jesus. In some situations the only way we can glorify God is to help with others' needs without having strings attached. But if all we accomplish is filling secular needs without ever glorifying our Lord or helping others to see Jesus, then we are not really serving God. Even if we are serving where God wants us to, we can still fail if we take our eyes off of the goal of glorifying God. On the other hand, even if we find ourselves working in a situation that God didn't call us to be involved in, we can still please our God if we start looking for ways to honor God in our situation. If our desire it to truly glorify God, then He will help us see the opportunities.

19. What is the most important element for us to know how we are to serve according to God's will? (John 12:26)

It always comes back to the same thing - our relationship with Christ. The more we walk with Him and the more we seek to know and to please Him, the more we will know His will for us.

20. Keeping in mind what we have learned in this lesson, how you would deal with the following scenarios?

A. You have been feeling convicted about serving in your church, but your schedule is already pretty tight, and you are not sure what you can or should do. Where do you go from here?

B. You have been serving in different ways, both in the community and in your church, but you are not feeling fulfilled, rather you are feeling used up. What things may you need to change to bring joy back into your service?

21. What does will it mean for you to walk by faith in service?

22. What is one way you can work at walking by faith in regard to service?

Life Examples
Andrew[17]

What does it mean for me to walk by faith in service to God? What has God taught me over the years about how to walk by faith in the area of service? One of the first major lessons God taught me about walking by faith with regard to service occurred with I was 17 years old.

I had been invited to go on a three month mission trip to Moscow, Russia. I was so excited! You see, God had been putting Russia on my heart for some time, and I had a strong desire to go there. The Iron Curtain had just come down not long before, and I had heard amazing testimonies about what God was doing in the hearts of the Russian people.

There was just one problem. I had almost no money, and the trip was quite expensive. My parents and I began to pray that if God wanted me to go He would provide the necessary funds. I wanted to serve God in Russia, but the cost seemed like an insurmountable obstacle. It was impossible! I could not raise so much money in such a short amount of time. But I learned something that year. "God's work, done in God's way, will never lack God's supply" (Hudson Taylor). As Scripture says, "My God shall supply all your need according to His riches in glory by Christ Jesus" (Philippians 4:19, NKJV). Money is simply not an obstacle to the Almighty God. Sometimes it may come as a shock, but the Creator of the Universe does not loose sleep worrying about inadequate resources! So I stepped out in faith and signed up to go, and money came pouring in! Through my church, my family, and others whom God used, He provided all the money needed for the trip.

But God did far more than meet my little step of faith halfway. God rewards even the smallest measure of faithfulness in service. I was too young and immature to even realize how unprepared I was to serve God in a foreign culture, and had no abilities or skills to be of any possible use to Him. Yet God found use for even me! I found so much joy in serving Jesus, even in the most seemingly menial tasks, and received the added bonus of seeing God use my frail efforts to impact people's lives for His Kingdom. I learned that God is not looking primarily for the most talented or skilled people to serve Him, He is looking for people who have willing and humble hearts, and who will do whatever tasks He gives them to do.

About a year-and-a-half later, I had the opportunity to go back to Russia as an English teacher. This time, however, I knew just how unprepared I was. I did not know Russian I didn't even know English well enough! Furthermore, I was not a trained preacher or Bible teacher, and I did not know how God could possibly use me. When I voiced my concerns to the group leader, he laughed at me. I still remember his next words, for they have made a lasting impression on my life. He said, "If we all waited until we felt ready to serve God, we would never get started." He was right. Although I did not feel very much like leaving my friends and family to go to another culture for an extended time, especially since I was certain there must be more qualified people available, I believed strongly that God had work for me to do there. I have since learned that service to God cannot be based on my feelings, whether I feel prepared or unprepared, able or unable, happy or unhappy. I am a servant. It is not given to the servant to pick and choose how or when he will serve his master, it is only given to the servant to listen and obey.

Throughout that year of ministry in Moscow, God again managed to somehow use me to serve Him and to further His Kingdom. Simply because I made myself available to God, regardless of my personal feelings, He blessed me and taught me so much about Himself. He even used me to lead several high school students to Christ. Sometimes I stop to wonder would they be in heaven if a simple country boy had not made himself available to serve God, in spite of his personal feelings?

A few years after the Russia trips, God began a new journey for me. He put it in my heart to begin to prepare for pastoral ministry. I had hardly gotten used to the idea, and hadn't even begun to think about what school to attend, when a local church asked me to consider applying to be their "part-time" youth pastor (I have since learned that nobody in service to God is part-time God calls us all, regardless of profession, to be full-time, whole-hearted servants of our Lord).

At this point, I had only taken a couple of Bible classes of any kind, and was definitely unqualified for the job. It was also way outside my comfort zone, and I did not even see myself at that time as being especially gifted with high school age students. But once again, God confirmed that He wanted me to do this ministry, regardless of my fears or my feelings of inadequacy. He would be the teacher. He would be the guide. Like Moses, and Abraham before him, all I had to do was stay close to God and He would reveal the way I should go.

Perhaps the most pertinent Scripture for me at that time was, " This is the word of the Lord to [Andrew]: Not by might nor by power, but by My Spirit,' Says the Lord of hosts" (Zechariah 4:6). In almost eight years of youth ministry at this same church, I have repeatedly seen the Spirit of God do amazing things that are far, far greater than I could ever accomplish. Sometimes people try to give me credit for what God has done, but all I can think is, "Can't you see I'm not smart enough or talented enough to do that? I just followed what the Holy Spirit told me to do, and this was the result. I had no idea this would happen, I just did what God seemed to be putting on my heart."

Of course, there have also been many times when I was not obedient to God, and I shudder to think of the blessings I have missed, and the ministry I've bungled, as a result. Sometimes I think my life is like a living demonstration of both the wonderful blessings that come when we walk in faithful service to God, and also the great suffering and grief of missed opportunities when we try to be our own masters. Over and over again, God has demonstrated to me that even when I don't understand no, especially when I don't understand, I need only to walk in obedience to Him, regardless of what I think the consequences might be, and He will accomplish His will in me and through me.

Through these experiences, I have repeatedly discovered that walking by faith in service is not about me, who I am, or what I can do. Rather it is all about GOD. Who He is, and what He can do through anyone who, regardless of their feelings, their abilities (or lack-thereof), or of the possible consequences, is willing to be obedient to Him. D.L. Moody, who became one of the greatest evangelists of the 19th century, was motivated by the statement, "The world has yet to see what God will do through one man (or woman) who is totally dedicated to Him." Will you be that person?

Chapter 11
FAITH IN DEALING WITH FAILURE
"Create in me a clean heart, O God, And renew a steadfast spirit within me." (Ps. 51:10)

The Question of Faith
Peter - John 21

I'm tired, so very tired. I feel as if there is a weight pressing upon me, squeezing the life from my limbs and my soul. I wish I could just curl up into a ball and shut the world out. If only I could escape the fear, the loneliness, and the failure. I thought for a while about killing myself, putting an end to it all. But that would just be one more failure added to the rest. Somewhere within me there was still a shred of pride that chided me, saying, "No, the easy way out is not for you. You don't deserve it. You must pay the price for your weakness." So I keep going, one step at a time, or as in my present situation, one hand over the other.

I sit in this boat, pulling in the net on more time, without much hope of any success. I came out here with James, John and some of the others. We have spent the night fishing, throwing our nets out, and drawing them back in. But we have nothing to show for our effort. We have caught nothing all night. My mind is dull from lack of sleep and my arms ache from the labor, but I can't stop. That same chiding voice keeps nagging at me, "Go ahead and give up. You're nothing but a failure anyway." Still I pull on. As I bring the net into the boat, I see it is empty yet again. Once again I have failed.

It is amazing how quickly things can change. It was just a couple of days ago that I had been so confident in what I could accomplish. Although, to be truthful, even then I was haunted by doubts, but I had been able to hide them behind a front of confidence. "Never!" I had said, "though all else leave You, Lord, I will never forsake You." I made Jesus this promise while we were sitting in an upper room sharing a Passover meal. Jesus just looked at me with a weary sadness, and said, "Truly, I say to you that this very night, before the rooster crows, you will deny Me three times."[1] I shook my head in disbelief, vehemently denying it. "Even if I have to die with You," I said, "I will not deny You." The other disciples agreed that they, too, would never fail Him.[2]

As we finished the meal and made our way up to the Mount of Olives, we had bragged to each other about what we would do if anyone tried to lay a hand on Jesus. "I have a sword," I told them, "and I am not afraid to use it. If they want Jesus, it will be over my dead body, and I'll take a few of them with me." Behind my bravado, I tried to bury my doubts. Would I really stand, or would I run? The others saw me as strong and confident, but I knew the man within. I knew how small he really was. It wouldn't be long before the others would see as well.

When we got to the garden of Gethsemane, Jesus instructed James, John, and myself to accompany Him. Moving a little off from the others, Jesus told us that He was extremely troubled, and He asked us to keep watch with Him. As Jesus went off to pray, I sat down by a tree. I had every intention of staying awake and being there for Him, but as I sat there, my eyes became heavy. I tried to blink away the sleep, but the next thing I knew Jesus was waking me up.

"So," Jesus said, "you couldn't even keep watch with me for one hour?"

As I sat up trying to rub the sleep from my eyes, my face felt flushed with embarrassment. I didn't know what to say.

"Keep watching and praying," He told us, "that you may not enter into temptation; the spirit is willing, but the flesh is weak."[3]

This time I was determined that I would stay awake. I sat up straight and even slapped my face a couple of times, but as the minutes dragged by my head began to nod, and once again I drifted off. The next time Jesus woke me, I knew He was disappointed with me. The fact that the others had fallen asleep as well was no comfort.

"Are you still sleeping and resting?" He asked. "Behold, the hour is at hand, and the Son of Man is being betrayed into the hands of sinners. Get up, let us be going; behold, the one who betrays me is at hand."[4]

It took me a couple of moments to shake the grogginess from my mind and get my wits about me. Suddenly there were lights and loud voices. When I staggered to my feet, I saw Judas pulling away from Jesus, and some other men reaching to grab Him. Instinctively, I grabbed my sword and struck out.

"Put your sword away," Jesus spoke in a commanding voice. "Those who use the sword will die by the sword." He reached out and with one hand, healed the man I had struck. I was confused and taken aback. Didn't He want me to try to protect Him? Jesus looked me in the eye, and as if reading my mind, He said, "Do you think that I can not ask My Father, and He would give Me twelve legions of angels? If I did so, how then would the scriptures be fulfilled that state that it must happen this way?"

Jesus turned back to talk to those who had come for Him, but I didn't listen. I couldn't understand what was happening. This wasn't how things were supposed to happen. It didn't make any sense. Why wasn't He even trying to resist them? I stood there watching in stunned disbelief. When they lead Jesus off, John and I followed behind. They went into the court-yard of Annas, the high priest. I stopped, but John came up beside me and whispered, "I know the gate keeper, and I think I can get us in." I wasn't sure I wanted to go in. Back in the garden I had acted out of instinct, but now I wasn't so sure I wanted to face all those guards. My courage seemed to have melted away. What if they recognized us and arrested us as well? But with John leading the way, I felt I had little choice but to follow.

After entering the outer courtyard, John continued on closer to the house, but this was as far as I was going. A slave girl stopped and looked up at me.

"Say," she said, "aren't you one of His disciples?"

Fear suddenly sprang up within me. I felt trapped. My eyes darted about as I quickly stammered, "No, I do not know what you are talking about." I moved away from her and over to a charcoal fire where some other men were warming themselves. From there I could see through a doorway into the inner courtyard where Jesus was being questioned. I was trying to see what was happening when one of the other men by the fire spoke up.

"You know," he said, "I believe I saw you in the garden. You're one of Jesus' disciples, aren't you?

I could feel all the eyes around the fire staring at me. "No," I said, "I swear to you, I don't know the man."

"No, you're one of them alright," said another, "I can tell by your accent."

It felt as if a circle of iron was tightening around me. Fear overwhelmed me. I began to swear and curse at them. "I do not know the man!" I shouted.

In that moment a rooster crowed, and Jesus' words sprang into my mind. "Before the rooster crows you will deny me three times." I turned and looked at Jesus, and He was staring right at me. Even at this distance I could see the sorrow in His eyes. The enormity of what I had done swept over me, and I found it hard to breath. I turned and fled out the gate. Tears streamed down my face and I ran in a blind stupor, careening off of anyone or anything in my path. I ran until I couldn't run any more. I found a dark hole, and crawled into it. There I curled up and cried. I had always prided myself on my strength. I had thought I could handle anything. But huddling there in the dark, I realized how wrong I had been. I wasn't strong, I was weak. I was scum. I was worth less than the dirt upon which I lay. I did not deserve to live.

Eventually I crawled out of my hole and went to find the others. I didn't really want to face them, but I had no place else to go. When I found them, they welcomed me. We clung to each other and cried. They told me how glad they were to have me with them, how they needed my strength. At that I nearly laughed. They did not know of my betrayal, and I could not tell them, though it ate away within me. I put on a mask of respectability and tried to hide my shame, but inside I knew. I knew.

Even later when I found that Jesus was truly alive again, it was not the same. True, I was happy to have Him back, but my shame continued to haunt me. I couldn't be free like the others to rejoice in His presence. I had denied Him. I had betrayed Him. While the others flocked to Him, I held back, not even sure if He would want me around Him anymore, I who had failed Him.

It was because I felt like such a failure as a disciple that I had decided to go fishing. I may be a failure at everything else, but at least I knew how to catch fish, or I had thought I did. Now as I sat here in the boat, I found I couldn't even do that right. We had fished all night and hadn't caught a thing. My heart was as cold and empty as the net which I held in my hands. I thought, "If I can't even fish, what am I good for?"

It was then, as the sun was posed to rise above the hills that someone called to us from the shore. We couldn't make out who he was, but he asked us if we had caught any fish. At our negative reply, he called out, "Cast the net on the right-hand side of the boat and you will find a catch."

We looked at each other and laughed, but then a thought came to me. I glanced at James and John. I could tell that they, like me, were remembering a time when Jesus had told us to cast our nets on the other side of the boat. John smiled, and shrugged as he said, "Why not?"

We threw our net on the right-hand side, and immediately we could feel it fighting against us. There were so many fish in it that it was all we could do to hang on. John turned to me with a smile on his face and a gleam in his eye, and said. "It's the Lord."

As He said this, I knew it to be true. Suddenly all my insecurities and emotions seemed to rise to the surface and all I wanted was to be free of them. I wanted, no, I needed to be with Jesus. I grabbed my cloak, jumped into the water, and started swimming for the shore. It may not have been very thoughtful of me to leave the others to deal with the work, but at that moment I didn't care. All I wanted was to see Jesus.

When I got to the shore, I found Jesus already had a fire going and was putting some fish over it. He looked up at me as I approached, and smiled.

"Peter, My friend," He said, "it is good to see you."

There were a thousand things I wanted to say. I wanted to explain, to apologize, to beg for His forgiveness. But as I stood there looking at Him, I could not find the words. Tears ran unhindered down my face and my mouth trembled, but nothing came out.

"Come," Jesus said, with a sympathetic smile, "sit here beside me and warm yourself."

I sat down beside Him as He finished arranging the fish and took out some bread. Where He got the fish and bread I had no idea, but I had learned not to question the things Jesus could do. When the boat reached the shore I went out and helped the others drag the net up on the beach. At Jesus' request we brought up some more fish, and there on the shore as the sun climbed into the sky, we broke our fast together.

The talk around the fire was light and lively. I could see the others were in a great mood, but I held back from joining in. I felt like such a hypocrite, sitting there beside Jesus. Then as the others were talking, Jesus turned and looked at me with that penetrating gaze of His.

"Simon, Son of John," He said, "Do you love me more than these?"

His question cut deep. I had claimed that though all else may fall away, I never would. I would die before I denied Him. But when it came down to it, I had denied Him, not only once, but three times. How could I say that I loved Him more than anyone else? I couldn't look Him in the eye as I responded, "Yes, Lord; You know I care deeply for You."

I didn't look up but I could feel His eyes boring into me. Then He said, "Tend my lambs."

I loathed myself and my duplicity. I silently pleaded for Jesus to turn His attention on someone else. But once again my luck failed me.

"Simon, son of John," He said again, "do you love Me?

"Oh, dear Lord," I thought. "Why do you torment me? Why don't you just curse me and be done with it?" But instead, still not meeting His eyes, I responded the same as before, "Yes, Lord; You know I care deeply for You."

"Shepherd My sheep," He said, still not turning away from me.

For a moment the silence hung between us then He spoke again. "Simon, son of John, do you care deeply for me?"

This was more than I could take. Three times He had asked me if my love was true, and this time He had used my own words. How deeply did I care for Him? Did I truly love Him? Yes, I did love Him. I knew I wasn't worthy of Him. I knew I didn't deserve His love or even His attention, but I did love Him.

Tears once again began to flow, but I paid them no heed as I looked up to His face. "Lord," I said, "You know all things; You know that I truly care for You."

Jesus smiled slightly and said, "Tend My sheep."

I whipped the tears from my eyes, and to my amazement, I saw there were tears in His eyes as well. I knew then that He knew what was going on inside of me. He knew my fears. He knew my failure, and His eyes told me that He loved me anyway.

It wasn't until then that I really paid attention to what He was telling me. He was directing me to help lead His people. He was asking me, the one who had failed Him, who had made a mess of things time and again. He knew what I had done, and He still wanted to use me. He still saw something in me that was worth loving. Jesus went on to tell me that when I had been young I was free to do as I pleased, but now things would be different. I would have face the things I that I feared- imprisonment and even death. There would be times when I would be weak and helpless, but while my strength had failed Him, my helplessness He would be able to use. Jesus looked me in the eyes and said, "Follow Me!"

I felt a joy and a hope surge up within me. Not only had Jesus forgiven me for denying Him, but He wanted to use me as well! Not only did He want me, but He had confidence that I would be able to stand and suffer for Him. I found I wasn't afraid any more. Not of prison, not of death, and not of Jesus. I knew I would undoubtedly fail again in the future, but Jesus knew that as well and He still wanted me.

I turned and saw John looking at us, and I asked Jesus, "What about him?"

"What happens to him," Jesus said, "is not your concern. You follow Me."

As Jesus turned to talk to some of the others I thought, "Okay Lord, if You will have me, then whatever the cost, I will follow You."

From here Peter goes on to become one of, if not the most influential of, the apostles and church leaders. Peter never achieves perfection in his Christian walk, but he is used by God in powerful ways. Peter's powerful personality is still seen in his preaching and willingness to stand up for Christ, but from this point on we also see a humility in Peter which demonstrates that he never forgets his unworthiness and his need for grace. This combination of boldness and humility is clearly shown in the way in which tradition tells us Peter died. In standing up for Christ he is condemned by Nero to die by crucifixion. Peter does not beg to be spared, but rather requests that he be crucified up-side-down. For he says that he is not worthy to even die in the manner in which his Lord died.

A Closer Look

How we handle failure often speaks more about our character and faith than how we deal with success. It would be nice if we did not have to deal with failure, if we just always did what we were supposed to do. Unfortunately, that is not reality. It is true that the best way to deal with sin is to avoid it in the first place. But when we fall to sin it is important that we know how to deal with it so we can move beyond our failure and get back to the freedom of walking with Christ.

One of the things that help us recognize the truthfulness of the Bible is that almost all of its main characters fail at one time or another. These are not make-believe people who never do anything wrong. Abraham, Moses, Elijah, David, Peter, and Paul were all men who failed at one time or another, and yet they are remembered as men of faith. Cain, Saul, Solomon, Jeroboam, Joash, and Judas were all men who started well, but ended up as spiritual failures. The difference was not that one group sinned, or failed, and the other ones did not. The difference was in the way they dealt with their failure.

For example, let us look at Israel's first two kings. Both Saul and David were chosen by God. They were both anointed by God's Spirit, and both faced difficulties and trials of faith. Scripture tells us that both of them failed at one time, and both were confronted by prophets of God. If we look at the sins committed by the men (Saul-disobeying God's directions,[5] David - adultery and murder[6]), we might think that David's sins were the more damaging and more likely to prevent him from being used by God. Who would you pick to lead your church? Someone who didn't always do all that God told him, or someone who was an adulterer and a murderer? Yet Saul had the kingdom and God's Spirit stripped away from him, while David continued on to be known as Israel's greatest king and a man after God's own heart.[7] It is true that David had to deal with some severe consequences because of his sin,[8] but God forgave him and continued to bless and use him. The key issue was not so much the size of their sin but how they dealt with their sin.

When Samuel confronted Saul with his disobedience, Saul sought to hide the truth. He made excuses for his rebellion and sought to put the blame on others.[9] When he did confess his sin, it was in an attempt to escape the consequences. When David was confronted by Nathan, he did not try to deny or excuse what he did. Rather, he openly confessed his sin.[10] Psalms 51, which David wrote at about this time, gives us a glimpse as to what was in his heart.

"Wash me thoroughly from my iniquity And cleanse me from my sin. For I know my transgressions, and my sin is ever before me . . . Create in me a clean heart, O God, and renew a steadfast spirit within me. Do not cast me away from Your presence and do not take Your Holy Spirit from me." (Ps. 51:2-3, 10-11)

David confessed, not to escape the consequences, but because he wanted to be right with God. He humbled himself before the Lord and sought His forgiveness. David placed himself back under God's authority and surrendered to His mercy. It is not your sin or your weakness that will keep you from being used by God, but how you deal with it.

We find some keys to dealing with sin and failure as we look at some other stories in scripture. In the story of the prodigal son we find, that in dealing with sin, sooner is always better. In Luke 15, a younger son demands his inheritance so that he can go off and live as he pleases. The father gives him what he demands, and the son takes off to a distant land where he begins to live it up. It is not here that the son begins to sin. He actually began that back when he was still at home. It was the attitude of rebellion and greed that the son allowed into his life that brought about his actions. Sin does not begin with a desire to do bad, but in becoming complacent in do good. It is when we neglect our relationship with our Father that we become open to sin. If the son had been willing to examine his attitude, and deal with it, he could have saved himself a lot of trouble.

The son thought that getting and doing what he wanted would make him happy, but he soon found out that it only led to sorrow. His life became miserable, but his pride would not allow him to go back home. He was sure that his father would reject him or respond to him in a negative way. It was not until he was starving to death that he finally came to his senses and turned back home. The son did not have to make it on his own all the way back to the father. The father met him part way. The father was waiting for him, but the son had to be willing to take the first steps. When he did the father was there to meet him, and far from rejecting the son, the father welcomed him with open arms.

What did the son gain by holding off from returning to the father? It gained him absolutely nothing, except for a lot of pain and misery. The love we see in the father's reception had been there all along. It was there when he left. It was there while he was out partying. It was there while he wallowed in the mire. It was there available to the son the whole time. But he could not benefit from it until he was willing to turn back to the father. When he did, the love he dared not hope for was waiting for him, and so was the forgiveness he longed for.

The father was ready to forgive him from the very start. Somehow we get the idea that if we sin, God will want us to suffer. There is nothing further from the truth. God does not want us to suffer. His desire is for our benefit. There may be times God will allow us to go through hard times either to prepare us for something ahead or to try to draw us away from something that is hurting us. But even that comes out of God's love. When we sin, it is always better to turn to God and seek His forgiveness right away.

In the account of Jesus meeting the woman caught in adultery[11] we find another key to dealing with failure - accept the grace but heed the warning. The woman in the story had been caught in the act of adultery. There was no question about her guilt. She was guilty. By law she deserved death. Jesus did not dispute her guilt or the fact that she deserved to die. Rather He said to her accusers, "He who is without sin among you, let him be the first to throw a stone at her."[12] In other words, Jesus agreed with them that she deserved to punished, only let the first person to throw a stone be someone whom did not deserve to be punished as well. We often want God to bring justice upon others who we feel deserve His punishment. But when it comes to us, we would prefer His mercy. In condemning her, they would be asking God to give them what they deserved as well.[13]

One by one the woman's accusers left, leaving her with Jesus. What did this woman expect from Jesus? Since He was a man of God and a Rabbi, she probably expected Him to scorn and despise her. But even though Jesus knew more about her sin than she realized, He showed neither scorn nor anger. In fact, I think Jesus smiled down at the woman as He helped her to stand. "Where are your accusers?" He asked. "Did not any of them choose to condemn you?" When she told them that they had not, He responded, "I do not condemn you, either. Go. From now on sin no more."[14]

We notice a couple of things here. First, it is not God's desire to punish us. He is not sitting up in heaven just looking for opportunities to show His wrath. The truth is that God has gone to a lot of effort to avoid punishing us. It is not God's desire that anyone should perish.[15] But God is also a God of justice. He cannot just ignore sin. Sin must be paid for, which is why Christ had to die on the cross - so that He might pay the price for our sins. He did this because it is His desire to forgive us. Secondly, this woman did nothing to earn Christ's forgiveness. She did not have to do any penance or make amends. Jesus forgave her because He wanted to, even in spite of what she did. Now keep in mind we are not talking here about salvation. Jesus did not say her sins were all forgiven or that she was now saved. For that, there must be faith. Jesus was just choosing not to give her the punishment she deserved for her sin.

So often we think we have to earn God's forgiveness that we need to somehow pay for our sins. In the Old Testament we do see this idea.

> "So it shall be when he becomes guilty in one of these, that he shall
> confess that in which he has sinned. He shall also bring his guilt offering
> to the LORD for his sin which he has committed, a female from the flock,
> a lamb or a goat as a sin offering. So the priest shall make atonement on
> his behalf for his sin." (Lev. 5:5-6)

To deal with sin, a person was to confess the sin and then make restitution. If the sin was just against God, then they were to offer a sacrifice. If the sin was also against a person, then in addition they were to make restitution, or do what they could to make it right with that person.

With Christ the sacrifice is no longer necessary because He has already paid the price. It is still important that we are willing to confess our sin, and when another person is involved, we are still to do what we can to make it right.[16] But there is nothing we can do or need to do to earn forgiveness from the Lord. It is good for us to do things for God, but it is not required for forgiveness, and does nothing to help bring forgiveness. That price has already been completely paid.

> "And their sins and their lawless deeds I will remember no more. Now
> where there is forgiveness of these things, there is no longer any offering
> for sin." (Heb. 10:17-18)

When we hold on to guilt or to the feeling that we must do something to fix it with God, we are saying to God that the blood of His son was not enough to pay for our sin. If we hear a voice reminding us of our sin, or telling us we need to do something to earn His forgiveness, we can know that voice is not God's but Satan's. When we confess our sins, He removes them and we start afresh from there.

What we do from there is very important. This is where we need to heed Jesus' warning, "Go. From now on sin no more." This is what it means to repent. It means to turn away from our sin or from the direction we were headed. If we ask forgiveness but just continue on willfully sinning, then we make Christ's sacrifice void.

> "For if we go on sinning willfully after receiving the knowledge of the
> truth, there no longer remains a sacrifice for sins," (Heb. 10:26)

The word "willfully" is important here. We may not find we have the power to resist sin, but if we are striving to be obedient to Christ, then even if we should be woefully inadequate, His grace still covers us. It is when we willfully choose to ignore God's will and go our own way that we take ourselves out from under the umbrella of God's grace. Even then we can be forgiven if we will just turn back to God. "Return, O faithless sons, I will heal your faithlessness . . ." (Jer. 3:22)

Another reason to heed Christ's warning is that we only make it harder on ourselves. The more we go back to a sin, the easier it is for Satan to draw us into that sin later, and the harder God is going to have to work to pull us out of that sin. This not only grieves God, it is harder on us. When we fall to sin, God will convict us of that sin. If we will respond to that conviction we can save ourselves a lot of trouble. Unfortunately, too often we ignore that conviction and continue on.

God does not give up on us, He will give us warnings. At first these may be minor. Something will happen that will give us a scare. We will be reminded that this sin is not a good idea. We may turn to God and ask His forgiveness and help. As with the woman caught in adultery, He is ready to forgive us, but the warning is there as well. "Sin no more." If we turn away from the sin then, we may find that the consequences of our sin are not too bad. But if we ignore the warning and go back to that sin, the next time the warning will be harsher and the consequences more severe. The more we ignore it, the worse things will get. We may end up losing our reputation, our job, our family, or even worse things may happen.

Part of this is because Satan is not interested in your well-being. He wants to destroy you. The further we follow his lead, the more damage it will to do our lives and the lives of those around us. Another reason is because the more we give into Satan, the more power we give him over our life. We force God to use more drastic means to reach us. The more we ignore God's warnings, the harder our hearts become. This may start in one area of our life, but it will affect our entire relationship with our Lord. We will find ourselves growing distant from God and may not know why. The harder our hearts get, the more severe the circumstances will have to be to break through. This is not God's desire. It hurts us and it hurts Him. But He loves us too much to just give up on us.

"There were those who dwelt in darkness and in the shadow of death, prisoners in misery and chains, because they had rebelled against the words of God and spurned the counsel of the Most High. Therefore He humbled their heart with labor; they stumbled and there was none to help. Then they cried out to the LORD in their trouble; He saved them out of their distresses. He brought them out of darkness and the shadow of death and broke their bands apart." (Ps. 107:10-14)

God's desire is for our freedom. It is Satan who wishes to bind us in our sin. God is ready and waiting to forgive us if we will just turn to Him, if we will just heed His warning.

"Seek the LORD while He may be found; Call upon Him while He is near.
Let the wicked forsake his way And the unrighteous man his thoughts;
And let him return to the LORD, And He will have compassion on him,
And to our God, For He will abundantly pardon." (Is. 55:6-7)

Digging Deeper

It is we, not God who is keeping us from receiving forgiveness and being free of sin and guilt. As we have seen, God is ready and waiting to remove our sin and help us to begin a new start. To deal with sin we first must understand its seriousness.

1. What are some of the consequences of sin?

Num. 14:30-33

Ps. 38:3-5

Is. 59:2

John 8:34

Titus 1:15-16

James 1:15

2. If a sin does not seem too serious to us, we may think that it won't do much harm. But what is the harm of allowing even small sins into our lives? (1 Cor. 5:6)

Once we allow Satan a foothold in our life, He will not be satisfied until He has complete control. If we deal with the sin, we can be freed from its control on our lives, but if we allow it to remain, it will hamper our relationship with God. This in turn makes us more susceptible to Satan's attacks in other areas of our life. Sin that is not dealt with will eventually contaminate our entire lives.

As stated earlier in this chapter, the best way to deal with sin is to avoid it in the first place.

3. What does scripture say about the possibility of avoiding sin? (1 Cor. 10:13)

4. How can we help ourselves avoid sin?

   2 Chron. 12:14

   Ps. 119:9-11

   Matt. 5:29-30

   Matt. 26:41

   1 Tim. 6:9-11

By fleeing from the things that cause us to sin and seeking the Lord, we can help ourselves avoid a lot of heartache.

But now we focus on what we should do once we have fallen to sin.

5. What do these passages tell us about how to deal with failure?

     A. 1 John 2:1; Heb. 4:15-16

     B. Ps.103:11-13

We need to remember that Christ is on our side. He knows how hard it is to deal with sin, and He wants to help us and God wants to forgive us. We do not have to convince Him or bribe Him. He is ready to receive us the moment we turn to Him.

     C. Rom. 5:8

Not only do we not have to work to earn God's forgiveness, we do not have to work to earn His love. There is nothing we can do to make God love us any more than He already does. Even when we fail Him, He still loves us completely. Our sin keeps us from experiencing that love but it is there waiting for us when we turn to Him.

     D. 2 Chron. 7:14

     E. Ps. 32:3-5; 1 John 1:8-10

It is important that we are honest with ourselves and with God. Until we are willing to face our sins and confess them before God, He can do nothing to help us. But when we humble ourselves before Him and confess our sins, He can then begin to wash and renew our spirit and bring healing to our soul.

     F. Ps. 119:58-60; 1 Kings 18:21

When we wait, we only end up hurting ourselves. When we sin we sometimes feel that we cannot come to God, because He is angry with us, or because we are unworthy. In truth we are unworthy, but that does not keep God from loving us and wanting us to turn to Him right away, the sooner the better. The sooner we confess our sin and seek His help and forgiveness, the sooner He can help free us from the hold of sin.

6. When we confess our sins, how long does God hold them against us? (Ez. 33:14-16)

7. How can others help us in overcoming sin? (James 5:14-16)

The word here for sickness can mean physical or spiritual weakness. It is good for us to find a Christian we respect, and ask them to pray for us and help keep us accountable.

8. What should we do once we have gotten right with God? (2 Peter 1:3-9)

It is important that we do not become lax once we have received God's forgiveness. We may not be very good at walking with the Lord, but we need to keep trying, and when we fail we need to get up, try again. God can deal with our sin. It is our attitude that often stands in the way. Self-pity, doubt, pride, and guilt are all tools of Satan to keep us from receiving the freedom God desires to share with us. The answer to sin is not strength, it is humility and faith.

9. What lesson did Paul have to learn to have victory over his weakness? (2 Cor. 12:7-10)

Paul's weakness could have been physical, or it could have been spiritual. We often get frustrated with God because He does not give us the spiritual strength to overcome some of our weaknesses. We pray to Him to remove these "thorns in the flesh," but continue to struggle against them. We beat ourselves up because we think we really ought to be stronger. But it is not our strength that God is looking for. It is our humility and our faith. It is not that we should just accept sin. God hates sin, and it hurts us. It is good for us to ask God to give us the strength to over sin. Sometimes He may give us that victory. Other times He will say, "My grace is sufficient for you, for power is perfected in weakness."[17] This is not because He does not care about us, nor is it because He does not care about sin. It is because He wants us to learn not to trust in our own strength, but in His strength and grace. This is where the true power of Christian living is found.

Sometimes we hold off turning to God because we do not think we will be able to live the way we know we should. We think, how can I ask for forgiveness when I know I will just fail again? God is not interested in our ability to do as we should. What God is interested in is our willingness to turn to Him. Humility is far more important than ability. Walking by faith in failure means we go forward even when we cannot see how it will work. We trust that God is willing to forgive our failures, and able to deal with our weaknesses. We take God at His word when He says, "My grace is sufficient for you."

10. Keeping in mind what we have learned for this chapter, answer how you would deal with the following scenarios?

     A. You have fallen once again to that same old sin that you have been struggling against for so long. You feel like such a failure, and you believe that God must be really angry with you. What should you do?

     B. You have confessed your sin and ask God for forgiveness, but are afraid you will just fall to the same sin again. You want to gain victory over the sin. What should you do?

11. What does will it mean for you to walk by faith in regard to your failures?

12. What is one area connected to failure that you can work on walking by faith in?

Life Examples
Steve[18]

     Faith has never been easy for me. I guess it isn't really easy for anyone, but I have come to realize that there are some things from my past that have made it even harder. It's hard for me to have faith in people I can see. It's harder still to have faith in a God I can't see. Some of this comes out of the way I was raised. It is not that my parents weren't good parents, they were and are, and I love them both. But my father has never been a believer, and his doubts have played a part in who I am. I have always been bothered by the fact that I never felt like I had my father's respect. I always felt that I had to measure up in some way, but never seemed to be able to achieve it. It is a feeling that continues to linger even today. When I became a Christian, it just made things worse. I felt like I was a failure in his sight. To him it appeared just wishful thinking. He thought I was wasting my time on things that weren't that important.

When I went to Bible College I thought faith would become easier, but instead it got harder. The simple faith that I knew seemed to get more complicated. There were professors I respected who attacked some of the things that were at the basis of my beliefs. There were people who were involved in ministry that appeared to have it all together, but who turned out to have feet of clay. Doubts began to creep in more and more about what was true and what wasn't. Was it enough just to believe there was a God and that I was going to heaven? Was this just wishful thinking, as my father thought? Surely there must be more. But nothing seemed clear. How could I rely on a God I couldn't understand?

I now realize that a lot of those doubts had more to do with me than with God. I struggled with things others seemed to have no problem with. Once again, I felt like I didn't measure up. My Christianity began to feel more like a show than a reality. Eventually I could no longer keep up the show. My doubts became more than I could deal with, so I turned away. This caused a lot of hurt and uncertainty with my wife and children, which only made things worse. I felt I was not only a failure as a Christian, but that I had failed my family as well.

What brought me back to the Lord? Hitting the bottom. Several things happened within a relatively short time, things within my family, my job, and within me. I came to a point where I saw life as being hopeless and meaningless. Without God, what is life but shallow relationships and empty things? I remember one night, lying in the bathtub long after the water turned cold. I came to the conclusion that life was no longer worth living. I had no faith in God. My wife did not love or respect me (Though, to her credit, I know most of the time she tried to do the right thing). It was I who drove her away. I felt that I was a failure as a husband, father, and man. I began thinking about how I could end my life, but make it look like an accident so my kids wouldn't have to bear the shame of having their father take his own life.

As I lay there, contemplating my death, Carolynn was away at a conference finding more life, joy, and peace than she had known in a long time. They helped her work through some of her struggles, and she came home happier than I had seen her in a long time. I envied her joy, but I could not share it. Her fullness only made my life seem emptier. When she couldn't share her new found love for life with me, she found someone else to talk to. This led her to be tempted to fall in a big way. When I learned of this I knew it was my fault, not hers. I had left her alone far too long. Knowing my sin could cause her, someone I saw as unshakeable, to stumble made me realize it was time for me to stop running from God and find some answers.

I went to the leaders of the seminar that she had attended and asked all of the questions I could think of that had been stumbling blocks to me. I wanted to know how a loving god could do some of the things we see in the Old Testament. I questioned, if God made the Bible to reveal Himself and to show us truth, then why was it so hard to understand, and why did so many people disagreed on what it meant? Why couldn't God have made it clearer? I had questions about heaven as well. How do we know what it will be like? How can we be sure?

The leaders helped me to understand some of these things, but mostly they helped me to understand that it was okay for me not to understand. These stumbling blocks I had were really only excuses and smoke screens I had used to avoid dealing with other things I found too painful to face. I didn't have to prove God for Him to be real. I realized I really did believe, and I just needed to say it out loud and ask for forgiveness. I also realized I didn't have to try to measure up for God. Even if I didn't understand Him, even if I was a failure, He loved me anyway. He loved me in spite of my failings and doubts. I decided to let go of my fears and insecurities and surrender myself back to God once again. And He was faithful and met me, as He always does when I come to Him broken and humble.

At that moment, it was as if there was a tremendous weight lifted from my shoulders. I was free. I didn't have to fight anymore. When I stopped fighting, God picked me up, and He loved me. I realize now that He loved me before, but for the first time in a long time, I could feel His love - and it felt good! Not only did God love me, but He changed me as well. The guilt and the sin that had been piling up was gone. I was still the same man, yet I wasn't the same at all.

When I got back home I shared with Carolynn what God had done in my life. We shared laughter and tears. I spoke to her of things I had long held locked within me. We decided that there were to be no more secrets between us. Good or bad, we would share them together. I can't say that our marriage was fixed overnight. There is a lot of damage to be undone, but God has begun a healing process that continues on today.

He is also helping me with other relationships as well. Even before I turned back to God, I started attending church with my family. I did it more for their sake than for my own. When I went I felt like an outsider. I couldn't feel what others seemed to feel. I kept myself aloof, afraid of letting anyone too close for fear they would see who I really was. I was afraid someone would cry out, "This man's a fake! He doesn't belong here." When Christ freed me from my fears, He freed me from this one as well. Finally I could open up and be who I was, for I knew that God loved me just as I was. When I opened up to others, I didn't find the rejection I had feared, but rather an acceptance, and a realization that most of them were not that much different from me.

It would be nice to say that all my doubts and my problems have disappeared, but it wouldn't be true. I still have to battle bad habits that I developed over many years of denying God. I still find myself trying to take care of problems, or solving things without first seeking the Lord's guidance. For so long this was just the way I operated. I still allow myself to get so busy with work that I don't make time for a relationship with my family or my God as I should. And I still have to battle the lies the enemy throws at me. "Nothing has really changed. You're not a real Christian. You don't belong. You are a fake. You should know so much more than you do. What you have to say doesn't really matter. You should just be quiet." I still have these struggles, but now at least I know how to fight them.

I still have questions, and God doesn't always make sense to me. But now, rather than looking for reasons to doubt God, I look for reasons to believe in Him. And there are so many to see. 1. The incredible and complex way the body is put together. 2. The fact that the mind is so wonderfully built, that it still is mostly a mystery to us. 3. The intricacy and the minute detail of nature. 4. The way the earth, sun and moon are placed in just the right way to enable us to survive. 5. The wondrous beauty of a bird in song. 6. The emptiness of a life without God. These things, and so many more, help me to know beyond a shadow of a doubt that God is very real, even if I don't always understand Him.

I have found that if I don't spend time in the Word, then I don't feel as close to my Lord. And I'm not just talking about reading the Bible so I can check a box in my reading program, but thinking about it and applying it to my life. I have also found that going to church is very important for me. It helps encourage me, and helps keep me accountable. I seem to need that.

What does it mean for a middle class American to say he has faith? We have jobs, insurance for our cars, our homes and our lives. We have Social Security, Medicare, Medicaid, IRAs, and pension plans, but where is our faith? We often don't have faith in people, groups, politicians, or even the government. Can we have faith in God?

I want to have a strong faith. I want to believe that Jesus is God's only begotten Son that He died, rose again and is preparing a place for us. I want to believe that He is interceding on our behalf, and that He sings over us. He has the hairs on our head numbered, and He weeps when we weep and rejoices when we rejoice. I want to believe He has a plan for MY Life. That life is more than working two jobs and paying the bills. I want to believe that I can make a difference, that what I do and say matters. I guess to me, this is what faith is about.

I am sure that it is abundantly clear that I still have a long way to go. Someday I hope and pray that faith will just become a part of my life, something I don't need to think about, worry over, or question. Until then I will keep praying, studying, and waking up every day deciding that I will believe.

Chapter 12
FAITH IN OUR UNITY
"Being diligent to preserve the unity of the Spirit in the bond of peace." (Eph. 4:3)

The Question of Faith
The centurion Julius - Acts 27

Much of my life has been spent leading men, but in the last few weeks I have learned a few things about what it means to be a leader. I have learned that leadership isn't just about authority and getting things done. It is about compassion as well. I have learned that if we are to survive, we must stick together. But I'm getting ahead of myself. Let me back up a bit.

As a soldier, I am most comfortable with my feet on solid ground. But as a soldier, I am also used to taking orders. Therefore, when I was given charge of a group of prisoners and told to transport them to Rome to stand trial, I began right away to make the necessary arrangements. I organized my squad of men to guard the prisoners. I made sure we had the money and supplies that would be needed, and planned out our travel rout, which included sea passage to Italy.

I looked over my list of prisoners and found they were a mixed lot. Some were potentially dangerous and would bear keeping a careful eye on. Others were political prisoners and the like. They, for the most part, were harmless. But then again, one never knew in these troubled times. One of the prisoners was a man named Paul. The governor had told me that his charges had to do with some disagreement with the Jewish religious law, and that I should treat him with some leniency. Paul had a couple of companions who requested to travel along with him. One of them was a doctor and I decided that he might come in handy along the journey. I told them they could come along, but they would have to cover their own costs.

The job of transporting the prisoners should have been an easy one, but things went wrong right from the beginning. We had delays in getting the supplies and in finalizing the travel arrangements. I'm not a man who likes delays, and I had to threaten to break some heads before we were finally ready to go. The journey itself started off well enough. We booked passage on a ship that was sailing north along the Palestine coast. We made good time the first couple of days, but then the wind backed and began to blow against us, which slowed our progress considerably.

After we rounded the point of Cyprus we turned west and sailed along the southern coast of Asia Minor. When we reached Myra at the southwest corner of Asia Minor, I arranged a transfer to a ship headed for Italy. The winds continued to be contrary and our progress seemed to inch along. We were forced to head south to sail under the shelter of the isle of Crete.

The journey was taking us much longer than I had anticipated, and my temper was getting short. I was anxious to complete my task. I had hoped to make it to Italy before it got too late in the year to continue the journey, but our slow progress was making that impossible. Soon the weather would bring sea travel to a halt. Even now it would be risky to go much further. The weather might hold fair for a number of weeks, but then again it might not. It could change in a matter of minutes, and turn a calm day into a nightmare.

We stopped at the port of Fair Havens for supplies, and there we had to make the decision as to whether to go on or spend the winter there. Fair Havens was not really suitable for wintering in and the pilot of the ship suggested that we continue on to the port of Phoenix, which was another fifty miles further up the shore of Crete. It was then that Paul asked to have a word with us. He told us that his God had revealed to him that we should stay here. It would be extremely dangerous to continue on, and if we did so there would certainly be great loss and damage.

By now, I had come to have a respect for Paul. There was something about him that spoke of an inner strength and wisdom. He was obviously some kind of holy man. I had heard him talk about his God a number of times. Now I am not much of a religious man, and I didn't know anything about his God, but when you are out on the sea at the mercy of the winds, you have a tendency to put more credence in such things. I was inclined to listen to Paul, but the pilot was adamant that we should go on. He was afraid that if we stayed in this unsheltered port, his ship would be vulnerable to the winter storms. It might get damaged or even sunk. He was sure that we could make it to Phoenix in a day or two. There we would be safe to wait out the winter.

Although the ship was his, I was on Caesar's business, so the choice was mine to make. To go on would mean to risk the lives of two hundred and seventy-six people. But I had my duty to think of. Phoenix was a larger town, and it would be easier there, to deal with my prisoners. It would also be more comfortable for my men and myself. I decided that if we got a favorable wind, we would take the risk.

The next day there was a moderate south wind, which would be just right to push us up to Phoenix. The pilot smiled at me and said, "See, I have prayed to my god and he has answered my prayers. He will protect us and see us safely to harbor." As we left Fair Havens, it seemed he was right. The wind continued to blow in the right direction for once.

I walked by where Paul was kneeling in prayer and said, "It looks like you were wrong about your God, or maybe He changed His mind."

Paul looked up at me with a calm resignation and said, "You will see." Then he bowed and continued to pray.

It was not so much the words that he said, but the matter-of-fact way he said them that made a chill run down my spine. "Surely he must be wrong," I thought, but the doubt lingered. The doubt became stronger when I felt the wind shift. It moved from south to northeast. "Still," I thought, "we should be okay."

But in a matter of minutes the wind went from a moderate breeze to a strong gale, and then turned into a real storm. The pilot shouted orders and the seamen rushed about the ship trying to secure the sails and regain control of the ship. The wind pushed us away from the protection of the coast and away from our destination. There was no maneuvering in this wind, so we gave way to it and let ourselves be driven along.

Within an hour, the sky was black with clouds and the seas became dark rolling mountains, tossing our ship about with ease. It became painfully clear that this was no small storm. This was the Euraquilo, or the Northeaster. When it came, men died. Paul was no longer the only one praying and the pilot was no longer smiling. Fear was written plainly upon his face while he did what he could to keep the ship afloat. He used supporting cables to undergird the ship, and let out a sea anchor to try to give us some control. As the storm continued through the night and into the next day the crew began jettisoning the cargo. Now the only goal was to survive. But more and more even that seemed to be an empty hope.

It is at times like these that a person's character can be most plainly seen. While some men despaired and others cursed, Paul continued on with a calm assurance that made it seem as if he were unaware of his danger. Of course he wasn't. One could hardly miss our peril with the roar of the wind drowning out all thought. The waves pounded against the ship, crashing over its sides and tilting it so that it seemed it would surely capsize. Then the ship would it righted itself and began the whole terrifying process all over again. Inside the ship we were tossed about, clinging to anything we could hold on to. Everyone was green with sea sickness, and Paul was as sick as the rest of us. Yet he continued to see to the needs of others and to encourage those around him. I had expected him to show anger over our disregarding his advice, and possibly even to try to foster discontent among the crew. Goodness knows that it wouldn't have been hard in the present situation. But Paul showed no animosity towards me, nor did he encourage any mutinous ideas.

After more than a week of relentless beating, the crew and passengers were so weary and sick that mutiny was the least of my worries. No one had eaten or slept since the storm had begun. A feeling of hopelessness had settled upon us, like condemned men waiting for the inevitable. Most of us, that is, except Paul and his companions. They, too, were sick and weary, but they continued to have about them a calm assurance. They would pray and sometimes even sing songs of praise. Most of the others thought they must have gone mad, but I knew there was something more.

One morning Paul stood up and signaled for our attention. Even in the ship's hold he had to yell to be heard over the thunder of the wind and waves.

"Men," He said, "you ought to have followed my advice and not to have set sail from Crete and incurred this damage and loss. Yet now I urge you to keep up your courage, for there will be no loss of life among you, but only of the ship. For this very night an angel of the God to whom I belong and whom I serve stood before me, saying, 'Do not be afraid, Paul; you must stand before Caesar; and behold, God has granted you all those who are sailing with you.' Therefore, keep up your courage, men, for I believe God and that it will turn out exactly as I have been told. But we must run aground on a certain island."[1]

This was the closest yet that I had heard Paul say, "I told you so." But I knew his point wasn't to show his superiority, but to remind us that his God had been right about the storm, and therefore we could have confidence that He would be right about our salvation as well. Paul continued to try to encourage those aboard, and the mood about the ship lightened a bit. But it wasn't until two days later that they began to show life again. About midnight, the sailors on the late watch became convinced we were nearing land. They conducted a sounding, and found that the water was indeed getting shallower. No one liked the idea of running aground at night, so we put out anchors at the stern and waited for the morning.

Some of the sailors began to let down the ship's boats. When I asked them what they were doing, they said they were going to lay anchors from the bow as well. Paul came up and warned me that these men were, in reality, attempting to escape and leave us behind. He told me that unless we all remained together, we would not survive. How Paul knew all this, I did not know, but I had already determined not to question his advice any longer. I gave the order to have the life boats cut away. There were only enough boats for a few people, and I thought it better to remove the temptation. Whatever happened to us would happen to us together.

As the sky began to lighten, Paul began to encourage us to eat. No one had felt like eating for two weeks. But now Paul said we should eat, for we would need our strength. "Not a hair from the head of any of you will perish," he assured us. And with that he led the way by taking some bread himself. We all watched as he gave thanks to his God. He then looked at us and smiled and started eating the bread. His confidence was infectious. The hours ahead would be filled with danger, but somehow he conveyed the feeling that we would be okay. We all began to eat, and to hope once again.

After we ate, we threw the rest of the stores overboard. The lighter the ship the better would be our chances of making it to shore. Besides, one way or another, we soon would have no need of them. As the sun came up, we let go the anchors and steered toward a sandy beach that could be seen in the distance. Just as our hopes began to soar, we were knocked off our feet by a sudden jolt. The ship had run aground on a hidden reef. We were stuck fast and the waves were pounding against the ship's stern. We knew it would not be long before the ship would begin to break up. It was time to abandon ship and try to make it to the shore. The general feeling was, "Every man for himself." My soldiers were concerned about the prisoners. If any escaped, we would each be held accountable. Many of them thought that it would be better if we killed them now rather than risk any getting away.

It was now in the midst of the chaos that I thought over what I had learned over the past few weeks. I knew for sure that I was not going to allow them to kill Paul. I knew little about his God, but I knew enough to know that I wanted to learn more. There was something about Paul that I needed for myself. But even more than that, I had learned that I had a responsibility for everyone aboard this ship. Every life was important. In the midst of the storm we had shared a common bond. Sailor, soldier, freeman, slave, each life was as important as the next. I couldn't guarantee their safety, but I could do my part to make sure we faced the dangers together.

I ordered everyone to quiet down, and even had to use some force to get them to listen. "This is how it is going to be," I said. "We are all going, and we are going together. No one is being abandoned or left behind. Those of you who can swim go head and swim for shore. The rest of you, look around for planks, boxes, or anything that will float. But most of all, work together. We can make it if we help each other and work together. Are you all with me? All right, now let's go!"

By following Paul's instruction, the entire ship's company makes it safely to shore. There while Paul is helping to build a fire, he is bitten by a viper. The people of the island think he must be cursed by the gods since he escapes a ship wreck only to be the victim of a deadly snake bite. They change their minds though when they see he suffers no ill effect from the bite. Through his witness and words, Paul is able to lead to Christ, not only many of his ship mates, but many of the islanders as well.

A Closer Look

Paul's journey

When we look at the story of Paul's sea journey, it may not seem at first to have much to do with unity. After all, it is not speaking about the church. It is speaking about a bunch of people on a ship. But there are many similarities for us to see.

1. We are all in the same boat. Paul makes this point, especially in the letters of Romans and 1st Corinthians. In both cases, he is writing to churches that are having problems with unity. There were groups within the churches that were struggling against each other.[2] It was not a matter of one group being right and the other being wrong, as much as it was seeing things from different perspectives. Paul wanted them to understand that they were all in this together.

In the church, we all have this same problem - sin.[3] We all need the same answer - grace,[4] which comes to us all the same way - through faith.[5] We all have the same head - Christ.[6] We are one body. What happens to one part of the body affects the rest.[7] We cannot separate our relationship with God from our relationship with each other. When there is a strain in our relationship with a brother or sister that interferes with our relationship with God.[8]

Through communion we see the corporate aspect of faith. We share in the blood and body of Christ, but we do not do it alone. The blood that Christ shed for me ties me to Him and that same blood connects me with my brother. When I hurt my brother, I wound Christ who died for me as well. Through baptism we are all joined to the same body.[9] In Christ there is no American, Russian, Iraqi, or African. There is no Baptist, Presbyterian, Charismatic, or Fundamentalist. We may have different abilities and different jobs, different preferences and different points of view, but we are to have the same goals - to build up the body[10] and to glorify God.[11]

2. We are to hold to God's truth. When God made it clear that they were headed for destruction, Paul did not hesitate to stand up and say so. While unity is important, what we are unified on is even more important. A group can be unified and yet be going in the wrong direction. It is important to preserve the unity, but sometimes we need to be willing to stand up and say, "We are going the wrong way." This is not done to prove we

are superior to anyone else but rather for the good of the body. It is also important that we make our determination of what is right and what is wrong not for our own personal opinions but rather from the Word of God. The church is the body of Christ. It does not belong to us, rather we belong to Him. Truth is determined by God, not what we choose to believe.

3. If we want God's grace, we must learn to give it as well. In the church, we are going to find that people are not always going to listen to us or agree with us, just as Julius did not listen to Paul at first. Paul was right and Julius was wrong. Paul could have held onto resentment, but instead he chose to try and help and let God take care of the situation. Because of Paul's attitude, and because of how God worked things, Julius was willing to listen to Paul later on.

4. Work to build up the body. Paul not only resisted getting angry, he worked to help the situation. He sought ways to encourage and to strengthen those around him. Jesus made it clear in Matthew 25 that serving our Lord is directly tied to how we serve our brothers and sisters in Christ. "Truly I say to you, to the extent that you did it to one of these brothers of Mine, even the least of them, you did it to Me."[12] Being a Christian in this world is not easy. From time to time we all need help, and God has called us to help one another. Whether we like it or not, we have a responsibility to each other.

5. Unity takes sacrifice. It would have been easier for Julius and Paul to have taken one of the boats for themselves and not worry about what happened to the rest. It would be easier for us just to focus on ourselves and not worry about those around us. It would be a lot easier to be a Christian if we did not have to deal with people who are in the church. There is a temptation to say, "Fine, you do your thing and I will do mine. Just leave me alone." That would be easier, but it is not what God has called us to do.

God has called us to be one, and not just with those we get along with. We are not going to agree on everything, but we still are called to work together. God wants His children to not only get along, but to work together. For this to happen it is going to take sacrifice, not only in time and energy, but in preferences and patience as well. Unity takes work, but it is worth it. For not only does it help others, it helps us as well. It helps us to become more than we are. We may wish to think that we do not need others, but we would be wrong. We cannot be pleasing to God unless we are willing to work with others.

> "Make my joy complete by being of the same mind, maintaining the same love, united in spirit, intent on one purpose. Do nothing from selfishness or empty conceit, but with humility of mind regard one another as more important than yourselves; do not merely look out for your own personal interests, but also for the interests of others." (Philip. 2:2-4)

Dangers to unity

Unity is important. It is important to God, and it needs to be important to us as well. But for us to be unified we must have something dependable upon which we can be unified about. Without something to be united on, unity loses its meaning. The church is to be unified in Christ and His Word. The way to promote unity is not to accept any idea that comes along, but to lift up the truth of God's Word, and to be united on that. Scripture warns of four things that we are not to allow to take root within the church, for they will end up destroying the church:

1. False teaching,

"Be on guard for yourselves and for all the flock, among which the Holy Spirit has made you overseers, to shepherd the church of God which He purchased with His own blood. I know that after my departure savage wolves will come in among you, not sparing the flock; and from among your own selves men will arise, speaking perverse things, to draw away the disciples after them." (Acts 20:28-30)

The question is, how do we know what is false teaching? Some people hold one opinion and others hold another. The test is not to be the opinion of man, but the Word of God. Man's opinion changes with the season, but God's Word holds true. It is the foundation that we are to be united upon.[13]

"For this reason we must pay much closer attention to what we have heard, so that we do not drift away from it." (Heb. 2:1)

The heart of Christianity is Jesus Christ and the gospel message. To deny or distort what the Word of God tells us about these two areas is to deny the faith.[14] For only the true Christ (God incarnate, who came down to earth, died on the cross for our sins and rose again), can bring us salvation. And salvation only comes to us by the means God has provided (by the grace of God that comes to us through our faith in Christ Jesus). Apart from Christ and the gospel, there is no salvation[15] and there is no unity.

There are other issues in the Bible as well. Some of which are hard to understand or accept. It would be a lot easier for us to pick and choose which we want to accept. But once we start down the slippery path of allowing man's wisdom to overrule God's, we lose any foundation to stand on. For one person's opinion becomes as good as another's. It would be like building a house upon the sand that shifts with each changing wind. We may not like everything we find in the Bible, but we must trust that God knows what He is doing. When God clearly speaks, we reject it at our own peril.

Now beyond this we find many teachings in Christianity that are not clearly stated in scripture. These are teachings we deduce or interpret from scripture. While we may believe that these teachings are true, we must be careful of making them issues of faith. Two people may equally believe God's Word, and yet disagree on how parts of it should be interpreted. In this case we need to rely on the grace of God and hold on to our unity. Paul tells us even if we think someone is wrong about an issue, we should accept them and withhold passing judgement.[16] Our job is to love them and let God deal with passing judgment.

2. Acceptance of sin. Jesus made it clear that He came to reach sinners, and that is the church's job as well. We are to welcome and accept sinners. If the church did not accept sinners, it would have to stand empty. But accepting the sinner does not mean accepting the sin as well. Paul chastised the Corinthian church for accepting sexual immorally among its members. In fact it seemed they were proud of their tolerance, but Paul warned them that they were being foolish.

"Your boasting is not good. Do you not know that a little leaven leavens
the whole lump of dough?" (1 Cor. 5:6)

The sin that was being tolerated was affecting the whole church. This was also the warning Jesus gave the churches of Pergamum and Thyatira in the book of Revelation.[17] The church, as the temple of God, is to be holy, and if we defile that holiness we will be held accountable.[18] It is true that none of us are perfect, but we are not to accept sin.

How, we may ask, does not accepting sin fit in with not passing judgment? Keep in mind, accepting something is just as much a form of passing judgment as condemning something. God has told us what is and is not acceptable to Him. It is not for us to add or delete from these. For instance, we may have our opinions on certain questionable behaviors. We may have verses that can be used to back up our opinions, and our opinions may be right. There is nothing wrong with expressing our opinions as long as we do not equate that with God's Word. Our understanding of a passage does not hold the same authority as something directly stated in God's Word. To say something is sin when the Bible does not, would be just as wrong as saying something is okay when the Bible says it is sin. It is not our job to convict the world of what we think is sin, that is the job of the Holy Spirit.[19]

God is also to be the judge in regard to each individual person. It is not for us to condemn or exonerate anyone. Only God can do that. We can and should condemn any sin that God has already passed judgment upon. If we do not warn others of the consequences of their sin, then we share in the responsibility of that sin.[20] Whether or not a person is involved in sin, we are still to love the person, but loving a person does not necessarily mean accepting their behavior if that behavior involves sin. When the behavior is harming that person or others, it is far more loving to refuse to accept the sin so that person might turn away from it. We are to love the person but hate the sin.

3. Division and strife. In truth, most people leave a church because of personality disputes more than doctrinal disputes. Someone says something and someone else gets offended. It is pride more often than not that destroys the unity of a church and grieves God. If we respond with resentment and pride, then we are in the wrong whatever the other person may have done. Jesus said that if we want God to forgive us, then we must be willing to forgive others.[21]

"Let no unwholesome word proceed from your mouth, but only such a word as is good for edification according to the need of the moment, so that it will give grace to those who hear. Do not grieve the Holy Spirit of God, by whom you were sealed for the day of redemption. Let all bitterness and wrath and anger and clamor and slander be put away from you, along with all malice. Be kind to one another, tender-hearted, forgiving each other, just as God in Christ also has forgiven you." (Eph. 4:29-32)

We are to be diligent to preserve the unity of the Spirit in the bond of peace.[22] This means to remove the things that destroy the church, and to work at the things that help to build it up.

Digging Deeper

When we talk about unity, we are talking about the church, for that is where Christian unity is found. It is not in our unity with the world, but in our unity with each other.

1. Scripture uses a number of different terms to describe the church. What are these terms and what do they imply for how the church is to operate?

Gal. 6:10

Eph. 2:19

Eph. 2:20-22

Rom. 12:5

Disagreement on how things should be done, have often cause damage to the unity of a church. This often happens not because one side or the other is right or wrong, but because they see things differently. But what we must understand is that God made us to be different on purpose.

2. How does God tell us to view people who see things differently than we do?
(1 Cor. 12:17-22)

What we find is that people who see things in a like manner have a tendency to gather together. This is natural, and is easier, but it causes problems as well. When the "hands" or the "feet" gather only with those who are like themselves, they may feel more comfortable, but they become less productive. They also get a warped perspective on what the body is about. When all the "hands" gather together, they may conclude that waving and clapping is what a body does, and walking or seeing is not that important. The "feet" may conclude that running and jumping is what a body does, and hearing or waving is not that important. When we choose to only work with those who see things like we do, we warp our perspective and limit our usefulness.

Within the church you have some people who want to get things done and others who like to talk things trough. Some are focused on the bottom line, while others are interested in building relationships. Some think the church should focus on evangelism, while others are interested in music, teaching or service. Some like new ideas. Others prefer the old ways. It can be very frustrating having to deal with people who see things so differently. But different is not necessarily wrong. In fact God made us different on purpose. Not only are others supposed to be different, but we need them to be different. Just as they need us to be as God made us. God made us different, and we are not meant to become like someone else, but we do need to learn to work with those who are different from us. A "foot" does not need to become a "hand" to be useful to the body, but it does need to be able to work with the hand or it will cripple the body.

This is also true in other areas as well. Some Christians have a charismatic leaning. They are more comfortable expressing their emotions and being spontaneous with the leading of the Spirit. This is good. It is how God made them. Other Christians have a more conservative leaning. They are more comfortable in using their intellect and having things lined out. This is good. It is how God made them. Some Christians have more of a social leaning, and are interested in righting injustice and improving social well-being. Still others have a doctrinal leaning, and are interested in being biblically correct. The problem comes when we only gather with those who see things the way we do. We lose perspective and become overly focused on things that interest us, and lose sight of the importance of the things that do not. We do not have to become like each other, but we do need each other, and we do need to work with each other. Separately, we become stilted and less than what God intends us to be. Together, we become stronger.

There are more than fifty different "one another" passages in the New Testament. These are passages where God directs us how to treat one another.

3. What is the most common "one another" direction given? (John 13:34)

Three times Jesus gives us the command to love one another. It is repeated by Paul, Peter, and John. We are to love fervently[23] and without hypocrisy.[24]

4. How are we supposed to demonstrate our love to each other within the church? (1 Cor. 13:4-8)

5. How else are we to treat one another?

       Rom. 12:10

       Rom. 15:7

       Gal. 5:13

       Eph. 4:2

       Heb. 3:13

Not only does scripture tell us how we are to treat one another, it also tells us how we are not to treat one another.

5. What are some of the ways we are not to treat one another, and how can we avoid them?

Rom. 14:13

Gal. 5:26

James 4:11

Col. 3:9

6. Keeping in mind what we have learned in this lesson, how you would deal with the following scenarios?

    A. The coach of your child's team is a Christian from another church. During a game you got angry because you did not feel he treated your child fairly. You said some harsh words to him and he turned and walked away. What should you do? What should you not do?

    B. You have been told by someone at work that a friend of yours at church is involved in an affair. What should you do? What should you not do?

7. What will it mean for you to walk by faith in Christian unity?

8. What is one area of unity you can work on walking by faith?

Life Examples
Mike[25]

I have been serving First Christian Church for more than 20 years. To my knowledge, I am the only person who has ever held all three positions the church offers - Youth Pastor, Associate Pastor and now, Senior Pastor.

Through the years we've experienced all phases of family life as a church. Growth, setbacks, trials, blessings, and victories have all been part of our life story. Through it all we have grown in numbers as well as maturity, but it has not been easy. In fact, I don't think Jesus ever promised us easy. With growth came an increased need for facility. We entered a capitol campaign through which we purchased 8 acres to build a new facility.

During that time there were some major changes taking place that stressed the church and began to fracture the unity of the body. We were changing our government, conducting a major stewardship campaign, calling a new senior pastor, discussing building a new facility and my wife was battling cancer. With so much going on, something had to give. Little schisms began to appear on our facade. Nothing earth shattering, but enough to let us know all was not well in paradise. An undercurrent of frustration and discontentment began to appear and replaced the atmosphere of joy which once pervaded our gatherings.

People became inwardly focused and gave into complacency. They felt like they had to let the staff know everything that was wrong with our church every time they saw us. I'm sorry, but that gets old, fast! Pretty soon the staff became a lightning rod for everything that was happening. We felt personally attacked on many fronts. There were days when it seemed the only solution was to see The Dalles in our rear view mirrors.

But there was something else I was hanging onto . . . I knew, beyond any shadow of a doubt, that God called me to be at this church . . . even if times were tough. When attacked I was tempted to fight back, and everything in me wanted to, but I was determined to let God be my vindicator. I tried to remain true to Eph. 4:3 in, "keeping the unity of the Spirit in the bond of peace." One of the hardest things I've ever done was to restrain my tongue instead of giving all the reasons why things weren't the way people were saying they were. I learned a valuable lesson about relying on God and His strength, power, and timing instead of trying to control things myself.

Finally, we as a leadership, decided to take the offensive to preserve the unity that God had placed in our midst. The elders decided to go to the source of every negative comment we were aware of to find out if it held any validity. If no, the parties involved were encouraged to be unified with the Body. Secondly, the staff started praying for every member of the church during their quiet times and wrote a personal note to them about what they prayed for. Third, we wanted people to know we have an enemy in common . . . and it's not us! The Body of Christ is all on the same side and we emphasized our unity around the Lord's Table.

Unity is something I can't control. Unity involves hard work and commitment from every member of the Body. Unity can cause you to stay when you want to leave. Unity says "we" not "I." We have learned all these lessons as we have felt the pains of growth within the Body.

The hard work and effort is now paying off. The Church is once again growing, and there is a feeling of freedom and joy that hasn't been there for a while. There is an excitement in seeing the hand of God working in the church, and the focus is once again upon "We," rather than "I." This feeling of freedom has blessed Mike as well. When he was willing to step back and trust God, he felt a burden lifted from him. He realized that he wasn't responsible for the things that only God could do. In letting go of control he has received the blessing of seeing the hand of God clearly demonstrated.

Chapter 13
FAITH IN OUR MISSION

. . . one thing I do: forgetting what lies behind and reaching forward to what lies ahead, I press on toward the goal for the prize of the upward call of God in Christ Jesus."
(Philip. 3:13-14)

The Question of Faith
Joshua - Joshua 1 & 3

"What do I do now?" This was the question that I asked myself. But I had no answer. My mind seemed to be at a loss as I sat in my tent and contemplated my future. Only it wasn't just my future. That was the problem. There were close to two million people out there, expecting me to lead them, to guide them in wisdom, provide for their needs, and lead them on to victory and prosperity. In short, they expected me to be Moses. There was only one small problem - I wasn't Moses. I was just plain old Joshua.

I didn't know how to lead God's people in the way they should go. It's not that I didn't know how to lead them. I had been Moses' second in command for forty years. I had learned a lot from him over those years. In truth, I had been in charge of much of the leadership responsibilities for some time. I knew how to organize the people into groups for travel and for war. I knew how to plan out a battle, and how to deal with the mundane requirements of a mass of people on the move. I knew all these things, but I also knew they weren't enough.

There was so much I didn't know. I didn't have Moses' wisdom. I didn't have his insight, and most of all, I didn't have his relationship with God. I knew that, more than anything else, what I needed was God's direction. When we walked with the Lord, He always provided for us. There had never been an enemy or obstacle that we couldn't overcome as long as the Lord was with us. But when we had turned way from the Lord, it had always led to trouble. It was essential that we follow God's way, but I didn't know what that way was.

When Moses had told me that it was time for Him to leave, I hadn't understood at first. When he explained that it was his time to die, I couldn't believe it. I knew that he was well over one hundred years old, but he still looked strong and vigorous. I tried to dissuade him from going. I even begged.

"We need you," I pleaded. "You must lead us into the promised land."

But he just smiled at me and said, "No, Joshua, you will lead them. God has spoken, so it shall be."

There was nothing I could say to change his mind. He called the people together, and before them all he laid his hands on me and blessed me. He told them that I was now to be their leader. Then he turned and began his solitary climb up Mt. Nebo. No one knew what to say. We all just stood and watched him slowly disappeared from our sight. We found it hard to believe that the man who had led us out of Egypt, and had been a father to us all, would no longer be with us. I didn't know how we could go on. It had always been Moses that had told us what God expected of us. It was Moses who had given us God's law. It was he who told us what we needed to do to please God and to receive the Lord's blessings. Moses had been the one we had relied on. It was he the people had looked to for direction. But now he was gone and they were looking at me.

It wasn't until Moses had been gone from my sight for some time that I finally turned and made my way back to my tent. And here I sat. Never in my life had I felt so alone. I felt small and inept, lost and confused. "What do I do now?" I asked myself once again, only louder this time. But still no answer came. My body shaking, I got down and prostrated myself on the floor.

"My Lord God," I prayed, "help me please! I'm afraid, and I don't know what to do. Show me Your way. Lead me Lord, for without You I am nothing." For a moment I just laid there, fearing that He would not answer me. But then I heard a voice. Only I heard the voice more with my heart than with my ears.

"Joshua, son of Nun," the voice said, and somehow I knew it to be the Lord's.

"Yes, My Lord," I replied, "I am here."

"Moses My servant is dead;" God said. "Now therefore arise, cross this Jordan, you and all this people, to the land which I am giving to them, to the sons of Israel. Every place on which the sole of your foot treads, I have given it to you, just as I spoke to Moses. From the wilderness and this Lebanon, even as far as the great river, the river Euphrates, all the land of the Hittites, and as far as the Great Sea toward the setting of the sun will be your territory. No man will be able to stand before you all the days of your life. Just as I have been with Moses, I will be with you; I will not fail you or forsake you."

"Be strong and courageous, for you shall give this people possession of the land which I swore to their fathers to give them. Only be strong and very courageous; be careful to do according to all the law which Moses My servant commanded you; do not turn from it to the right or to the left, so that you may have success wherever you go. This book of the law shall not depart from your mouth, but you shall meditate on it day and night, so that you may be careful to do according to all that is written in it; for then you will make your way prosperous, and then you will have success. Have I not commanded you? Be strong and courageous! Do not tremble or be dismayed, for the LORD your God is with you wherever you go."

I got up off the floor shaking, only this time not from fear, but with excitement and wonder. I still felt small and inept, but now I was no longer afraid. I now knew what I needed to do. Or rather, I knew that as long as I walked with the Lord, He would tell me what I need to do. I could feel the Spirit of the Lord upon me, and it gave me a strength and hope that I had never known. I walked out of my tent and looked about me. I saw everything with a new light. I looked at the tents spread out before me, and at the people milling about. These were God's people, and He would lead and protect them. I just needed enough courage to follow His lead.

I gathered the leaders of the people and told them, "Prepare your people to move, for in three days we will cross the Jordan and we will take the land, for the Lord your God is giving it to you to be your home. The promise is at hand. The Lord is with us!" A cheer arose amongst the people. We would surely miss Moses, but God was leading us on. I walked through the camp, conferring with the leaders and encouraging the people. I could feel the sense of excitement building. The heads of the tribes came and told me that they would follow me as they had followed Moses.

A moment of apprehension passed over me as I felt the enormity of the task ahead. I knew I could never fill Moses' sandals. But God's Spirit spoke to my soul. I didn't have to fill Moses' sandals I just had to follow God's lead. How we were to cross over the Jordan River while it was running at flood stage, I had no idea. Nor did I know how we were to deal with the obstacles on the other side. But I knew that God had a plan, and He would reveal it when the time came. My job wasn't to solve the impossible. My job was to prepare the people to follow the Lord. He would do the rest.

The day before we were to cross the Jordan, I called the people together. "Consecrate yourselves," I said, "dedicate yourselves to the Lord, and put away all that is unclean. For tomorrow the Lord will perform wonders before your eyes."

That night the Lord spoke to me again. He assured me that He would be with me, and He would show His power through my leadership. He instructed me to have the priests carrying the Ark of the Covenant go out before the people. The priests with the ark were to stand in the Jordan so that the people could cross the river.

That was last night. This morning I woke up early. I climbed up a hill that looked down upon the Jordan. The river swollen from the spring rains and mountain run off. It surged over its banks as a seemingly unstoppable force. Standing there I gazed across the valley to where Jericho lay, only a few miles distant. The walls of Jericho would be our first test, after we make it across the Jordan, that is. I looked at the hills that rose up from the valley floor and stretched to the high country beyond, the top of the hills just now being caressed by the rays of the sun peaking up behind me. There lay our destiny - the Promised Land, our hope and our future.

No, I remind myself, our hope lay not in the land or in the riches that it held. Our hope is in the Lord. He, and He alone, holds our future. I know that we are here for a reason that was much bigger than just our happiness. We are a part of God's plan, and we have our role to play. The battles lay before us, whether it be with a river, a city, or ourselves. The obstacles that face us are varied and complex, but our mission is simple - follow where God leads and be obedient to His call. Conquering this land is more than we can handle, but we can follow God, one step at a time. That we can do. I turn and walk back down to the people.

"Come to me," I call, "and hear the words of the Lord your God. Today you shall know that the living God is here among you. He will drive out your enemies before you, and He will establish you in the land He swore to your fathers. He will fulfill His promises, and it will start today. The priests who carry the Ark of the Lord shall lead us down to the river. There they shall step out upon the Jordan. When the soles of their feet touch the water, the Lord will stop the rushing torrent and we shall cross over on dry land. Come now and let us see together the salvation of the Lord."

At the sound of the trumpets, the priests lead the way. You could feel the sense of excitement, mingled with a touch of fear. Would the waters really stop? Would God truly show His power? As the priests come to the water's edge, they hesitate for a moment, and then the lead priests step out. As their feet touch the water, the thought runs through my mind, "It all begins with a step of faith."

We are told by scripture that the waters stopped when the priests' feet stepped upon the water. Joshua led the people across, and continued to lead them until the day he died. Through his leadership the people overcame incredible obstacles. They learned to deal with success as well as failure, and the key was always the same. If they wanted to succeed, they needed to keep their trust in God and be obedient to His will. Joshua knew he did not have the ability to lead the people or to deal with the problems which faced them, but he also knew that victory would be theirs as long as the walked with God.

A Closer Look

As we have seen, walking by faith is no small thing. It involves every area of our life. It pushes us beyond our comfort zone and asks of us more than we can manage. We find this to be especially true when viewed from the context of the world we live in. There is a continual pressure upon us to conform to the pattern of those around us, and to become one with the world. Satan attacks our mind and spirit. Age or sickness attacks our body. Sometimes it seems that the best we can do is to hold on and survive. This can be true both for the individual and as well as for the church. But we have not been called to survive. We have been called to conquer.[1]

The church is not just to withstand the attacks of Satan. It is to break down the gates of hell.[2] We are not just to survive the world. We are to overcome the world.

"For whatever is born of God overcomes the world; and this is the victory
that has overcome the world--our faith." (1 John 5:4)

Faith and love are the two most powerful forces in the world. Faith can move mountains. But our own faith can often seem more like a ninety pound weakling.

Part of the problem is that we have a tendency to lose sight of our goal. It is easy to get discouraged when you feel lost and that your life has no purpose. Proverbs tells us that when people do not have direction they fall away.[3] The best thing to do when you are trying to make your way through a wilderness is to pick out a goal and keep working your way towards it. Now, there are all kinds of goals we can set up for ourselves, and many of them may be good goals. But walking by faith in regard to our mission is not about having faith in our goals, or even about choosing good goals. It is about seeking God's goal for our life, and striving to be faithful as we rely upon His strength and wisdom to go forward.

The specifics of God's goal for us will change from person to person and from situation to situation. There is no set formula for determining God's will. If we seek the Lord and strive to be obedient in that which we already know God would have us do, then

He will make His will known to us when we need to know it. We may not know what God's will for us will be in the future, but we can know is that it will always be in line with His ultimate goal for us - to become like Christ. Whether we are talking about a church or an individual, His mission for us is to be conformed to the image of Christ.[4]

Therefore, we can determine two things about what our goal or mission is, or will be. First, it will always be in line with the ultimate goal of becoming like Christ. If we feel we must go in a direction contrary to what Christ has shown or directed us in order to achieve our goals, then our goals are in opposition to God's will. Second, the way in which we are to act in achieving our goal is always to conform to the example or instruction of Christ. If our attitude is wrong, then even if our goal is correct, we will not be pleasing to God.

If we keep in mind God's ultimate goal for us, then even if we do not know what God's "mission" for us is yet, we can still walk in confidence. For as long as we are trying to conform our life to the image of Christ, we can know that we are at least headed in the right direction. And when He does revile His will to us, we will be where we need to be to go forward with it. When we look at what it means to walk by faith in regard to our mission in life, the key is Christ. He is the begriming and the end.[5] He is the one who leads down the right path,[6] and in Him we find the strength to go on. And no matter what the specifics of our mission might be, Christ is always to be our goal and the means by which we check ourselves. He is our guiding star.

Now when we consider the holiness and purity of Christ, and contrast it with our meager efforts, it might seem that having Christ as a goal would be rather discouraging. But the truth is, keeping our eyes on Him is what gives us the strength we need. As long as Peter kept his eyes on Christ, his faith enabled him to walk on water. But when he took his eyes off of Christ, Peter's faith failed him.[7] Keeping our eyes on Christ not only gives us a goal worth striving for, but it also supplies us the power we need to continue.

The mission God has set for us is more than our own power or ability is able to achieve. I t is not ability, but faith that is needed for us to reach the goal. For when we act in faith, God brings about the change.

> "For it is God who is at work in you, both to will and to work for His good pleasure." (Philip. 2:13)

The truth is that God is already working in you. You would not be reading this if God was not working in you. And He will continue to work in you. Even though we are weak and sinful, we can have confidence that God is not going to give up on us. He will continue to work within us and will complete the work He has begun.[8]

We may feel that God will never be able to complete the work in us because we are just not strong enough. It seems we will always fall short of the goal. We will always be lacking. But our completeness comes not from what we are able to achieve, but from Christ living in us.[9]

"and in Him you have been made complete, and He is the head over all rule and authority;" (Col. 2:10)

How can God take imperfect people who are definitely incomplete, and make them complete in spite of their imperfections? This is indeed a mystery. But the answer to that mystery is Christ. When He is Lord, He makes us complete.

When we choose to commit ourselves to Christ and strive to live by faith a number of things happen. 1. We receive God's grace. Our sins are removed. When we give our life to Him, our sins belong to Him as well. And since Christ has already paid the price for those sins on the cross, they are cancelled out, wiped clean. 2. Because we belong to Christ, and because He lives within us, God now receives us as He would Christ. We become acceptable to God, not because of what we do, but because Christ lives within us. His fullness completes that which is lacking on our part. Our completeness in the sight of God comes from Christ. 3. Christ begins to work within us to help us conform to His image. It is not by our power, but by His working within us. But for it to work, it requires faith.

We must be willing to put our trust in God's plan for our life, rather than try to manipulate things to our will and thinking. And we must be willing to be faithful to that which God has called us to do. God knows that the goal of becoming like Christ is too much for us to grasp. So He has helped us by mapping out smaller goals that will lead us in the direction we need to go. God's Word lays out these directions, and His Spirit will help us to understand and apply them. But we must choose to follow.

God also knows that we have a hard time following this path. We are not strong, and Satan is continually trying to draw us away. So God not only points us down the path we should go, but through Jesus Christ, He walks that path with us. The key to achieving our mission is our relationship with Christ. The closer we walk with Him, the more sure we can be that we are on the right path. When things get too rough for us, it is our relationship with Christ that gives us the strength we need. Walking with Christ is not just what leads us to our goal, it is the goal. For the more time we spend with Christ, the more we become like Christ. Our goal is not achieved when we reach the end of the path. It becomes a reality as we walk the path with Jesus.

Walking with Jesus involves putting our trust in Him and striving to be obedient to His will. It all comes back to the same thing we have been talking about from the beginning - faith. Our willingness to step out and act in faith, in spite of our doubts and weaknesses, is what opens the door for the power of God to work within us. To God, the importance of our efforts is not in what they may achieve, but in the faith which they demonstrate. This is why actions that are not of faith, but come out of our own motives (pride, legalism, recognition, etc.), do not please God.[10] If they are not of faith, then no matter what they may achieve, they bring us no closer to our goal. On the other hand, if our actions come out of faith, then whether or not they achieve what we think they should, they are still pleasing to God. Christ can still use our efforts to conform us to His image, even if we see those efforts as a failure.

What does all this have to do with our mission (to become like Christ)? It means that our mission is obtainable. It is not something way out ahead of us that we can never reach. It is right there in front of us. Every time we choose to go forward in faith, Christ will use that to shape and mold us. And because faith opens the door for His presence in our life, He then completes in us that which is lacking in the sight of God. Christ's presence within us makes us complete and acceptable to God.

This is why a new Christian, who is immature in his or her walk, can be just as acceptable to God as a Christian who is much more knowledgeable and does "greater" things for God. The criteria for acceptance is always the same - faith. This is also why we can never reach a point where we can relax and say we have done enough. We will always be called to walk by faith. Without faith, it is impossible to please God.[11]

On any journey it is important that we know two points- our starting point, and where we need to be to achieve our goal. If we know those two positions, it will tell us what we need to do next. Our starting point is where we are at right now. It is not somewhere back behind us, because each day starts anew. It is not somewhere beyond us, because God is willing to start with us right where we are at. We do not have to fix up our life before we can start a walk with the Lord. He is willing to take us right where we are at. We do not have to be ashamed or embarrassed. We just need to turn to Him.

Where ever we are is an acceptable starting point, but it is not acceptable for us to stay there. God always calls us forward. He will always require that we walk in faith. Whether as an individual or as a church, our goal is not just to survive. When we stop reaching forward, we begin to die. This was Christ's warning to the church in Sardis.

> "To the angel of the church in Sardis write: He who has the seven Spirits of God and the seven stars, says this: 'I know your deeds, that you have a name that you are alive, but you are dead. Wake up, and strengthen the things that remain, which were about to die; for I have not found your deeds completed in the sight of My God. So remember what you have received and heard; and keep it, and repent. Therefore if you do not wake up, I will come like a thief, and you will not know at what hour I will come to you." (Rev. 3:1-3)

To become like Christ is our goal. God has not placed our goal far out of our reach. It is always right before us. To find it we need only ask, "God, what is Your desire?" In that question we will find what our next step is to be. What is His desire in our relationships? What is His desire in our work? What is His desire for our finances? What is His desire in our church? To be acceptable to God and to become more Christ - like, we do not have to know all the answers. We just have to be willing to genuinely ask the right questions, and then step out in faith.

If we seek the Lord, He will show us what the next step is to be. It will probably be more than we can achieve, but it will not be more than He can achieve working through us. It will not be the same for each person, for each of us is at a different point.

What will be the same is Christ. He will call us to come walk with Him one step at a time. That step will always be going forward, and it will always require faith.

Digging Deeper

As servants of Christ, we are not to go through life aimlessly. Nor are our goals to be the same as the world around us. We have been bought with a price. We are not our own, we belong to Christ.[12] We have a mission.

1. What do we need to do to achieve that mission? (Heb. 12:1-2)

We need to keep our eyes on Christ because He is the mission. Our goal is to become like Christ.

2. What are some things the Bible tells us are involved in becoming like Christ?

Rom. 13:13-14

Gal. 2:20

Philip. 2:3-8

If our mission is to become like Christ, then one place to look is at the things Christ did while He was here on earth.

3. What are some things Christ demonstrated were priorities to Him?

Luke 4:18-19

Mark 10:44-45

4. How can we follow His example in our lives?

5. How can we follow His example in our church?

The next place to look in becoming Christ-like is in the commands He has given us.

6. What are some instructions Christ has given us?

Matt. 5:16

Matt. 28:18-20

John 4:23

John 13:34

7. What do we need to do to demonstrate faithfulness in these areas within our lives?

8. What do we need to do to demonstrate faithfulness in these areas within our church?

9. Is there a difference between acting in obedience and acting in faith, and if so, what is it?

While acting in faith involves being obedient to God's direction, sometimes we connect obedience to our abilities. We do what we can to be obedient, and that which is beyond our abilities we do not even try. Walking in faith is not confined to our own abilities. Rather, we seek God's desire, and we step out in faith trusting that He will supply what is needed.

10. Through this study over the last 13 weeks, what area of faith have you found most challenging?

11. Is there any area you have purposely worked on, and if so, have you seen any results?

12. Keeping in mind what we have learned in this lesson, how you would deal with the following scenarios?

    A. You are a Christian that desires to walk by faith, but you are not sure what you are supposed to do. Where would you start?

    B. Your church is a church that desires to operate by faith and not by sight. What are some questions your church may need to ask itself to make this come about?

13. What does will it mean for you to walk by faith in following God's mission for your life?

14. What does will it mean for your church to walk by faith in following God's mission for it?

15. What is one area in regard to mission that you can work on walking by faith in?

16. What is one area in regard to mission that your church needs to work on walking by faith in?

Life Examples
Karina (Keeky) [13]

In May, 1995, I asked God to show me His purpose for my life. I wanted a verse to stand on. God used a Bible teacher to lead me to Isaiah 58:12.

> "Those from among you will rebuild the ancient ruins; You will raise up
> the age-old foundations; And you will be called the repairer of the breach,
> The restorer of the streets in which to dwell." (Is 58:12)

God would use my life to rebuild the foundations of the wasted places and of the ruined generations. At the time I was working with troubled youth and families through the Institute in Basic Life Principles.

Then in August of 1997, I became very ill. Doctors couldn't explain the cause nor provide a cure. They stated that they could not tell whether I would ever walk normally or work again, but that I certainly would never travel. A friend gave me a small paper with a phrase, which I read over and again, sometimes with tears, until I was able to embrace it, "God has every right, and my permission, to do with my life whatever would bring Him the greatest glory."

On January 26, 1999, I was on my knees, reading and agreeing with Psalm 116.

> "I love the LORD, because He hears My voice and my supplications.
> Because He has inclined His ear to me; Therefore I shall call upon Him as
> long as I live." (Ps 116:1-2)

As I was thanking Him for the truth of this passage, the Lord spoke to me, "Karina, we are coming out of this valley for now." Improvement began immediately; slowly, but surely. By summer of that year, I started nursing school. On graduation, I was unanimously chosen to receive the "Nursing With Excellence" award.

Shortly thereafter, July of 2002, by miraculous means God brought me to Uganda, Africa, for a short term mission. I was in a public canoe on Lake Victoria, on the way to Lingira Island, when God spoke to me once more, "Karina, look around you. This is your home." I went back to the States to an incredible job at The Oregon Burn Center, but knowing that it was not to be my future. Rather, it was preparation for what God had in store on the islands.

By the time I arrived back on the island base for Youth With A Mission (YWAM), October of 2003, their funding had been cut and the clinic closed down. With a lot of zeal and a good deal of ignorance, I plunged into the work, opened the clinic and came face-to-face with the cycle of poverty and disease of the third-world.

Through the work at the clinic, I began seeing many inter-related needs. I saw that it was not enough to deal with the medical problems. We need to address the root causes that lead to these problems, such as polluted drinking water, poverty, lack of spirituality and lack of education. I consulted with some of the pastors in the area, one of whom is a man known as Uncle Samson. Under his leadership and that of YWAM, in early 2005 we began a clean water project and a discipleship program.

But still there was a feeling of helplessness among the young people of the island. With extreme poverty and little opportunity to make any money added to a life expectancy of only the early 30's, they saw little hope in the future. Why stay in school in the early years when there was no opportunity to continue that education beyond the primary school level? On February 6, 2006, we started Lingira Living Hope Secondary School, one of only two secondary schools serving all 52 of the Buvuma chain islands.

Back in 2005, I had gone to visit Pastor Robert of Lingira, who was in university in Kampala, Uganda. He told me how God had shown him the many things I was doing and that I needed to form an umbrella organization under which the ministries could run efficiently. Then he mentioned the name, Shepherds Heart. I shrugged it off, stating that I was working with Youth With A Mission and promptly forgot about it.

In December of 2006, during Christmas holidays, I went to Pastor Moses to pray for direction. My time of commitment to YWAM was ending. Now what? During that time, the Lord impressed me with the example of Christ, who became one of us, even to the point that He was unashamed to be identified as our Brother. Although I didn't know what I would do, I knew it was time that I should move outside YWAM but continue my involvement with the community and church there on Lingira Island.

I was still at Pastor Moses' when I was called to a meeting regarding the Clean Water Project. Through the meeting, the men began asking what I was going to do and strongly urged me to start an NGO (Non-Government Organization) which would encompass the various ministries on and off the islands. They didn't accept my refusals. Finally I stated, "I am not the one to lead any ministry for two reasons. First, I have no interest in controlling others. I just want to empower those who have visions. Secondly,

I am not interested in making a name." At that, Father Alfred spoke for the first time. "Keeky, that is just the kind of leader which God wants."

I left that meeting very troubled. I went back to the place I was staying, Alice Kisolo's. I found there a group of intercessors in prayer. Soon after I joined them, a woman began speaking, "I see as if we are in a boat, in a storm. The waves are high and like Jesus' disciples we have been straining to stay afloat. Yet Jesus is coming towards us, walking on the waters. He wants us to be like Peter and to say, 'Lord, if it is You, tell me to come.' You must get out of the boat," looking directly at me she continued, "even if the winds were too strong while you were in the boat, you must get out into the waves and go to Jesus . . . "

On Christmas Sunday, Pastor Robert preached a message aimed straight at me, though he didn't know it. He spoke about Mary's role in carrying the child, Jesus, to term. "She could have refused or aborted for many reasons: How would she explain to Joseph or others? Wouldn't they believe this pregnancy was a result of her own iniquity, not Divine intervention? Wasn't she young and inexperienced? Nine months was long and tiring . . . If you think carrying the baby is bad, wait for the labor pains. What would have happened had Mary aborted? We would have all missed the Messiah. Now we have forgotten her pain because we rejoice in the birth." Pastor Robert then likened Mary's role to ours when God gives us a vision. If we abort the vision because of fear of people's reaction, or because of tiredness or pain, we are destroying the blessing that God has designed for those around us. If we persevere, the vision will come to fruition. Even those who spoke ill will forget their words and will rejoice. He went on to say, "What if God has given a vision to Keeky, yet it was never fulfilled because we refused to stand with and support her, as Joseph did for Mary?"

Afterwards I asked Pastor Robert why he had spoken so directly. Had God shown him what was happening with me? I had not yet spoken anything of what was going on in my heart. As I shared with him and asked him to pray about being a part of whatever it was God was starting, Pastor Robert reminded me of the time I had visited him at the university. "I told you then that this is what God was doing, but you did not hear it." For sure I had completely forgotten.

Later, when we asked Uncle Samson to consider being the third director, he asked me to consider what God had shown me in the dream years ago. I had forgotten that, too. This ministry must focus on rebuilding the foundations of the wasted generations around us. Coming up with a name was the next struggle. We struggled on our own, but when Shepherd's Heart International Ministry (SHIM) was mentioned, it just fit. We submitted several names officially, but immediately SHIM was chosen.

When Pastor Moses heard, he chuckled. "If you were to leave me here and go talk with my wife, Florence, she would tell you that I had already spoken that it was time for Keeky to start her own organization for the sake of island ministry and that it needed to be independent from other existing organizations or churches so it would be free to inter-relate with all."

One of the first things we did was to go to Kenya for a time of prayer together. While there, it was decided that we needed land. A specific area between the Kyoya and

Katonga camps was mentioned. On arriving back at Lingira, God again used Pastor Moses to bring confirmation. "You need your own land. You need the place between the Kyoya and Katonga. Actually, God had already spoken to me about it and I put down some money to reserve the area."

In April 2007, we took a few days to meet with "the team," including the island pastors and some others who would shortly be involved in Shepherd's Heart. It was incredible to hear each one explain what they felt God was doing and how they were to be a part of that. Pastor Waboka, of the new church in Kyoya, shared how the church's vision corresponded directly with the vision and objectives of SHIM. The excitement and unity was contagious as we prayed and discussed what God is doing on the islands.

During that meeting, we formulated our vision: Shepherd's Heart International Ministry exists to glorify the Lord Jesus Christ and to further God's kingdom by empowering indigenous leaders to help their own people promote the spiritual, economic, educational, and physical development. As an umbrella organization, we link resources, channel funds, network, give legal coverage and coordinate volunteers/teams. It is not our desire to control or own every project under SHIM but to help individuals or programs to recognize and achieve their God-given potentials.

SHIM was officially organized in 2007. Currently, some programs are directly under SHIM, such as the Water Projects, Economic Development, Discipleship Training, Pastoral training, Child Development, Family Training, Agriculture Training, etc. Others are being encouraged or supported through partnering together, like the Lingira Living Hope Secondary School, which now has 11 teachers and over 150 students, and the Buvuma Islands Savings and Credit Association. In the short time that SHIM has been in existence God has blessed it in many ways. Not only has God blessed the ministry but God has blessed Karina as well. In 2007 a young man named Andew Smith came to the islands on a short term mission trip and not only fell in love with the people and the area, he fell in love with Karina as well. In 2008 they were married and are now beginning to raise a family as they continue to follow God's ministry for their lives on the island of Lingira.

ENDNOTES

Introduction:
1. Matt 17:20
2. Spiros Zodhiates, Th.D. (Compiler), Illustrations of Bible Truths, (Chattanooga, TN: AMG Publishers, 1991) p.79

Chapter 1:
1. Webster's New Collegiate Dictionary, (Springfield, Massachusetts: G.& C. Merriam Company. 1979) p. 408
2. Webster's New Collegiate Dictionary, (Springfield, Massachusetts: G.& C. Merriam Company. 1979) p. 408
3. Rom. 4:5, 11; 2 Cor 4:13; Gal 2:16; 3:22
4. Mark 16:16; Acts 15:11; Rom 10:8
5. Gen. 45:26; Ex. 4:1, 5, 8, 9; 19:9; Num. 14:11; etc.
6. Job 39:12
7. Num. 12:7; Deut. 7:9; 1 Sam. 2:35; 22:14; 2 Sam. 20:19; etc.
8. Eph. 2:8; 1 Peter 1:9
9. John 1:12; 3:15-17; 6:47; 11:25-26; 20:31
10. Acts 2:38; 3:19
11. Acts 2:38; 1 Peter 3:21
12. Matt. 7:21; John 3:36; Heb. 5:9; 1 John 5:1-5
13. Rom. 10:9-11
14. Matt. 24:13
15. Gal. 2:16; Rom. 3:27-28; 9:32
16. Rom. 1:5; 16:26
17. Rom. 6:2
18. Rev. 3:1-2
19. 1 Tim. 6:21
20. 1 Tim. 1:19
21. Jer. 3:22
22. Bob Peterson, missionary to Uganda with Global Outreach
23. Eph. 2:8
24. Matt. 7:21-23

Chapter 2:
1. Ps. 57:1
2. Ps. 23:4
3. Ps. 57:2-3
4. Deut. 13:1-3; 2 Chron. 32:31; Dan. 12:10;
5. James 1:13
6. Gen. 3:1-6; 1 Chron. 21:1; Matt. 4:1; 2 Cor. 11:14; Eph. 6:11; 1 Thess. 3:5
7. James 1:2-4, 12; 1 Peter 1:6-7
8. Rom. 13:1-2; 1 Peter 2:13-15
9. Lev. 2:2-12; Deut. 26:17-18; 30:15-16; 1 Kings 2:3; Ez. 20:19
10. Jer. 7:23; Dan. 9:10
11. Deut. 30:15-16

12. 1 Kings 8:61
13. Josh. 22:5
14. Gen. 5:22; 6:9
15. Heb. 11:5, 7
16. Derek Kinder, Psalms 1-72, Tyndale Old Testament Commentaries, ed. D. J. Wiseman, no. 14a (Downers Grove, Illinois, 1973) p. 110.
17. John 10:4
18. 1 John 5:13
19. Eph. 2:8; Rom. 5:2
20. Gal. 3:26
21. Acts 26:18; Heb. 6:12
22. Matt. 9:22
23. James 5:15
24. Heb. 11:3
25. Eph. 6:16; 1 John 5:4
26. Is. 26:2
27. Acts 15:9
28. Rom. 3:26; Gal. 2:16; 3:24
29. Acts 26:18
30. Gal. 3:26
31. Lev. 26:3-9; Deut. 7:12-16; 30:16
32. 1 Kings 2:3
33. Gal. 3:2, 14
34. Lev. 26:3-12; Ps. 101:6
35. Prov. 12:22
36. Deut. 26:17-18
37. Ex. 20:12
38. Ps. 103:13
39. Eph. 5:25
40. 2 Tim. 2:11-12
41. 2 Cor. 5:14-15
42. Deut. 28:15
43. Deut. 32:20
44. Rom. 14:23; Lev. 6:2
45. Is 59:2
46. Deut. 5:9
47. Deut. 5:10; 7:9
48. Joe Hover, missionary to Guinea with Pioneer Bible Translators

Chapter 3:
1. 1 Chron. 16:11; Is. 55:6
2. Ps 55:16-18
3. Dan. 6:26
4. Dan. 1:9
5. Dan. 1:8
6. Dan. 2:28; 6:22
7. Dan. 5:11-12
8. Rom. 13:1-2
9. Rom. 3:27
10. 1 Cor. 9:21; Gal. 6:2
11. 1 Cor. 5:12-13
12. Dan. 4:1-37
13. Tom Harris, school custodian in Dufur Oregon

Chapter 4:
1. Henry T. Blackaby and Claude V. King, Experiencing God:

Knowing and Doing the Will of God (Nashville Tennessee: Life Way Press, 2001), 96.
2. Heb. 13:8
3. John 3:16; Rom. 5:8
4. 1 John 4:8-10
5. Jer. 31:3
6. Is. 59:2
7. Prov. 3:11
8. Gen. 1:1; Jer. 10:12-13
9. Col. 1:16-17
10. Luke 1:37; Matt. 19:26
11. 2 Chron. 16:9
12. Josh. 24:15
13. Rom. 8:35-39
14. Matt. 26:38
15. Luke 22:44
16. Ex. 9:13-17
17. Ps. 107:10-14
18. Ps. 22:1
19. Virginia Albrecht, school administrator in Dufur Oregon

Chapter 5:
1. 1 John 4:20
2. Luke 10:30-37
3. Luke 6:27-28
4. Eph. 2:8-9
5. Prov. 15:1; 25:15
6. Prov. 14:30; Is. 40:30; Gal. 6:9; Heb. 10:36
7. Ps. 10:17; Prov. 11:2; 15:33; 22:4; Matt. 18:4; 23:12
8. Prov. 28:20
9: John 16:28
10 . Matt. 15:4-6
11. Carolynn Harkins, housewife in Spanaway Washington

Chapter 6:
1. Matt. 6:32
2. Luke 14:33
3. Matt. 25:14-30
4. 1 Cor. 3:18-19
5. Luke 6:20, 24
6. Matt. 19:23
7. Matt. 19:26
8. Luke 12:16-21; Prov. 11:4
9. Matt. 6:19-20
10. 1 Cor. 3:18-19
11. 1 Cor. 16:1-2
12. Matt. 7:11
13. 2 Cor. 8:3
14. 1 Cor. 7:23
15. 1 Cor. 7:21
16. 1 Tim. 6:11
17. Matt. 5:3
18. Luke 16:10-12
19. Jerry Peterson, camp ministry missionary in Wamac Oregon

Chapter 7:

1. Gen. 28:15
2. Gen. 26:3
3. Ps. 27:14; 37:7; Prov. 20:22
4. Zeph. 3:8
5. Ps. 13:1
6. Ps. 35:17
7. Ps. 89:46
8. John 10:24
9. Ex. 10:3
10. Ex. 16:28
11. Jer. 13:27
12. Henry T. Blackaby, Claude V. King. Experiencing God: Knowing and Doing the Will of God (Nashville, Tennessee: Life Way Press, 1990). p. 119.
13. Ex. 8:20-24
14. Gen. 16:7-9
15. Gen. 15:1
16. Gen. 28:10-13
17. Dan. 4
18. Ex. 19:16-19
19. Matt. 12:38; 16:1; 24:3
20. Stan Peterson, Pastor of Monmouth Christian Church in Monmouth Oregon

Chapter 8:
1. Otto Koning, The Pineapple Story, Tape one in The Pineapple Story Series , (Oak Brook, Illinois: Institute in Basic Life Principles, 1997)
2. Matt. 6:12-15; 18:21-35; Mark 11:25-26; Luke 17:3-4; Rom. 12:17-19; 2 Cor. 2:7; Eph. 4:29-32; Col. 3:12-13
3. Rom. 12:19
4. Eph. 4:30-31
5. Eph. 4:26
6. Matt. 18:23-35
7. Matt. 5:38
8. Col. 2:12-14
9. Heb. 10:18
10. 1 John 1:9
11. Num. 12
12. Josh. 7
13. 1 Sam. 15:35
14. The names have been changed for the sake of privacy.

Chapter 9:
1. 2 Kings 16:3

2. 2 Kings 17:31
3. 2 Kings 16:3; Ez. 16:20-21; Jer. 32:35
4. Lev. 19:21
5. Ex. 13:2
6. Lam. 1:8
7. Matt. 10:37
8. Matt. 19:29
9. Gen. 37:5-9
10. Ex. 3:16-17; 4:30-31
11. 1 Sam. 16:12
12. Michelle Peterson, missionary to Uganda with Global Outreach

Chapter 10:
1. Luke 6:20
2. Matt. 19:24
3. Mark 1:15
4. Luke 18:16
5. Matt. 21:43
6. Matt. 13:44-46
7. 1 Cor. 1:26
8. Eph. 2:10
9. Eph. 4:11-12
10. The parable of the talents (Matt. 25:14-30), the parable of the ten virgins (Matt. 25:1-13), the parable of the faithful and evil slaves (Luke 12:35-40), the parable of the faithful steward (Luke 12:42-48)
11. Rev. 3:1-13
12. James 2:26
13. Mark 4:14
14. Matt. 25:23
15. Rick Warren, The Purpose Driven life (Grand Rapids, Michigan: Zondervan, 2002), 237.
16. 1 Cor. 10:31
17. Andrew Smith, missionary in Uganda with Global Outreach

Chapter 11:
1. Matt. 26:34
2. Matt. 26:35
3. Matt. 26:40-41
4. Matt. 26:45-46
5. 1 Sam 13:6-14; 15:1-9
6. 2 Sam. 11:1-27
7. Acts 13:22
8. 2 Sam. 11:11, 14
9. 1 Sam. 15:13-21
10. 2 Sam. 12:13
11. John 8:1-11

12. John 8:7
13. Matt. 7:1-2
14. John 8:10-11
15. 2 Peter 3:9
16. Matt. 5:23-24
17. 2 Cor. 12:9
18. Steve Harkins, paramedic in Tacoma Washington

Chapter 12:
1. Acts 27:21b-26
2. 1 Cor. 1:11-13
3. Rom. 3:22-24
4. Eph. 2:8-9
5. Rom. 5:1-2
6. Col. 1:17-18
7. 1 Cor. 12:26
8. Matt. 5:23-24
9. 1 Cor. 12:13-14
10. Eph. 4:11-12
11. Matt. 5:16
12. Matt. 25:40
13. Eph. 2:19-21
14. Gal. 1:8; 2 John 9
15. Acts 4:12
16. Rom. 14:1-4
17. Rev. 2:14-16, 20-23
18. 1 Cor. 3:16-17
19. John 16:7-8
20. Ez. 3:17-21
21. Matt. 6:14-15
22. Eph. 4:3
23. 1 Peter 1:22
24. Rom. 12:9
25. Mike Wilson, Pastor at First Christian in The Dalles Oregon

Chapter 13:
1. Rom. 8:37
2. Matt. 16:18
3. Prov. 11:14
4. Rom. 8:29
5. Rev. 21:6
6. Ps. 23:3
7. Matt. 14:28-31
8. Philip. 1:6
9. Col. 1:26-28
10. Rom. 14:23
11. Heb. 11:6
12. 1 Cor. 6:19-20
13. Karinia Smith, missionary in Uganda with Global Outreach
14. Prov. 3:5-6

BIBLIOGRAPHY

Benge, Janet & Geoff. Christain Heroes: <u>Then & Now, George Muller, The Guardian of Bristol's Orphans</u>. Seattle, WA: YWAM Publishing, 1999.

Blackaby, Henry T., Claude V. King. <u>Experiencing God: Knowing and Doing the Will of God</u>. Nashville, Tennessee: LifeWay Press, 1990.

Canfield, Jack, Mark Victor Hansen, Patty Aubery, Nancy Michell Autio, eds., Chicken Soup for the Christian Family Soul. Letters to a Stranger, by Susan Morin. Deerfield Beach, Florida: Health Communications, Inc., 2000.

Holladay, William L. <u>A Concise Hebrew and Aramaic Lexicon of The Old Testament</u>. Grand Rapids, Michigan: William B. Eerdmans Publishing Co, 1989.

Kinder, Derek, Psalms 1-72, <u>Tyndale Old Testament Commentaries</u>, ed. D. J. Wiseman, no 14a. Downers Grove, Illinois, 1973.

Koning, Otto. <u>The Pineapple Story</u>, In The Pineapple Story Series , Oak Brook, Illinois: Institute in Basic Life Principles, 1997.

Warren, Rick, <u>The Purpose Driven life</u>. Grand Rapids, Michigan: Zondervan, 2002.

<u>Websters New Collegiate Dictionary</u>, Springfield, Massachusetts: G.& C. Merriam Company. 1979.

Zodhiates, Spiros, Th.D. (Compiler), <u>Illustrations of Bible Truths</u>, Chattanooga, TN: AMG Publishers, 1991.

www.ingramcontent.com/pod-product-compliance
Lightning Source LLC
Chambersburg PA
CBHW080554090426

42735CB00016B/3229